RESTRICTING
THE
CONCEPT OF
FREE SEAS
MODERN MARITIME LAW REEVALUATED

RESTRICTING
THE
CONCEPT OF
FREE SEAS

MODERN MARITIME LAW
RE-EVALUATED

GEORGE P. SMITH II

ROBERT E. KRIEGER PUBLISHING CO., INC.
HUNTINGTON, NEW YORK
1980

Original edition 1980

Printed and Published by
ROBERT E. KRIEGER PUBLISHING CO., INC.
645 New York Avenue
Huntington, New York 11743

Printed in the United States of America.

Library of Congress Catologing in Publication Data

Smith, George Patrick, 1939-
    Restricting the concept of free seas.

    1.   Maritime law.   I.   Title.
JX4411.S49   341.44'8   79-15020
ISBN 0-88275-998-1

CONTENTS

The historic function of the law of the sea has long been recognized as that of protecting and balancing the common interests, inclusive and exclusive, of all peoples in the use and enjoyment of the oceans, while rejecting all egocentric assertions of special interests in contravention of general community interest.

M. McDougal & W. Burke,
The Public Order of the Oceans (1962)

About the Author

The author was the correspondent for the American Bar Association Journal *to the 1976 session of the Law of the Sea Conference held at the United Nations Headquarters in New York City and to the 1979 session in Geneva, Switzerland. He was also a correspondent for the* Journal *at the United Nations Conference on the Human Environment held in Stockholm the summer of 1972 as well as a conferee at the international meeting,* Pacem In Maribus, *held on Malta during the summer of 1970. Professor Smith, who holds a J. D. from Indiana University and a LL.M. from Columbia University, has studied at the Hague Academie de Droit International in the Netherlands, lectured in ocean law at the Graduate School of Public and International Affairs at the University of Pittsburgh, served as special counsel for environmental-maritime affairs to the late Winthrop Rockefeller, and acted as a legal advisor in the Foreign Claims Settlement Commission of the United States Department of State. He is a professor of law at The Catholic University of America, Washington, D.C., and a visiting scholar at The Kennedy Institute, Georgetown University, Washington, D.C.*

To
William W. Bishop, Jr., Edwin D. Dickinson Professor
of Law Emeritus, University of Michigan—
with respect, admiration, and enduring appreciation

FOREWORD

The Third United Nations Conference on the Law of the Sea has been the international legal event of overriding concern during the 1970s. Whatever ultimately emanates from these lengthy and complicated deliberations is likely to remain the object of international negotiation and dialogue well into the twenty-first century. As the Conference itself moves toward conclusion, those who have reason to examine retrospectively the course of the proceedings will confront an unusual situation. The duration, diverse locations, changing personnel, *modus operandi*, and documentation of the Conference have combined to make it exceptionally difficult to follow or comprehend the interplay of interests and the compromises struck as a preliminary to the consensus-developed single, unified, and composite draft texts which have emerged.

One source of illumination in the passage of time will be the recollections of the participants themselves. Another, of which Professor Smith's book is an example, will be the reflections of informed lay observers who have attended the Law of the Sea Conference in unprecedented numbers and indirectly perhaps, in some instances, been involved informally in the corridor diplomacy so essential to consensus negotiation. Professor Smith attended the 1976 and 1979 sessions of the Conference as an observer from the legal profession and has been inspired to reflect on a very wide range of recent literature, as well as on the very origins of "free seas," in the light of the issues discussed during the proceedings. His observations are a useful and constructive contribution that will interest both layman and lawyer alike; they doubtless represent a species of commentary on the Law of the Sea Conference that in its own way augments the formal record of the Conference itself.

Freedom of the seas, as Professor Smith rightly stresses, remains a core concept of modern maritime law, notwithstanding the very considerable and often very necessary attenuation of that concept in recent decades. If the Conference on the Law of the Sea should succeed, a total revision of the entire body of the law of the sea is in prospect; should the Conference fail to reach consensus or if its agreed texts do not secure the requisite level of acceptance, the law of the sea in any event is likely to be strongly influenced by patterns of state practice flowing from the Conference deliberations — the two-hundred-mile fishing zone already is one example. As the types of ocean use expand, it will become increasingly essential to be explicit about the relationship of these respective uses to one another and perhaps to be more precise about prohibited uses. All components of the freedom of the seas as presently defined cannot enjoy a coequal relationship indefinitely. International solutions are likely to be the preferred means for adjusting these competing uses, despite constant pressures for unilateral measures.

The issue is no longer one of "freedom of the seas" being "disminished" but rather how various freedoms and rights are to be evaluated and ranked among themselves. These are questions of vital importance not only to the

international lawyer or those concerned with national defense or foreign affairs but also to scientists, enviromenta-
lists, commercial entrepreneurs, and others.

WILLIAM E. BUTLER
PROFESSOR OF COMPARATIVE LAW
UNIVERSITY OF LONDON

ACKNOWLEDGMENTS

The research facilities of the Ocean Policy Library at the Johns Hopkins School of Advanced Studies in Washington, D.C., and those of the United Nations Library in New York City greatly aided me in the preparation of this book. Additionally, the research facilities at Cambridge University, which I used during the summer of 1975, the winter of 1976, and the spring of 1978, and particularly the Squire Law Library, University Library, the Law Library at Jesus College, and the library of the Institute of Advanced Research of the University of London were of considerable assistance. The library of the Cosmos Club in Washington, D.C., provided me with a refuge for maritime cogitations pertinent to the book's completion, and Ambassador Rudolf E. Schoenfeld's interest, encouragement, and professional perspective were also a positive influence.

I would be totally remiss if I did not acknowledge the kindness of my friend and colleague Dean Emeritus John L. Garvey of the Law Faculty at The Catholic University of America, and his understanding and encouragement which allowed me to continue researching and writing this book over the past two years. A debt of gratitude must also be recorded to the Honorable Edward D. Re, Chief Judge of the United States Customs Court, for his exciting introduction to the field of international law in 1966 and for his many kindnesses over the years.

To President Emeritus Dr. W. Taylor Reveley II of Hampden-Sydney College, Hampden-Sydney, Virginia, and to his charming wife, Marie, I express my sincere thanks for having provided me with a quiet, congenial atmosphere conducive to the completion of this book at Cambridge, England, during the spring of 1978.

Finally, I thank the *University of Pittsburgh Law Review* for permission to draw upon and develop certain themes and ideas which appeared in my article on the politics of international maritime law in volume thirty-seven of the *Law Review* in 1976.

INTRODUCTION

The history of maritime law is a saga of the long-continuing efforts to balance and where feasible to resolve conflicting interests arising principally between coastal states and the international community.[1]

No two states share precisely the same treaty relations and therefore do not have the same rights and duties under international law; yet in certain areas of shared concern there are bases for "community interest" that often serve as strong stabilizing forces both in promoting and maintaining compatible international relations among all nations. Even within the area of community interest, however, there has not been one unified response to the law of the sea.[2] Strains of discord and incompatibility have arisen in efforts to assure coastal states that their needs for greater sources of economic growth and for protection will be satisfied and at the same time to assure the major maritime interests that their need for freedom both in their military and commercial undertakings will continue.[3] This struggle, then, is the quintessential issue in the history and development of maritime law. Today, with stability in world order virtually nonexistent, any efforts to regulate the use of the seas are especially difficult.

Political activity is the arena in which lawmaking is undertaken. Within the international system, governments of states are the major participants who shape and reshape law, and their policies are most often influenced and, indeed, directed by domestic, transnational, and international forces. Which of these forces independently influence, combine as prime movers of, or act as dependent variables affecting policy formulation is determined by the actual scope of political situations as they develop and subsequently mature. Thus, when new law emerges, it may be correctly viewed as the result of complex influences and forces — or vectors of force.[4]

Central to an understanding of the emergence and development of maritime law is an analysis of the concepts of free seas and sovereignty. Such an analysis, undertaken with an emphasis on the political underpinnings of the concepts, reveals a study in conflicts and compromises in which the politics of tension is seen. The very principle of freedom of the seas reflects tensions at play; it responds to sporadic exercises of tension and acts independently of it. Both the concept of free seas and sovereignty are inextricably intertwined with the concept of territorial seas. Some view the formation of the concept of territorial seas as but a reaction to the concept of the freedom of the seas, with the recognition of coastal state rights emerging only after basic conflicts were resolved. Others assert that the recognition, maintenance, and expansion of sovereignty were the principal factors responsible for shaping the historical perspective of territorial waters. What follows in this investigation and reevaluation of maritime law shows that both the politics of freedom and the concept of sovereignty have shaped and continue to shape thinking about the freedom of the seas and territorial waters. Because modern thinking incorporates both views about the development of territorial seas, there has often been confusion and difficulty in pursuing permanent solutions to conflicts in this area.

In contrast, innocent passage and free transit—internationally recognized rights—present fewer problems. Complexities and tensions, however, arise in interpreting these rights when some states become dissatisfied with the presently enforced right of innocent passage because of what they consider to be weaknesses in the operation of this right. They thus seek to modify or to transform completely the right of passage into the broader right of free transit through certain carefully prescribed territorial waters in international straits without regarding coastal state needs. Other states maintain that there can be neither a reevaluation nor a modification of this long-established right of innocent passage—and for that matter the right of free transit—until an accord is reached concerning the extent of expanded fishing rights and rights for full exploration of seabed minerals. Moreover, the very determination of the exclusive and inclusive limits of the territorial sea is inextricably related to an equitable resolution of these two issues. Regardless what the territorial seas are defined as including, the right of innocent passage will continue to be assured and recognized by the states of the world community. The present need to clarify and reevaluate the parameters of the rights of innocent passage and free transit as codified in the 1958 Territorial Sea Convention cannot, however, be fully undertaken until these related issues are first settled and defined in a treaty subscribed to by the world community.

The present efforts of the Third United Nations Law of the Sea Conference to raise the issues of innocent passage and free transit to a cognizable level of compatible coexistence, free from misunderstanding and misconception, are being met with qualified success. Yet, a study of the diplomatic tactics of the delegates to the conference reveals the striking and pervasive influences of geopolitics in the international lawmaking process, the interplay of a variety of vectors of force, and the depth of frustration that is occasioned by crowding an agenda with ancillary issues that almost defy consensus and detract from the final resolution of basic issues. The hard and fundamental decisions that must eventually be made regarding the need to make new law or to continue the present laws of the sea will, in the final analysis, be made upon an evaluation of the basic cost and advantage of either course of action to individual national interests.[5] Stated otherwise, ultimate decisions will be based upon a consideration of the gravity of the harm occasioned by the continuance of the status quo versus the functional utility of the good that should be incurred by developing new law.

NOTES TO INTRODUCTION

1. P. JESSUP, THE USE OF INTERNATIONAL LAW 13 (1959).
Wolfgang Friedmann suggests two basic challenges face mankind in the remaining years of this century: 1) can man develop an ability to cope with an environment that threatens to overcome him and 2) will nations continue in their competitive races for power and wealth or seek an ordered cooperation in building an international order that serves mankind. W. FRIEDMANN, THE FUTURE OF THE OCEANS 1 (1971). See generally, W. JENKS, THE COMMON LAW OF MANKIND (1958).

2. O. LISSITZYN, INTERNATIONAL LAW TODAY AND TOMORROW 9, 110 (1965). See McDougal & Burke, *The Community Interest in a Narrow Territorial Sea: Inclusive versus Exclusive Competence over the Oceans,* 42 CORNELL L.O. 171 (1960); McDougal, *The Impact of International Law upon National Laws: A Policy-Oriented Perspective,* 4 S.D.L. REV. 25 (1959).

3. There are some Afro-Asian states that wish to maintain a wide territorial sea because they believe maintenance of a 3-mile rule would allow major powers to exert psychological pressures at critical moments by an ostentatious display of naval force slightly beyond the 3-mile limit. The major maritime powers, in contrast, are for less encroachments of sovereignty on the seas and freer exercise of the principle of freedom. In this way, maritime commerce and military exercises, of a defensive strategy, may be undertaken expeditiously. A 12-mile territorial sea is acceptable to the major powers if, as will be discussed in greater length, they are assured rights of free transit through international straits. M. AKEHURST, A MODERN INTRODUCTION TO INTERNATIONAL LAW 213 (1970); D. BOWETT, THE LAW OF THE SEA 7 (1967).
The common objectives of ocean action undertaken by coastal states are power, wealth, enlightenment, well-being, respect, skill, solidarity, and rectitude. McDougal & Burke, *Crisis in the Law of the Sea: Community Perspective versus National Egoism,* 67 YALE L.J. 539, 549, 550 (1958). See also,

McDougal, *The Law of the High Sea in Time of Peace,* 25 NAVAL WAR COL-
LEGE REV. 35 (1973).

The usual interests states have in the oceans can be categorized as accessibil-
ity, investment, dependence, and control. Alexander, *Indices of National Interest in the Ocean,* 1 OCEAN DEVELOP. & INT'L L.J. 21, 23 (1973).

Freedom of the seas has been used in two principal ways: 1) as freedom from
the sovereignty of any nation, and 2) as freedom of navigation and trade in
peace and in war. P. CORBETT, LAW IN DIPLOMACY 131-133 (1959). Basically,
freedom of the seas means that "one nation cannot prevent the vessels of others
from going their way." L. HENKIN, HOW NATIONS BEHAVE 22 (1968). See also,
J. M. KENWORTHY & G. YOUNG, FREEDOM OF THE SEA (1928).

4. Henkin, *Politics and the Changing Law of the Sea,* 89 POL. SCI. Q. 46,
47 (1974); See also, P. JESSUP, TRANSNATIONAL LAW 2 *passim* (1956).

5. E. BROWN, PASSAGE THROUGH THE TERRITORIAL SEA: STRAITS USED FOR
INTERNATIONAL NAVIGATION AND ARCHIPELAGOS 141 (1973); HENKIN, HOW NA-
TIONS BEHAVE 84 (1968); Henkin, *International Law and the Behavior of Na-
tions,* 114 RECUEIL DES COURS 171, 192 (1965). See generally, K. HJERTENSSEN,
THE NEW LAW OF THE SEA (1973); W. BURKE, TOWARDS A BETTER USE OF THE
OCEANS (1969); THE SEA: UNITED NATIONS, LEGAL AND POLITICAL ASPECTS — A
SELECT BIBLIOGRAPHY (1974).

Chapter 1

MARITIME JURISDICTION AND THE FREEDOM OF THE SEAS

Shaping the Concept of Free Seas

An understanding of the historical underpinnings of the concept of free seas is important to any complete appreciation of current problems. By reviewing this history we can learn about the early politics of lawmaking and understand how the politics of freedom and the principles of sovereignty have shaped the very concept of freedom of the seas.

Romans were the first to set forth the concept of freedom of the seas as a principle of law. They characterized the sea as *commune omnium*, the common property of all, both as to ownership and use, and they considered it as *usus publicus*, as a public utility. Hence, the Romans viewed the seas as *res nullius* in that they could not belong — in a possessory sense — to any one person or nation. When Rome ruled the Mediterranean, control of—or sovereignty over—the seas was not of especial importance; at least the issue was not seriously contested by other powers.[1]

In the Middle Ages, however, when Venice became a center of commerce and a maritime power, nations began to compete for the use of the seas. Venice's claim of sovereignty over the entire Adriatic Sea was followed by the Republic of Genoa's claim to dominion over the Ligurian Sea. Other Mediterranean states soon adopted policies by which they asserted control over or appropriation of waters in which they were interested. Appropriation was normally effected by force and "legalized," if at all, subsequent to the appropriation.[2] Since the seas were the source of food, navigation, and commerce, control over the seas thus translated into wealth, power, and economic growth, which were the necessary prerequisites of territorial expansion or a means of strengthening the political position of ruling sovereigns. Territorial supremacy then, perhaps more than today, was synonymous with sovereignty.[3] Spain and Portugal were notable among the nations which, supported by authority from the Roman pontiff, made extravagant claims to colonial discoveries in the New World. Britain was equally notable for resisting such claims.[4]

Free Seas: A Politics of Freedom

To study English history—particularly its maritime history—is to study the principle of freedom and its dynamic application. The early politics of freedom—not sovereignty—shaped the English concept of freedom of the seas. Although not as significant today, the politics of freedom still has a definite influence in determining maritime policy.

To provide for a "liberty of fishing," Edward III (1327-1377) entered into the first formal treaty on fishing in 1351 with the king of Castile. Henry IV (1399-1413) followed Edward's practice, and in 1403 he made an agreement with the king of France that was to be the first of many agreements guaranteeing the freedom to fish for herring in the narrow seas between their countries. For nearly two hundred years, in fact into the middle of the sixteenth century, England sought with its neighbors to guarantee freedom of fishing in the waters off its coast. No license was required of nor any tribute levied upon fishermen in the English seas. The freedom to fish at sea was so generally recognized in England during the fifteenth century that the principle could rightly be regarded as a part of English international policy and custom.[5] Scotland, however, did not promote such freedom. As early as the twelfth century, the Scottish kings were making exclusive claims to their coastal waters and the abundant sources of herring they yielded.[6]

North Sea routes and those through the English Channel were important to a good number of European countries. Free navigation through them was of especial importance to Holland, France, and Spain — all of which had significant fishing and commercial interests. The national policy of Britain was to leave its sea boundaries undetermined and thereby to avoid frequent, costly wars over territorial boundaries. Thus, when the British navy was strong and efficient, and suitable occasions arose, any pretensions to maritime sovereignty could be posited and used as an instrument of political force. A vague notion of maritime boundaries also allowed pretensions of ocean sovereignty to lapse quietly when naval strength was inadequate, and thus there was no risk of jeopardizing the "national honour." Tension and exercises of force were thus kept to a minimum.[7]

Elizabeth I (1558-1603) established herself as champion of a national policy of free seas long before Hugo Grotius and his ideas of *mare liberum* became popular. Elizabeth's motives were not directed toward a betterment of mankind. Rather, she was intent on maintaining freedom of trade and fishing for her nation. As noted, Spain and Portugal were threatening these freedoms under various claims to sovereignty over parts of the seas.[8]

It is important to understand that English fisheries, apart from their obvious economic and commercial value, were considered indispensable in maintaining power and security. Indeed, fishermen and their vessels constituted a "considerable part of the naval force available for the defense of the kingdom, for offensive operations and the transport of soldiers."[9]

Yet during the English Reformation, the fisheries began to decay. As long as Englishmen were required by the Church of Rome to observe numerous days of fasting from meat they obeyed. But once this ecclesiastical burden was lifted with the dissolution of the Roman Church in England under Henry VIII (1509–1547), the English preference for meat was reinstated.[10] The phenomenal growth of the Dutch fisheries and commerce also had a pronounced effect on the general decline of the English fisheries. After Holland gained its independence from Spain in 1581, it took immediate and successful steps to make the deep-sea herring fisheries "the chief industry of the country and principal gold mine to its inhabitants."[11]

Political Tensions Arise

The first note of England's jealousy of the fleets of foreign fishing vessels from Zealand and Holland was recorded in 1570, when the Privy Council received a petition requesting that restraints be imposed on these fleets. Unemployment in the English fishing industry at this time was high, and the shipping industry was having difficulty sustaining itself. Elizabeth was unwilling, however, to interfere with the freedom or "liberty" of fishing by foreign nations. Rather, she chose to increase popular consumption of fish through the passage of laws requiring it, and she sought at the same time to restrain the importation of foreign fish. For a time, England considered establishing a National Fishery. None of these efforts, however, succeeded in reviving the fishing industry.[12]

In 1609, James I (1603-1625) exercised sovereignty over the British seas by prohibiting foreign fishermen from fishing in them without first being licensed and paying a tribute. He did this to protect English freedom of the seas from foreign encroachments.[13]

In February 1609, Grotius enunciated a simple thesis: the sea could not be occupied; it was by nature intended to be free to all — *mare liberum*. This was not a new idea. Its attractiveness was found in its appeal "to the sense of justice and conscience of the free peoples of Christendom to whom it was dedicated."[14]

John Selden, upon the request of James, undertook to prepare a response to Grotius entitled, *Mare clausum seu de dominio maris*. This piece was prepared in 1618, but was withheld from publication until 1635. Selden's major thesis was that the sea was not common to all men but, indeed, could be dominated and owned, and that the king of England was the "proprietor" of the surrounding sea "as an inescapable and perpetual appendix of the British Empire."[15]

James I made no assertion of total maritime sovereignty during his reign. Rather, to ensure freedom on the seas he established boundaries of neutrality in the waters off the coast of England. Within the waters of some twenty-six bays surrounding England called "King's Chambers" — the extent of which varied with the geography of the coastline — belligerents were prohibited from engaging in hostile acts. The very establishment of these bays was antagonistic to claims of extensive maritime sovereignty, since they "restricted a most important attribute of such sovereignty to a comparatively narrow space in the adjacent sea, though a space much greater than that now comprised in the so called territorial waters."[16]

James's imposition of a license requirement upon all foreign fishermen on the British seas which he rescinded in 1610 for political reasons, was but an exercise in the politics of freedom. For the English to enjoy the freedom of fishing in English waters, it was necessary — as observed — to restrict all foreigners, particularly the Dutch, from their unrestricted use. English statesmen and economists, alike, saw the Dutch fisheries off their coasts as a menace to their nation's power and wealth.[17]

Charles I (1625–1649), after making countless unsuccessful attempts to strengthen the fisheries (including the establishment of a National Fishery Association), engaged the Dutch in war. Numerous sea encounters followed, and the Dutch established their supremacy of the seas in 1639. They continued to dominate the seas until a decade later, when Oliver Cromwell (1599–1658) reasserted and at last established British sea supremacy.[18]

The closing years of the seventeenth century witnessed a diminution of claims to exclusive sovereignty over extensive sea areas and the emergence of policies determining exact boundaries of ocean control for various special purposes. These claims were normally validated by the execution of international treaties. This emergence of the concept of a territorial sea as a reaction to free seas will be explored more fully later. Interestingly, from about 1689 in England, definite boundaries were specifically determined for fishing.[19]

In the eighteenth century, the British pretensions to ocean sovereignty were — as other similar national claims had been previously — abandoned. It was not until 1817, however, that Selden's theory was officially repudiated by the courts. In that year, Lord Stowell declared in the *Twee Gebroeders* case that all nations "have an equal right to the unappropriated parts of the ocean for their navigation."[20]

The principle that emerged in the eighteenth century and which carried over into the nineteenth and even into the middle of the twentieth century was that the oceans were free and open and could not be appropriated. It was also established, even though never universally agreed, that all states possessed sovereign rights in those parts of the sea that touched their shores. Although the precise extent of these rights was not determined, a three-mile limit was regarded as the most practical extent to which a state could exercise effective control.

Sovereignty

Sovereignty of the sea, although defined differently over the course of history, may commonly be understood as a mastery or supremacy over the seas achieved by force of arms. This sovereignty was, in a strict sense, a "political sovereignty," and its existence was understood as a matter of right comparable to the sovereignty enjoyed by a state on land. At sea as well as on land, the maintenance of sovereignty quite often depended upon an exercise of force or a threat of the use thereof.[21]

Philip Jessup states that sovereignty should be understood as "a freedom to perform governmental acts to the exclusion of all other authority, subject to such limitations as are self imposed or imposed by international law." Thus, in a strict sense, international law is viewed not only as a restriction upon but also as an actual denial of absolute sovereignty.[22] Julius Stone lists as the chief obstacle to the development of the rule of law among nations the intransigence of states that insist on the historical prerogative of sovereignty.[23]

Today, unlimited sovereignty is clearly no longer regarded as a desirable attribute or prized possession. The independence once exhibited by states is increasingly giving way to interdependence and ordered cooperation. Under such circumstances, sovereignty is regarded as fraught with confounding ambiguities, too ideological, and—in a word—terribly overrated. Responsibilities far outweigh rights in the modern view of sovereignty.[24]

and—in a word—terribly overrated. Responsibilities far outweigh rights in the modern view of sovereignty.[24]

The Territorial Imperative

Territorial supremacy is "the nexus around which the distribution of legal competences among states is achieved."[25] Even though the concept of territory is not a dominant factor in foreign policy, every valid foreign policy objective may be thought of as assuming the integrity and inviolability of the national territory. The concept of internal sovereignty is related to territoriality. A nation is master in its own territory only insofar as limited by international law or treaty.[26] And the boundaries of a nation are effective only if respected by other states or territories. Thus, claims made by a state are recognized only to the extent that such claims are firmly established, effective, or are obeyed.[27]

The terms, "territorial seas," "territorial waters," "jurisdictional sea," and "marginal or littoral sea" have been used interchangeably over the years to denote "all waters within three marine miles of low water mark off the coast, including ports and harbors."[28] All of these phrases have normally been regarded as embodying the acceptable legal principles of effective state control of the seas or oceans around it.[29]

The history of the territorial seas presents a rich study of usages, rules, and maxims, none of which can be placed in any established order; some coexist, others clash.[30] What this history shows, however, is the formation of the concept of territorial waters emerging from the political struggles that shaped the principle of free seas. The claim to territorial waters arose as a consequence of the need to determine boundaries for sea fisheries. As already shown, the need to establish these fishing boundaries was essential to maintain a part of the liberty or freedom of the seas that had been historically guaranteed and subsequently to maintain national wealth and power.

In 1625, Grotius published what is believed to be his greatest work — *De jure belli ac pacis.* In it he modified his previous position on freedom of the seas and maintained that the sea could be occupied "by him who is in possession of the land on both sides. . . ." He also advocated what may be understood as a right of transit and of innocent passage through marginal or occupied waters.[31]

Perhaps the most practical approach to the territorial seas was suggested in the early seventeenth century by an Italian, Paolo Sarpi. He stated that reason and justice should determine the extent of the territorial sea, which, he contended, should be made proportionate to the requirements of adjoining states without violating the rights of other people.[32]

In 1702, Cornelis van Bynkershoek restated and popularized the so-called cannon shot rule in his *De dominio maris.* Under this rule, a state was given authority to exercise its jurisdiction over a maritime belt extending seawards from its shore up to the extreme range of a cannon shot — a distance commonly held to be three miles. What Bynkershoek did in his theory was to place all ships lying off the coast and covered by the actual guns of actual ports or fortresses of a territorial sovereign under the *protection* of the sovereign.[33] This theory presented a happy medium for nations which, although unwilling to acknowledge that free and common seas touched their seas, found it impracticable to assert their sovereignty over vast oceans.[34] Interestingly, Thomas Jefferson, as secretary of state in 1793, acknowledged the acceptance by the United States of the three-mile limit of territorial waters.[35]

The Emergence of Coastal State Rights

As the conflicts over ocean sovereignty more or less resolved in the latter part of the seventh century and in the early eighteenth century, the emerging rights of coastal states become more clearly defined. Recognition of the new principle of freedom of the seas, as it came forward in the nineteenth century, was met at once with a new demand for its modification. Coastal states asserted their rights to protect their own territory and citizens from "attack, invasion, interference and injury."[36] Health and commerce also had to be protected. The extent to which the coastal state furnished this protection was determined by the extent of the state's *power to control* the areas of concern.

Under a variety of labels, such as "contiguous zone," "customs area," "defensive area," "conservation zone," and "zone of neutrality," states exercised an acknowledged competence to declare the existence of these zones and to function within them. Some states chose to claim these zones as extensions of their territorial waters. Others merely sought to safeguard certain special rights over parts of the seas through them.[37]

The contiguous zones are traditionally imposed today and similarly recognized for safeguarding sanitary regulations, protecting a state's fiscal or revenue programs, and more especially for preventing smuggling activities. The width of the zones varies.[38] Their creation does not extend the state's territorial sovereignty, for the waters within the zones remain part of the high seas.[39] Customary international law dictates that the acts of the coastal states within the zones are always to be of a reasonable nature.[40]

A Modern Application of the Contiguous Zone

Based on the contiguous zone theory, an Act to Amend the Territorial Seas and Fishing Zones Act was passed into law in Canada in 1970.[41] By this law, Canada proclaimed its right to exercise jurisdiction over the seas contiguous to but outside its territorial waters for one hundred miles for purposes of controlling pollution on the high seas. The

Canadians claimed they took this action as an execution of the right of a coastal state to defend itself against serious threats to its environment.[42] Accepted and developed by other less responsible states, a one-hundred-mile contiguous zone for pollution could become a signal for the creation of other contiguous zones to meet any imaginable purpose. The Canadian experiment here, without more, is a significant step in eroding the principle of freedom of the seas.

Justification for the Canadian action was also tied to what Canada believed to be its responsibility as a coastal state to the international community in general; a responsibility to prohibit ships from using the seas in a way violative of reasonable standards. What is seen, then, is a reliance upon the *principle of custodianship* by the coastal state. But "until there exists detailed internationally agreed regulations to which it can be harnessed and which could also have the effect of bringing flag jurisdiction and coastal state jurisdiction into double harness instead of having them pull in different directions," the concept of custodianship will mean little or nothing.[43]

Britain's Continuing Fishing Crisis

"The British fishing industry is today struggling for survival. Only two years ago it was enjoying an unprecedented boom."[44] These words were written neither in the late 1500s nor in the early 1600s; they were written in 1975. This crisis has been precipitated as a consequence of the development of two situations. First, the American markets have taken less fish from Iceland and Norway and more from Canada. The fish that normally would go to America is now flowing into Britain, depressing the market, and thus lowering fish prices. Second, fuel costs remain unchecked, and wages and dock charges continue to rise. In the present era of inflation, twenty percent of total costs are now tied to expenditures for fuel.[45]

The predominant fear of the British trawling associations is that the British fishing industry will not be able to sustain itself if the government does not place stronger curbs on fish imports and enforce a two-hundred-mile fishing zone. Both Norway and Iceland are planning to establish fishing zones of this dimension. When they do, fishing vessels that would normally use the waters of these two countries for fishing will be diverted to relatively "free" waters surrounding Britain. Under the 1964 Fisheries Conference Convention, England declared an exclusive fishing zone of from six to twelve miles.[46]

The important point today is that England is being forced to preserve and protect its original freedom or "liberty" of the seas to fish as a consequence of world economic pressures. The politics of freedom is the focal point today as it was in 1351, when Edward III signed the first treaty with the king of Castile for assurance of free fishing rights on the seas. No pretensions of ocean sovereignty are involved.

CHAPTER 1—NOTES

1. E. JONES, LAW OF THE SEA 6 (1972); S. SWARTZTRAUBER, THE THREE MILE LIMIT OF TERRITORIAL SEA 10, 11 (1972); P. POTTER, THE FREEDOM OF THE SEAS IN HISTORY, LAW AND POLITICS, chs. 11, 12 (1924); C. MEURER, THE PROGRAM OF THE FREEDOM OF THE SEA 6, 107 (1919); P. FENN, JR., THE ORIGIN OF THE RIGHT OF FISHERY IN INTERNATIONAL LAW 23 (1926); Smith, *Apostrophe to a Troubled Ocean*, IND. L. REV. 267, 271 (1972). See generally, J. REDDIE, AN HISTORICAL VIEW OF THE LAW OF COMMERCE (1841).

The sea laws of the Rhodians and their general philosophical view of the seas heavily influenced the Roman law. A. SCHOMBERG, A TREATISE ON THE MARITIME LAWS OF RHODES 7, 19, 38 (1766). See also, THE RHODIAN SEA LAW (W. Ashburner, ed. 1909).

2. JONES, *supra* note 1; T. FULTON, THE SOVEREIGNTY OF THE SEA 3 (1911).

3. W. COPLIN, THE FUNCTION OF INTERNATIONAL LAW 37 (1966).

4. Pope Nicholas V, in his bull *Romanus Pontifex* issued in 1455, gave Portugal an exclusive right to African lands from Cueta to Guinea. Pope Alexander VI, by a series of bulls beginning on May 3, 1493, with *Inter Caetera*, in essence assigned all future lands discovered thenceforth in the New World to Spain. Portugal disputed these grants and because of numerous conflicts promoted the Treaty of Tordesillas, which was signed in 1494. Under its pro-

visions, a more equitable division of New World territories was effected. SWARTZTRAUBER, *supra* note 1. See also, C. COLOMBOS, THE INTERNATIONAL LAW OF THE SEA 48 *passim* (6th rev. ed. 1967); C. FENWICK, INTERNATIONAL LAW. 22 (4th ed. 1965).

5. Fulton, *supra* note 2, at 67 *passim*.

6. Scotland, because of its geography, favored little agricultural development, and therefore herring were of greater *relative* importance there than in England. England possessed many rich agricultural assets and was basically considered an agricultural economy. *Id.* at 76.

7. *Id.* at 20, 105. Because of the numerous uncertainties introduced into the flow of commerce as a consequence of warfare, wars were avoided whenever possible. It was believed more profitable to obtain "security for one's own trade than to rely upon the destruction of the trade of others." P. JESSUP & F. DEAK, 1 NEUTRALITY; ITS HISTORY, ECONOMICS AND LAW 10, 11 (1935). The authors note that economic needs led to the development of new legal rules. A compilation of Mediterranean sea law, *Consolato del mare,* was published in 1494. The earliest full statement of neutral maritime rights is found in this work. Interestingly, the development and acknowledgment of the legal rights of neutral commerce was merely one phase in the development of the whole law merchant; *Ibid.* See generally, T. A. CLINGAN, JR. & L.M. ALEXANDER, HAZARDS OF MARITIME TRANSIT (1973); McDougal, *Law and Power,* 46 AM. J. INT'L L. 102 (1952).

8. FULTON, *supra* note 2, at 86 *passim*. See also, supra note 4. For the same reasons, Denmark emerged as a threat to England under Elizabeth's reign. See generally, D. JOHNSTON, THE INTERNATIONAL LAW OF FISHERIES (1965).

9. FULTON, *supra* note 2, at 58, 86. Fish was consumed equally — or in excess in some ports of the realm — with beef, mutton, or pork. Fish was used as a staple in feeding the armed forces and as a meat substitute in winter. The marketing of it was unusually efficient. *Id.* at 58.

10. *Id.* 87. In 1548, Parliament passed an Act for Abstinence from Flesh and sought to impose fines on those who did not observe certain "Fast" days along the same nature as those required by the Roman Church, when it was recognized in England. The English people were directed to eat fish 153 days a year. This "political lent" was largely a failure. *Id.* at 89.

11. *Id.*

12. *Id.* at 87, 95, 115.

13. *Id.* 116. Lapidoth, *Freedom of Navigation—Its Legal History and Its Normative Basis,* 6 J. MARITIME L. & COMM. 259, 265 (1975).

14. FULTON, *supra* note 2, at 341, 342. Fulton notes that Grotius drew heavily upon the ideas of the writings of a mid-16th-century Spanish monk, Francis Alphonso de Castro. Ferdinand Vasquez's ideas also assisted Grotius in formulating his *Mare liberum.*

Grotius wrote *De jure praedae* — of which ch. 12 was subsequently published as *Mare liberum* — under pay by the Dutch to prove, primarily to the Portugese, the Dutch right, to engage in trade in the East Indies. The month following the publication of *Mare liberum,* the Treaty of Antwerp, which recognized this Dutch trading right was signed.

Jurists and commentators, largely regarded Grotius's views in *Mare liberum* as minority ones until the early 18th century. Many commentators responded negatively to *Mare liberum.* John Selden, Sir John Burroughs, William Welwood, Alberico Gentili, and Paolo Sarpi were among the principal writers who opposed Grotius's thesis. FENWICK, *supra* note 4, at 498.

15. The work was not publicly released by the king because of what he considered the offensive tone of several passages regarding his "friend" the Danish king. O'Connell, *The Juridical Nature of the Territorial Sea*, 45 Brit. Y. B. Int'l L. 303, 305 *passim* (1971). O'Connell asserts that only one theory of the nature of the territorial sea was predominant until the middle of the 19th century; that theory was that the governance of coastal waters depended upon coastal states having property in the sea. He skillfully discusses other theories used from time to time — police, competence, servitude, and sovereignty.

16. Fulton, *supra* note 2, at 118-120.

17. Sir Walter Raleigh observed that "whosoever commands the sea commands the trade; whosoever commands the trade of the world commands the riches of the world, and consequently the world itself." *Id.* at 136.

In 1620, John Keymer wrote that about 3,000, Dutch ships and 50,000 Dutchmen were employed in fishing off the English, Scottish, and Irish coasts. It is believed these figures are somewhat exaggerated. *Id.* at 127.

18. *Id.* at 246-337.

19. *Id.* at 523, 524.

20. *Id.* at 537. P. Jessup, The Law of Territorial Waters and Maritime Jurisdiction 4 (1927) [hereinafter cited as Jessup, Law of Territorial Waters].

21. Fulton, *supra* note 2, at 2., Sovereignty exercised over territorial waters is distinct from the jurisdiction that many states exercise for various purposes over a zone of waters outside the territorial zone, the contiguous, or adjacent zone. Sovereignty implies jurisdiction, but jurisdiction does not automatically imply sovereignty. J. Vanderlee, Divergencies in International Law with Special Reference to the Law of Territorial Waters 6 (1951).

22. Jessup, Law of Territorial Waters xxiv, n. 6.

23. J. Stone, Of Law and Nations 445 (1974).

24. P. Jessup, A Modern Law of Nations 2 (1948); G. Schwarzenberger, International Law and Order 57 (1971). See generally, H. Lauterpacht, The Development of International Law by the International Court 297 *passim* (1958), for a discussion of the recognition of sovereignty and of the restraints placed upon it.

25. W. Coplin, The Function of International Law 30, 31 (1966). See also, Lauterpacht, *supra* note 24, chs. 25, 26; R. Jennings, The Acquisition of Territory in International Law, chs. 1, 4, 5 (1963). For a discussion of Lauterpacht-Kelsen views regarding the concept of territorial waters, see Lauterpacht, *Review*, 29 Brit. Y.B. Int'l L. 509 (1952).

26. L. Henkin, How Nations Behave 18 (1968).

27. H. Kelsen, Principles of International Law 213 (1952). See also, J. Fawcett, The Law of Nations, ch 5 (2d ed. 1968).

28. Jessup, Law of Territorial Waters xxvii.

[29]. J. Moore, 1 Digest of International Law 698 *passim* (1906); 2 *id.* 886 *passim*; Coplin, *supra* note 25 at 35.

30. J. Oudendijk, Status and Extent of Adjacent Waters: An Historical Orientation 10 (1970).

31. Fulton, *supra* note 2, at 348.

32. *Id.* at 547. Sarpi elaborated his point by observing that a country or city possessing large and fertile territories that provided adequate subsistence for the inhabitants would have little need of the fisheries in the neighboring sea, whereas one with small territories that drew a large part of its subsistence from the sea ought to have a much greater extent of the sea for its exclusive zone. *Id.*

33. Walker, *Territorial Waters: The Cannon Shot Rule*, 22 Brit. Y.B. Int'l L. 210, 212 (1915).

34. JESSUP, LAW OF TERRITORIAL WATERS 7.

35. *Id.* at 6. Puffendorf maintained in his *Law of Nature and Nations* published in 1672 that dominion over narrow seas belongs to the sovereign of the surrounding land, and if there are several sovereigns, they divide dominion among them. O'Connell, *supra* note 15.

In 1758, Vattel, in his *Droit des gens,* repeated Grotius's argument on freedom of the sea and added that natural law gave no man a right to appropriate inexhaustible and useful sea waters. FENWICK, *supra* note 4.

The net result of the Grotius-Selden controversy was, eventually, a universal response of acceptance both of the principle of freedom of the seas realized as such, through *res communis,* and the balancing principle under which littoral state territorial waters were protected. P. JESSUP, THE USE OF INTERNATIONAL LAW 14 (1954). See also, JOHNSTON, *supra* note 8, at 307 for his conclusions regarding the Grotius-Selden debates and their basis in maritime political ambition.

36. JESSUP, LAW OF TERRITORIAL WATERS 5; FULTON, *supra* note 2, at 549.

The Permanent Court of Arbitration in the North Atlantic Coast Fisheries Arbitration in 1910 acknowledged that the marginal strip of territorial waters, based originally on the cannon shot, was founded on the necessity of the riparian state to protect itself from outward attack; this strip of water provided something in the nature of an insulating zone. 11 U.N. *Reports of the Int'l Arbitral Awards* 167 at 205.

In Church v. Hubbard (2 Cranch 187 (1804), Chief Justice John Marshall declared that a nation's power to secure itself from injury might certainly be exercised in the marginal seas beyond the limits of the territorial waters. See Dickinson, *Jurisdiction at the Maritime Frontier,* 40 HARV. L. REV. 1 (1926).

37. W. MASTERSON, JURISDICTION IN MARGINAL SEAS 377 *passim* (1929).

38. Address by W. Bishop, "The Exercise of Jurisdiction for Special Purposes in High Seas Areas beyond the Outer Limits of Territorial Waters," Inter-American Bar Association Conference, Detroit, Mich. (1949), pp. 3, 4, 5. Bishop notes that various liquor treaties concluded with the United States during the prohibition years (1924-1930) allowed the United States government the right to control and prevent the smuggling of liquor in foreign vessels within one-hour's sailing distance from shore. In 1935, the United States Anti-Smuggling Act (49 Stat. 517) allowed the federal government to enforce its customs laws against the vessels of those countries having no liquor treaties with it to the extent of 62 nautical miles from shore.

Upon the outbreak of World War II, the American republics signed the Declaration of Panama wherein they declared that their status of neutrality extended to several hundred miles off their shores. Bishop, *supra.*

Hovering laws existed not only in the United States but also in England. They found justification in the "Theory of interest" which in essence, declared that the state must exercise jurisdiction in adjacent coastal waters in order to protect its various interests — one being revenue sources. Thus, prevention of illicit trade from the sea was the objective. Such laws had no application to vessels engaged in lawful enterprise. MASTERSON, *supra* note 37, at 380. See also, Henkin, *Changing Law for the Changing Seas, in* USES OF THE SEAS 69, 73 (E.Gullion, ed. 1968).

39. Bishop, *supra* note 38, at 2; MASTERSON, *supra* note 37, at 377. One authority has suggested that the nature of coastal state rights in adjacent waters cannot be properly evaluated or determined within the concept of sovereignty. He asserts these rights differ from country to country depending upon the state

of constitutional law. O'Connell, *supra* note 15. See also, JESSUP, LAW OF TERRITORIAL WATERS 82.

40. JESSUP, *supra* note 39, at 95 and ch. 2; M. McDOUGAL & W. BURKE, THE PUBLIC ORDER OF THE OCEANS, ch. 6 (1962); M. WHITEMAN, 4 DIGEST OF INTERNATIONAL LAW 480-498 (1965).

41. 18 & 19 Eliz. 2 C. 47 (Can.).

42. Bilder, *The Canadian Arctic Water Pollution Prevention Act: New Stresses on the Law of the Sea*, 69 MICH. L. REV. 1, 12 (1970); Morin, *The Quiet Revolution: Canadian Approaches to the Law of the Sea*, in THE CHANGING LAW OF THE SEA (R. Zacklin, ed. 1974); Green, *Canada's Jurisdiction over the Arctic and the Littoral Sea*, in LIMITS TO NATIONAL JURISDICTION OVER THE SEA 207 (G. Yates, J. Young, eds. 1974). See generally, Kiselev, *The Freedom of Navigation and the Problem of Pollution of the Marine Environment*, 6 GA. J. INT'L & COMP. LAW 93 (1976); Johnston, *Facts and Value in the Prevention and Control of Marine Pollution*, in TOWARDS WORLD ORDER AND HUMAN DIGNITY: ESSAYS IN HONOR OF MYRES S. McDOUGAL, ch 14 (W. M. Reisman, B. H. Weston, eds. 1976.)

43. Jennings, *A Changing International Law of the Sea*, 31 CAMB. L.J. 32, 48 (1972). Bilder, *supra* note 42, at 30. See generally, Pharand, *Innocent Passage in the Arctic*, 6 CAN. Y.B. INT'L L. 3 (1968).

44. Burton, *Crisis in the Fishing Industry*, 263 ILLUSTRATED LONDON NEWS 31 (Aug. 1975).

45. *Ibid.*

46. JOHNSTON, *supra* note 8, at 189.

Interestingly, in the Soviet Union there is no international rule concerning the breadth of the contiguous zone. The government acknowledges that in meeting its responsibility to regulate navigation it may establish zones or areas in which foreigners are prohibited from navigating or fishing — among other activities — in Soviet territorial waters. W. BUTLER, THE SOVIET UNION AND THE LAW OF THE SEA 76 (1971).

In the fall of 1975, Iceland announced that it was establishing a 200-mile fishing limit and prohibiting all foreigners from fishing inside it. In the past, there had been a 50-mile fishing limit. Norway also indicated it would follow Iceland's move. Miller, *200 Mile Limit by Iceland*, Daily Telegraph (London), July 16, 1975, p. 1. See also, Petty, *Collapsing Fish Industry Seeks 200 Mile Limit, id.*, p. 6; *Iceland Breaks Relations With Britain Over Fishing*, New York Times, Feb. 20, 1976, §C, p. 3, cols. 7-8.

In June 1976, Britain signed a conditional 6-month agreement with Iceland wherein it agreed to send no more than 24 fishing trawlers per day into Iceland's 200-mile zone, to respect certain specific areas as fish conservation areas, and to permit Icelandic patrol vessels to halt and inspect British trawlers suspected of violating the agreement. Basically, under the agreement the British fishermen are limited to taking about 30,000 tons of cod annually from the disputed area compared with 130,000 tons last year. Some 1,500 British seamen and 7,500 shore workers may eventually lose their jobs because of the reduced cod catch. Britain was pressured into taking this action principally by the United States, because Iceland threatened to resign from the North Atlantic Treaty Organization (NATO) unless Britain acquiesced in some type of agreement. Time, June 14, 1976, p. 37. Interestingly, on Oct. 30, 1976, the foreign ministers of the European Economic Community (EEC) agreed that member states should extend their fishing limits in the North Atlantic and North Sea to 200 miles as of Jan. 1, 1977. FACTEL, Br. Info. Services, No. 669, Dec. 1976, *Classification* 5 (d)/7(c).

In Jan. 1977, Iceland was banned from Britain's new 200-mile fishing zone in force around its shores. A number of members of the Common Market have asserted that it is for the members — not for Britain — to decide on regulations governing fishing in what is the Common Market community's 200-mile limit. This ban on Icelandic fishing affected at the most but a dozen Icelandic trawlers. It was intended to last until the Reykjavik government announced the number of British trawlers it was prepared to readmit while a long term agreement was negotiated with the EEC. Recently, the British issued a denial that a secret agreement had been reached concerning the EEC's common fishing policy. Times (London), May 16, 1978, p. 16, col. 3.

Today, an *impasse* still exists between Iceland and Britain concerning fishing rights. No British fishing vessels are in Icelandic waters, and the British ban on Icelandic vessels is still in existence. Basically, what is happening is that Britain has "given up" on reaching a specific accord with Iceland and is instead trying to work out long-term fishing agreements with the EEC. This, too, is proving to be fraught with hazards. Telephone conversation between author and Ian Soutar, British Embassy, Jan. 23. 1979, Washington, D.C. See generally, Koers, *Participation of the European Economic Community in a New Law of the Sea Convention*, 73 Am. J. Int'l L. 426 (1979).

Every EEC country is — under the equal process or provisions of the common fishery policy — allowed to continue fishing in the 200-mile zone. Norway, the Faroes, Finland, East Germany, Poland, Portugal, Spain, Sweden, and the Soviet Union will be allowed to fish in Britain's zone for several months in order that the EEC can negotiate with them on future reciprocal arrangements. More specifically, as regards the internal regime of the EEC waters, under arrangements of the present Common Fisheries Policy, all member countries may restrict fishing in areas up to 6 miles off their coasts to vessels traditionally fishing these waters (Art. 100 of the Treaty Concerning Accession under which Britain acceded to the EEC, Cmnd. 5179, Jan. 1973). In addition, the rights of other member states to fish within Britain's 6-to 12-mile belt are limited — quite broadly — along the lines of the arrangements that existed before Britain's accession to the EEC (Art. 101). Britain, as might be expected, has indicated its refusal to be ultimately satisfied with 12-mile coastal bands. FACTEL, Br. Info. Services, *supra*.

Britain's biggest problem with its new fishing zone is the enforcement of the prohibition against fishing within it. Only frigates are able to catch any of the marauders who violate the prohibition; the Royal Navy has very few such vessels to reassign from national defense purposes to patrol of the fishing zone. Palmer, *Britain Hits Iceland with Fishing Ban*, Guardian (London), Dec. 30, 1976, p. 2, col. 5. Steers, *Communist Trawlers Beat 200-Mile Limit*, Sunday Telegraph (London), Jan. 2, 1977, p. 1, col. 7.

In an effort to preserve dwindling stocks of herring, the Brussels Commission proposed a total ban on herring fishing in the North Sea for 18 months. Osborn, *Herring Bans Supported*, Daily Telegraph, July 15, 1977, p. 4, col. 2.

John Silkin, British minister of agriculture, recently attacked the EEC for wishing to keep British fish stocks open to their fishermen as long as the fish lasted without giving any interest to preserving fishing industries for the future or to observing a common fisheries policy. This attack was prompted because of a move by the EEC to lessen protection of British fishing waters. Silkin charged that the present EEC fisheries policy was hastily devised in 1970 to benefit Germany, France, and the Netherlands at the expense of Britain and Norway. Svend Jacobson, the Danish minister, called upon the EEC to take Britain to the International Court of Justice if it followed through with plans to widen the area covered by the ban on Norway pout fishing off the coast of Scotland. Brian Lenihan, Irish fisheries minister, said Irish vessels would ignore the ban on herring fishing in the British sector of the Irish Sea, and he warned the British authorities not to harass Irish fishermen. Michael Hornsby, *Mr. Silkin Attacks EEC Attitudes on Fisheries,* Times Sept. 26, 1978, p. 6, col. 8.

International negotiations are presently underway in an effort to study and develop ways to protect against the over-exploitation of fish in Antarctica. Some estimates suggest that the potential yield from harvesting shrimp-like creatures called krill, which are found in great abundance in Antarctica, may exceed the current annual catch around the world. Krill is the staple diet of a wide range of Antarctic animals — penguins, seals, and whales. There is a growing realization that without some type of conservation agreement unregulated commercial harvesting of the krill could deplete this as a source of food for the marine mammals and destroy the entire ecological balance of the area. Rulless, *Fishing Parley in Canberra Soon: Environment Groups Seek Stiff Antarctic Rules,* Washington Post (D.C.), Feb. 7, 1978, § A, p. 5, col. 1. See also, Sullivan, *13 Nations Support a Curb on Krill Fishing in Antarctica,* New York Times, Mar. 24, 1978, § A, p. 8, col. 1, where a report of a draft document designed to set annual catch quotas — possibly to take effect at the end of the year — is discussed. This report is a survey of the Canberra Fishing Parley. See generally, Note, *Thaw in International Law? Rights in Antarctica under the Law of Common Spaces,* 87 YALE L.J. 804 (1978).

Chapter 2

THE CONCEPT OF
INNOCENT PASSAGE
IN INTERNATIONAL LAW

Early Attempts to Balance Competing Interests

In 1894, the Institute of International Law posited rules, one of which allowed states to regulate the passage of ships through their territorial or marginal seas primarily with the view of protecting or, if necessary, defending the territorial interests of the coastal sovereign.[1]

The 1930 Hague Conference for Codification of International Law sponsored by the League of Nations made a careful study of the marginal sea and the various extents thereof. No agreement was reached, however, on the breadth of the marginal sea; nor were there any successes recorded to efforts designed to draw a convention that would reflect what the present law was commonly understood as prescribing.[2] Nonetheless, a dialogue had been initiated among the members of the international community, and the task of continuing it fell to the International Law Commission of the United Nations subsequent to the establishment of the United Nations in 1945. The Commission issued its final report on July 4, 1956, which served as a blueprint for action at the 1958 Geneva Law of the Sea Conference sponsored by the United Nations.[3]

New Sea Law Directions
before the 1958 Convention

Thirteen years before the 1958 Geneva Conference, new directions in the law of the sea began to emerge. With President Harry Truman's Proclamation on the Natural Resources of the Subsoil and Sea Bed of the Continental Shelf in 1945, the United States sought to stake out a claim to ocean resources.[4] Many small, weaker states endeavored to assert similar interests, resulting in coastal states undertaking expansion more and more as an element of economic self-determination.[5] Such an expansion obviously runs afoul of freedom of navigation on the sea, historic fishing claims, and the principle of common heritage stressed under the international rubric of "free use" by the world community itself.

The First Conference

The First United Nations Law of the Sea Conference held at Geneva lasted from February 24 through April 27, 1958, attracted seven hundred delegates from eighty-six countries, and produced four conventions, nine resolutions, and an optional protocol.[6] Of importance to this discussion is the fact that the requisite twenty-two states necessary for ratification of the Convention on the Territorial Sea and the Contiguous Zone gave their assent, and the treaty came into effect on September 10, 1964.[7]

Although declared a "successful conference" by one

optimistic authority,[8] the conference failed to act effectively on the most crucial aspect — defining the territorial seas — even though such seas were generally acknowledged to be no greater than twelve miles.[9] What emerged, then, from the Conference was a reaffirmation of essentially traditional law. Since many states realized their rights were untouched by the various conventions, they refrained from adhering to them, although by doing so they did not necessarily reject them.[10] In 1960 the Second United Nations Law of the Sea Conference was called for the sole purpose of defining the territorial sea. It failed to accomplish this purpose.[11]

Codifying Freedom of the Seas in the 1958 High Seas Convention

A half century ago the classic dispute between appropriated seas and free, open seas appeared to have been resolved. Under a form of dualism, the coastal state was acknowledged as having sovereignty over a belt of waters, denominated "territorial water," subject to the right of innocent passage. The high seas beyond these territorial waters were recognized as *res communis*; thus they were not subject to acquisition by title or extension of asserted coastal state subject to acquisition by title or extension of asserted coastal state sovereignty. Rather, they were subject to an international regime structured in terms of "freedom" to be enjoyed by the flags of all nations. These freedoms were, subsequently codified in the 1958 Geneva High Seas Convention.[12] Article 2 of the convention provides:

> *The High Seas being open to all nations, no State may validly purport to subject any part of them to its sovereignty.* Freedom of the high seas is exercised under the conditions laid down by these articles *and* by the *other rules of international law.* It comprises, inter alia, *both for the coastal and non coastal states:*

1. Freedom of Navigation.
2. Freedom of Fishing.
3. Freedom to lay submarine cables and pipelines.
4. Freedom to fly over the high seas.

> These freedoms, and others which are recognized by the general principles of international law, shall be exercised by all States with *reasonable regard* to the interests of other States in their exercise of the freedom of the high seas.[13]

The influence of the politics of freedom is obvious in this article. The particular problem of a legal system which is defined in terms of "freedoms" is that it is not "transformed into a system of government and regulations of the kind needed to find long term, adequate solutions to the law of the sea problems."[14]

What might at first have appeared to be a total triumph for the principle of free seas was actually not such a triumph. As will be seen, the extension of coastal state sovereignty over the seas was assured and even given impetus as a result of the 1958 Geneva Conferences. But the Territorial Sea Convention and the High Seas Convention did not, as originally hoped, achieve a balance between interests.

Political Interest Groups at the 1958 Conference

Four interest groups were loosely indentifiable among the states at the 1958 Geneva Conference: seafaring states, security-conscious states, sedentary-fishing states, and what might be termed specific-interest states.[15]

Most of the Western European states, such as Britain, the Netherlands, and English-speaking members of the British Commonwealth, composed the first group. The United States identified with this interest group but shifted on occasion to the security-conscious group. This group endeavored to gain in their negotiations the most unlimited right of innocent passage as possible. They sought objective criteria for determining questions that arose over the innocence or noninnocence of passage, a right of innocent passage for warships, and a right of free transit through international straits. They also endeavored to restrict both the civil and the criminal jurisdiction of the coastal state.

Within the second group were most of the security-conscious Afro-Asian states, such as India, Indonesia, and the Arab states, and the members of the Soviet bloc. The Arab states quite often shifted from this group to the specific-interest group with comparative ease. For those states in this second group coastal state security needs were of greater concern and importance than expansion of the right of innocent passage. They were opposed to innocent passage for warships, advocated the use of subjective criteria in determining innocence of passage, and did not favor the recognition of a right of free transit through international straits.

The Latin American states largely comprised the third interest group, which was primarily concerned with protecting and expanding the sedentary fishing grounds adjoining their coastlines. They too advocated that subjective criteria be used to determine whether a passage was innocent or noninnocent. Their particular concern was that fishing vessels would take advantage of the coastal states by continuing to fish during passage through their territorial waters. Consequently, the coastal states within this group strongly favored the imposition of rules and regulations designed to safeguard their econmic interests in their territorial waters. They had no uniform policy regarding innocent passage for warships or their free transit through state territorial waters.

The fourth group, the specific-interest states, was composed of Israel and the Arab states. Israel sought recognition of a right of access to Elath through the Straits of Tiran. The Arabs fought to deny this recognition and sought support from the security-conscious states. "It was a struggle to gain a political solution within a context of law codification."[16] The votes on this issue were not only expressions of a position on the principle of freedom of the seas but also indications of a political attitude over the Arab-Israeli conflict. Article 16 (4) of the 1958 Territorial Sea Convention was specifically designed to resolve, among other matters, situations like this. It provides that there "be no suspension of the innocent passage of foreign ships through straits that are used for international navigation between one part of the high seas and another part of the high seas or the territorial sea of a foreign state." Regrettably, it has not resolved the conflict.

A careful reading of the Record of the Conference — especially the plenary sessions — discloses that innocent passage as an internationally accepted principle and right was never really in issue at the 1958 Law of the Sea Conference. What was in contention, however, was the relative weight to be given under particular circumstances to coastal state sovereignty and to the right of freedom of navigation. The outcome, as observed, although perhaps not fully appreciated at the time, was to accord to the coastal states new rights of expanded sovereignty and to erode the very principle of freedom of the seas. Article 1 of the 1958 High Seas Convention may be thought of as the hallmark of the plan to extend coastal state legal powers, for it defined the high seas as all the parts of the seas that were "not included in the territorial sea or in the internal waters of a state." Stated otherwise, the seaward progression of coastal state jurisdiction started with the unhinging of "the frontier between the zone of exclusive national jurisdiction and sovereignty and the part of the sea which is *res communis.*"[17]

The vast and often highly exaggerated coastal state expansions being undertaken might well appear to place the Selden thesis in the forefront of ocean diplomacy today.[18]

Regrettably, neither the theories of Selden nor Grotius comes to grips with the "basic revolution in man's spatial relationship to the oceans."[19] The "egoism of the poor" emerging nations combines with their jealousies and distrust of the established members of the world community to frame the modern saga of freedom of the seas. As its central task at this moment, the international community faces the need to find a means of curtailing the seemingly restricted use of the oceans and national sovereignty over parts of it.[20]

Reconciling the various conflicts, which began in 1945 and were not satisfactorily resolved in 1958, is a herculean undertaking. There have been many disturbing losses and few total victories in the attempt to find a new, appropriate balance. Indeed, there has of late been more take and less give in ocean diplomacy than in most other current international problem areas. The politics of freedom is one born of force and sporadic tension; it reacts strongly against limitations. Under a solidarity not normally seen among smaller (and some underdeveloped) states, territorial sovereignty over the seas is vigorously asserted as a counterforce to the politics of ocean freedom.

Innocent Passage

Striking a Reasonable Balance

As has been made apparent thus far, an analysis of innocent passage as a right and as a legal principle is tied in essence to an analysis of the extent of coastal state authority over access to the territorial sea. Innocent passage is firmly established in international law and needs little supporting argument for its justification. It owes its existence to the need to maintain freedom of navigation on the oceans thereby to promote commerce. It is also the result of an effort to allow the coastal or littoral state a right to pursue policies of territorial sovereignty.[21] The term itself—"innocent passage"—not only describes the nature but also the limitations of the right. It is, in the first instance, a right of passage or right to use the waters as a highway between two points outside them. Second, the passage of the vessel in question must be *innocent*. That is to say, the vessel is allowed to exercise the right only as long as it respects the coastal state regulations regarding navigation, pilotage, safety, and other matters of local coastal state concern associated with maritime navigation. Nothing may be done that would disturb or threaten the tranquility of the coastal state.[22]

To test state standards regarded as excessive abridgments of the right of innocent passage, the general criterion of reasonableness is applied. When conflict arises over the validity of state standards, an attempt is made to strike a balance between promoting international needs for unrestricted and unburdened navigation and protecting the sovereign integrity of coastal states. It is fair to suggest that such a balance should accord to the coastal state a fair amount of discretion in determining the scope of protection necessary to assure its security. Yet, the state should not be allowed to act with whimsy or caprice. If challenged on its determination that the passage of a particular vessel through its territorial waters would not be innocent, the state should be required to show that the interest it seeks to protect is important and the substance real, that the passage of the vessel in question would present a substantial risk to or abridgment of that interest, or that a reasonable expectation exists that harm would be inflicted upon the coastal state if passage were not prohibited.[23]

Problems in Application

General Scope

The right of innocent passage applies to ships not aircraft. Aircraft may of course, upon consent, enter the airspace above a coastal state's territorial sea. The coastal state is thus recognized as having exclusive sovereignty over the airspace above its territorial sea. Regimes of flight for the accommodation of foreign aircraft in this space are often established, thus ensuring the protection of the sovereign interests of the coastal state and promoting air commerce. There has been considerable academic discussion over the issue of whether rights of innocent passage over straits for civil and military aircraft are recognized in international law. One view is that in the absence of treaty stipulations to the contrary no right of passage exists in the air above the territorial waters of international straits.[24] However, international law recognizes a right of passage for civil and military aircraft in the superadjacent air over international straits.[25] Practices within individual coastal state airspace are usually prescribed by treaty—bilateral or limited-multilateral. Treaties of this nature are enforced widely, and thus largely resolve conflicts that might otherwise occur.[26]

Article 14 of the 1958 Territorial Sea Convention clearly provides that the rights of innocent passage extend to "ships of all States," so long as the passage is innocent and does not prejudice "the peace, good order or security of the coastal State." The coastal state is accordingly allowed considerable latitude in determining the innocence or noninnocence of a particular passage. Even though no act has been committed against a coastal state's peace, good order, or security, this standard allows a state to classify, for example, passage of an oil tanker or nuclear-powered vessel as being *ipso facto* prejudicial to the state's security and therefore noninnocent. What is lacking here are objective criteria for determining what acts by a vessel will jeopardize its right of innocent passage.[27]

Foreign fishing vessels are allowed innocent passage as long as they obey all coastal state laws and regulations that are normally designed to prevent fishing during the passage.[28] Submarines must navigate on the surface and show their flag.[29] Merchant ships may not be hindered in their use of innocent passage by being assessed or charged fees for that passage. Charges may be levied only for specific services rendered to the ships.[30] Government ships that are being operated for commercial purposes are also protected by provisions of the convention.[31]

Warships

Some commentators maintain that warships have no unlimited right of innocent passage through territorial waters under the Territorial Sea Convention.[32] Others assert warships do have such a right.[33] The decision in the *Corfu Channel* case by the International Court of Justice in 1949 held that in time of peace the right does exist for warships to pass through straits. The court specifically held:

> It is . . . generally recognized and in accordance with international custom that States in time of peace have a right to send their warships through straits used for international navigation between two parts of the high seas without the previous authorization of a coastal State, provided the passage is innocent. Unless otherwise prescribed in an international convention, there is no right for a coastal State to prohibit such passage through straits in time of peace.[34]

Subsection A of Section III of the 1958 Territorial Sea Convention includes a general declaration of a right to innocent passage. The subsection is entitled, "All Ships," which would presumably include warships. Subsection C deals with different types of government ships, which are made subject to the general right of innocent passage by *specific reference*. Subsection D concerns warships. By omission of any specific reference to right of innocent passage for warships, it is argued that the provisions under it *preclude* recognition of a general right of innocent passage for warships.[35] The other side of the argument is that a general reading and broad interpretation of these same specific provisions do allow warships the right of innocent passage.[36]

Assuming, for the sake of argument, that the general right of innocent passage does exist for warships using international straits within territorial waters during peacetime, the significant issue then becomes whether the concerned coastal state is entitled to prior notification by the warship of its intended passage.[37] Again, there is disagreement. It may be contended that special circumstances surrounding the passage being absent, there should be no reason for a warship to be required to give prior notification of its intended passage.[38] Although the convention does not authorize the coastal state to make passage of warships subject to previous authorization, neither does it forbid action of this nature. Since the Record of the Conference reveals that a clear majority of the states participating in the 1958 Geneva Conference favored such a right of prior notification, nothing should be interpreted in a way that would deprive a coastal state of this right.[39]

In the Soviet Union, there is continuing debate over the nature of actions—such as innocent passage—which are thought to be limitations of state sovereignty. Russia does not recognize an effective principle of innocent passage for warships. National legislation exists now that operates in effect to deny—rather than to restrict—a right of innocent passage to warships. The Soviet requirement that a warship submit a thirty-day notice prior to passage has the practical effect of precluding an effective use of innocent passage.[40]

The United States recognizes the right of innocent passage for military vessels. It requires no notice from foreign warships in its territorial waters, and it gives no such notice when its vessels enter the national waters of other states. Despite the United States practice, which is followed by a majority of states, it must be concluded that no universal acknowledgment of the right of innocent passage for warships through territorial waters during peacetime, including those which comprise straits, can be understood as existing.[41]

Civil and Criminal Jurisdiction

A merchant vessel that enters a foreign port becomes subject to local law. At the same time, it remains subject to the law of its flag. Although concurrent jurisdiction thus exists, in actual practice few conflicts arise because of a rule of convenience and comity that is applied. Specifically, local authorities will not interfere in matters of purely international concern to the ship; to do so could well be construed as contrary to customary rules of international law.[42] Whether, and on what grounds, coastal state authorities are entitled to arrest foreign ships that merely traverse territorial waters is an unsettled issue.[43] The generally accepted view is that if a foreign vessel either passes through territorial waters with the purpose of entering a port or hovers in such waters it no longer is acknowledged to be exercising a right of innocent passage and it becomes fully subject to the laws of the coastal state. It may, accordingly, be boarded, searched, and even arrested.[44]

Innocent passage does not guarantee to vessels exercising it what might be considered a total immunity from the local laws. The flag state may only protest when coastal state action amounts to an unreasonable interference with navigation.[45] Article 20 (1) of the 1958 Territorial Sea Convention states that a coastal state "should not" exercise its civil jurisdiction in relation to foreign shipts that pass through its territorial waters. Article 17 requires foreign ships to comply with all coastal state laws and regulations when passing innocently through the waters. Article 17 does not explicitly allow coastal states to enforce their laws in the territorial sea, but there appears little doubt that this was one of its objectives. Indeed, the general attitude of states at the 1958 Geneva Conference was that their civil jurisdiction did most assuredly extend to those ships that passed in their territorial waters.[46] The words "should not" in Article 21 (1) are thus interpreted as a mere exhortation rather than a mandatory command for the coastal state to refrain from exercising its civil jurisdiction. In any event, the most desirable policy would be to limit the occasion for interference by the coastal state. Interferences always interrupt the expeditious flow of commerce.[47] Regarding a coastal state's criminal jurisdiction, Article 19 (1) of the same convention states again—in exhortation—that it "should not" be exercised on board foreign ships that pass through territorial waters.

Regina v. *Keyne*, decided in 1876, held that the extent of criminal jurisdiction of the British Admiralty did not include acts that were committed by foreigners on board foreign ships on the high seas.[48] The case arose as a result of a collision two and one-half miles from the beach of Dover, England. It involved a British steamer, *Strathclyde*, and a German vessel, *Franconia*. As a result of the collision between the two vessels, a passenger aboard the *Strathclyde* was killed. Keyne, the commanding officer of the *Franconia*, was tried for manslaughter in the Center Criminal Court in London and found guilty by a jury. On appeal, his conviction was overturned. The Territorial Waters Jurisdiction Act was passed by Parliament less than two years after this case was decided. By the terms of the act, jurisdiction was conferred upon the Admiralty for crimes that were "committed on board or by means of a foreign ship in the territorial waters of England defined as any part of the ocean sea within one marine league of the coast measured from low water mark."[49]

Today it is acknowledged that the law of the land is paramount to the law of the flag. In England, if an act designated as a crime under English law is committed aboard an English ship, the offender may be tried and punished—regardless of his nationality—in England. Whether such a situation is also of concern to the coastal state is a decision only the local authorities can make. General practice records noninterference here. Yet, the coastal states do enjoy a legal right to take such an offender and try him under their own laws.[50]

In *Wildenhaus'* case, Chief Justice Morrison Waite, by way of defining the scope of criminal jurisdiction in 1887 said:

> By comity it came to be generally understood among civilized nations that all maters of discipline and all things done on board which affected only the vessel or those belonging to her, and did not involve the peace and dignity of the country or the tranquility of her port, should be left by the local government to be dealt with by the authorities of the nations to which the vessel belonged, as the laws of that nation or the interest of its commerce should require. But if crimes are committed on board of a character to disturb the peace and tranquility of the country to which the vessel has been brought, the offenders have never by comity or usage, been entitled to any exemption from the operation of the local laws for their punishment if the local tribunals see fit to assert their authority.[51]

Thus, in the absence of treaty provisions to the contrary, a foreign merchant vessel in port has no legal right to protest against any exercise of jurisdiction whatsoever on it by the local sovereign.[52]

Warships are held to be within the rule that all ships in a port are subject to the law of the land. Yet, there is one important reservation. The law of the port cannot be enforced against any person on board for actions on the ship nor can the ship, itself, be libeled or held for any action under the ordinary processes of law. This privilege is often understood as an application of the principle of extraterritoriality. The real basis of the immunity that is extended to the warships is found in the principle that "one sovereign state will not assert any coercive jurisdiction over the public agencies of another which are within its territory unless by mutual consent."[53] Interestingly, all state-owned vessels in the Soviet Union are — for Soviet legal purposes — "assimilated to warships" in that they are accorded total immunity from all but flag state jurisdictions.[54] Thus, such vessels, their crews, and passengers, while subordinate to the laws of the flag state, enjoy its defenses and protection.

Archipelagos

Innocent passage through archipelagic waters has always presented a contentious problem that is tied, very simply, to coastal security of the individual islands that comprise the archipelagos. Archipelagos have been defined as formations of two or more islands which, because of connecting geographic features (i.e., islets or rocks), might well be considered as a whole. There is, generally, little uniformity of geographic measurement possible because of the varying size of the islands and the size, shape, and very position of the archipelagos.[55] What formula to use in determining the internal waters, then, becomes a problem of initial importance.

The Philippines and Indonesia have asserted a right to draw a perimeter around their outermost waters and to claim those waters as internal waters, with the territorial waters extending outward from straight baselines set by them. Indonesia proposed a twelve-mile limit to its territorial sea, and the Phillippines set a varying limit. At the 1958 Geneva Conference, Indonesia's position was the passage through the archipelagos with full freedom of navigation would be allowed as long as there was no evidence of danger to the security interests of that country.[56]

To require consent from the archipelagic state before

passage can be gained through its internal waters — many of which waters are declared to be high seas under customary international law — is considered a too burdensome restriction to place on international commerce today. The better approach is for the archipelagic states to recognize a nondiscriminatory right of passage through certain designated ocean corridors wherein selective, not absolute, control could be imposed.[57] Any policy established here should seek an equitable balance between the needs of the international community to expedite commercial intercourse and the needs to provide adequate coastal security.

NOTES—CHAPTER TWO

1. C. HYDE, INTERNATIONAL LAW 518 (2d rev. ed. 1945). Neutrals were acknowledged as having a right to regulate passage only of vessels of war. It was generally assumed, however, in spite of this interpretation by the Institute, that a neutral state enjoyed both the right to prevent and to regulate the passage through its marginal sea of belligerent ships of any nature.

2. *Id.* at 453. At the last meeting of the Conference, an expression of sentiment — without formal vote — regarding desired jurisdictional limits of a state's territorial waters revealed that: 20 states, including Britain and the United States, preferred 3 miles (with some accepting, on condition, a contiguous zone); 12 states preferred 6 miles (with several of them requiring a contiguous zone); and 4 states declared 4 miles. C. COLOMBOS, THE INTERNATIONAL LAW OF THE SEA §116 (6th rev. ed. 1967).

The issue of the territorial sea framed at the 1930 Hague Conference was: if the territorial sea is only a portion of the high seas, the coastal state has only a *police right* over it — limited in its exercise by the principle of freedom of the seas; but, if the territorial sea is within the territory of the coastal state, the state has the same rights in respect to the sea as it possesses over its territory. O'Connell, *The Juridical Nature of the Territorial Sea*, 45 BRIT. Y.B. INT'L L. 304 352 (1971) [hereinafter cited as O'Connell, *Juridical Nature of the Territorial Sea*.].

3. COLOMBOS, *supra* note 2, § 118. The International Law Comm'n, *Report*, U.N. GEN. ASS. OFF. REC. 11th Sess., Supp. No. 9 (A/3159) (1956), covered the regime of the high seas, territorial waters, contiguous zones, the continental shelf, and the harvesting and conservation of the living resources of the high seas. See also, Jessup, *The International Law Commission 1954 Report on the Regime of the Territorial Sea*, 49 AM. J. INT'L L. 221 (1955).

The Harvard Draft legislation prepared in anticipation of the 1930 Hague Conference for Codification of International Law, the first of such conferences, is important as a background work in the area of drafting law of the sea conventions. See, 23 AM. J. INT'L L. 243 (Supp. 1929) for this work.

4. Exec. Order No. 2667, Sept. 28, 1945, Fed. Reg. 12303 (1945); 59 Stat. 884. Exec. Order No. 2668 involved coastal fisheries in relation to the high seas; it differentiated jurisdiction over conservation zones in the water column

from that over seabed resources. See, Hollick, *U.S. Oceans Policy: The Truman Proclamations*, 17 VA. J. INT'L L. 23 (1976).

5. Henkin, *Politics and the Changing Law of the Sea*, 89 POL. SCI. Q. 47 (1974) [hereinafter cited as Henkin, *Politics and the Changing Law of the Sea*].

6. Jessup, *The United Nations Conference on the Law of the Sea*, 59 COLUM. L. REV. 234 (1959) [hereinafter cited as Jessup, *United Nations Conference*]. See also, Fitzmaurice, *Some Results of the General Conference on the Law of the Sea*, 49 AM. J. INT'L L. 221 (1955).

The 4 conventions executed were: the Convention on the High Seas, the Convention on the Territorial Sea and the Contiguous Zone, the Convention on Fishing and Conservation of Living Resources of the High Seas, and the Convention on the Continental Shelf. See 2 YEARBOOK OF INTERNATIONAL LAW COMM. pt. 2, at 67 (1971) for a wider discussion of the conventions.

7. Slonim, *The Right of Innocent Passage and the 1958 Geneva Conference on the Law of the Sea*, 5 COLUM. J. TRANSNAT'L L. 96 (1966). This article presents an exceptionally solid review of the *travaux preparatoires* of the Conference. The report of the International Law Commission on the work of its 8th session is, however, the chief document to be consulted here. See *supra* note 3. See also, E. BROWN, PASSAGE THROUGH THE TERRITORIAL SEA: STRAITS USED FOR INTERNATIONAL NAVIGATION AND ARCHIPELAGOS (1973).

As to the 3 remaining conventions, the Convention on the High Seas came into effect on Sept. 30, 1962; the Convention on Fishing and Conservation of Living Resources of the High Seas came into effect on Mar. 20, 1966; and the Convention on the Continental Shelf came into effect on June 10, 1964.

All 4 conventions drawn at the 1958 Geneva Conference have secured an average of only approximately 40 ratifications from the total of over 150 sovereign states in the world today. It is therefore a moot point whether these conventions, which passed into law with such a few number of ratifications, can be correctly viewed as representing either the will or interests of the great majority of the members of the international community. Amerasinghe, *The Third United Nations Conference on the Law of the Sea*, 6 UNITAR NEWS 2, 3 (No. 1, 1974).

8. Jessup, *United Nations Conference* 234.

9. Henkin, *Politics and the Changing Law of the Sea*, 46, 50.

10. Ibid. Perhaps one of the most significant accomplishments of the 1958 Geneva Conference was its acceptance of the straight baseline for delimiting the territorial seas, even though this method of delimiting the sea was to be used only in exceptional cases. G. VON GLAHN, LAW AMONG NATIONS 306 (1965). See also, Art. 4 of the 1958 Convention on the Law of the Territorial Sea and the Contiguous Zone printed in Appendix 1.

11. Henkin, *Changing Law for the Changing Seas*, in USES OF THE SEAS, 69, 73 (E. Gullion, ed. 1968); Bowett, *The Second United Nations Conference on the Law of the Sea*, 9 INT'L & COMP. L.Q. 415 (1960).

At the 1958 Conference, the United States proposed a basic 6-mile territorial limit on the sea with a 6-mile fishing zone beyond. Of course, both proposals failed. The Soviet Union proposed what it termed a "flexible rule" for determining the width of the territorial sea at the 1960 Conference. Under it, each state would have been permitted to select its own extent of territorial limitation anywhere on a scale from 3 to 12 miles. An exclusive fishing zone was allowed beyond the territorial sea limit. A bloc of Afro-Asian nations followed suit with a proposal similar to that submitted by the Soviets. The United States and Canada then sought a compromise, which if accepted would have in turn compromised American fishing claims in order to force a consensus agreement on a

6-mile territorial sea limit. Dean, *The Geneva Conference on the Law of the Sea: What Was Accomplished?* 52 AM. J. INT'L L. 607 (1958); Jessup, *United Nations Conference* 234; VON GLAHN, *supra* note 10, at 305 *passim.*

12. Jennings, *A Changing International Law of the Sea,* 31 CAMB. L.J. 32 (1972) [hereinafter cited as Jennings, *A Changing International Law of the Sea*]. See generally, Lauterpacht, *Sovereignty over Submarines,* 37 BRIT. Y.B. INT'L L. 376 (1951).

13. 13 UST 2312, 2314, TIAS No. 5200. Italics added by author.

The character of the coastal state's territorial sea has been largely determined by the extent to which it has executed two of these rights: 1) the exclusive jurisdiction over resources (i.e., exploitation), and 2) the right to preserve its national defenses. Farer & Caplovits, *Towards A New Law for the Seas: The Evolution of United States Policy,* in THE CHANGING LAW OF THE SEA 40 (R. Zacklin, ed. 1974).

14. Jennings, *A Changing International Law of the Sea* 40. Both the coastal "control" approach to expanded jurisdiction and the freedom of the seas approach are *laissez faire* in their execution. That is to say, they allow each member of the world community the freedom to share in the ocean's benefits — without regulation — insofar as the exercise of the right does not injure others who seek to exercise a similar right. The distribution of the benefits under the control approach is left to accidents of geography which, under freedom of the seas, is guided by varying technological capacities and military or economic power. Hargrove, *New Concepts in the Law of the Sea,* 1 OCEAN DEV. & INT'L L.J. 5, 7 (1973).

15. Slonim, *supra* note 7, at 125.

16. *Id.*

17. Jennings, *A Changing International Law of the Sea* 33, 34. The 1958 Conference also gave to the coastal states new exclusive rights over their continental shelf, contiguous zone jurisdiction, and — as noted — allowed the straight method of demarcating the territorial sea in locations either deeply indented or on the fringe of islands. *Id.* at 32.

18. Friedmann, *Selden Redivivus: Towards a Partition of the Seas?* 65 AM. J. INT'L L. 763 (1971).

19. Brown & Fabian, *Diplomats at Sea,* 52 FOREIGN AFFAIRS 301, 315 (1974).

20. Henkin, *Old Politics and New Directions,* in 3 NEW DIRECTIONS IN THE LAW OF THE SEA 5 (R. Churchill, K. Simmonds, J. Welch, eds. 1973); Friedmann, *supra* note 18.

21. M. McDOUGAL & W. BURKE, THE PUBLIC ORDER OF THE OCEANS 179, 180, 232 (1962); M. AKEHURST, A MODERN INTRODUCTION TO INTERNATIONAL LAW 210 (1970); P. JESSUP, THE LAW OF TERRITORIAL WATERS AND MARITIME JURISDICTION 120 (1927) [hereinafter cited as JESSUP, LAW OF TERRITORIAL WATERS]. Jessup recognizes the right of innocent passage as a servitude. *Id.* at 119. See also, McDougal, *The Law of the High Seas in Time of Peace,* 3 DENVER J. INT'L L. & POLICY 45 (1973).

Schwarzenberger observes that on the basis of numerous treaties, a rule of customary international law began to develop which gave to foreign merchant vessels a limited right of innocent passage through coastal state territorial waters. G. SCHWARZENBERGER, A MANUAL OF INTERNATIONAL LAW 104 (5th ed. 1967).

Grotius, in THE RIGHTS OF WAR AND PEACE (1625), recognized rights of innocent passage. See T. FULTON, THE SOVEREIGNTY OF THE SEA 348 (1911). VATTEL, IN HIS LAW OF NATIONS (1760) — published 135 years after Grotius's work — observed that "a state cannot refuse access to vessels from innocent use without violating its duty. "M. VATTEL, 1 THE LAW OF NATIONS, ch. 23, §288 (1760). At sec. 289, Vattel states that the dominion of a state over neighboring seas extends so far as necessary in order to promote its *safety*.

O'Connell states that the problem of rationalizing a right of passage through the territorial sea was remedied by disengaging the concepts of territory and jurisdiction. About 1840, territory ceased to be regarded as a spatial area within which the faculties of sovereignty could be exercised. Police powers could be exercised outside this spatial area to the extent that international law permitted, and hence jurisdiction ceased to be spatially coterminous with territory. It thus became possible to speak of "jurisdiction" over coastal waters without importing the notion of territory to justify it. At the same time, such jurisdiction, being limited with respect to occasions and objects, was easily reconciled with innocent passage, which had become the dominant concept now that neutrality was no longer practically relevant and free trade was more significant than mercantilist protectionalism. O'Connell, *Juridical Nature of the Territorial Sea* 325.

The issue of whether innocent passage is an independent right on a par with that of coastal state sovereignty or is to be viewed as a subordinate right in the nature of a grant made by the coastal state has been considered frequently. The majority practice among states is to view innocent passage as an exercise of sovereignty. The authority of the coastal state in regulating innocent passage was, in fact, considered as an exercise of sovereignty at the 1930 Hague Conference. The minority position denies the territorial character of the maritime belt. It concedes to the coastal state only powers of control that are exercised in the interest of *security*, not sovereignty. Slonim, *supra* note 7, at 97. For a discussion of the basic weakness of the concept of innocent passage — namely its subjective, rather than objective, direction — see Burke, *Contemporary Law of the Sea: Transportation, Communication and Flight,* 2 YALE STUDIES IN WORLD PUB. ORDER 184, 210 (1976).

22. J. BRIERLY, THE LAW OF NATIONS 180 *passim* (5th ed. 1956).

See Waldock, *The Release of the Altmark's Prisoners,* 24 BRIT. Y.B. INTL'L L. 216 (1947), where the author concludes that apart from the duration of passage, a course through territorial waters to escape an attack is *not* mere passage under the protective assurances of the right of innocent passage.

The innocence of passage depends upon the situation under which passage is undertaken. In Vietnam, all North Vietnamese vessels entering South Vietnamese territorial waters *before* the peace, were treated as hostile and force was employed against them. O'Connell, *International Law and Contemporary Naval Obligations,* 44 BRIT. Y.B. INT'L L. 19 (1970).

The pertinent provisions of the Territorial Sea Convention delineating the scope of the right of innocent passage are printed in Appendix 1.

23. McDOUGAL & BURKE, *supra* note 21, at 231, 232, 291. See Appendix 1, Arts. 14 (4) *et seq.* See also, AMERICAN LAW INSTITUTE, RESTATEMENT OF THE FOREIGN RELATIONS LAW §45 *passim* (2d ed. 1965).

24. Jennings, *International Civil Aviation and the Law,* 22 BRIT. Y. B. INT'L L. 191, 196 (1945).

25. M. WHITEMAN, 4 DIGEST OF INTERNATIONAL LAW 459, 560 (1965).

26. *Id.* at 345. P. BARABELYA et al., 1 MANUAL OF INTERNATIONAL MARITIME LAW 25-27 (1968).

Airspace over the high seas — as opposed to over territorial waters — is free to aircraft of all states; it is not subject to any state's jurisdiction. O. LISSITZYN, INTERNATIONAL AIR TRANSPORT AND NATIONAL POLICY 365 (1942). This time-honored principle in international law does not appear to meet the prevailing practice of states, however. The states assert occasional, exclusive competence for state purposes in the airspace over the high seas. McDougal & Burke, *supra* note 21, at 787-790.

Freedom of the air is, very practically, an opportunity to compete. "Competition leads to economic management and a maximum rate of economic progress and technological development." H. Wassenbergh, Aspects of Air Law and Civil Air Policy in the Seventies 7 (1970).

See also, Akehurst, *supra* note 21, ch. 14; T. Buergenthal, Law Making in the International Civil Aviation Organization 80-85 (1969). See generally, Lissitzyn, *The Treatment of Aerial Intruders in Recent Practice and International Law,* 47 Am. J. Int'l L. 559 (1953).

The Soviet Union does not recognize the right of innocent passage for foreign aircraft over Soviet waters. Flights of foreign aircraft in Soviet airspace is to be allowed only in accordance with specific international agreements to this effect with the Soviets. W. Butler, The Soviet Union and the Law of the Sea 100 (1971).

27. Brown, *supra* note 7, at 16.

28. Art. 14 (5), printed in Appendix 1. It has been judicially determined that the right of hot pursuit may be commenced within the United States contiguous fisheries zone (the 9-mile-wide belt of sea extending seaward from the outer limit of the 3-mile territorial sea of the United States) for violation of United States exclusive fishing rights in that zone. United States v. Fishing Vessel Taiyo Maru No. 28, 395 F. Supp. 413 (D. Me. 1975). See also, Fidell, Hot Pursuit from a Fisheries Zone, 70 Am. J. Int'l L. 95 (1976); Meron, *The Fisherman's Protection Act: A Case Study in Contemporary Legal Strategy of the United States,* 69 *id.,* 290 (1975). This act provides for reimbursement by the federal government for United States vessels seized by a foreign nation.

29. Art. 14 (6), printed in Appendix 1. See O'Connell, *The Juridical Nature of the Territorial Sea* 40 *passim,* for a thorough discussion of modern submarine problems in the territorial sea and innocent passage. O'Connell observes that in some naval circles, Art. 14 (6) of the Territorial Sea Convention, which states that for submarines to enjoy innocent passage they must navigate on the surface and show their flag, is to be strictly construed with Art. 16 of the same convention. Under Art. 16, the coastal state may take whatever steps it believes are necessary to prevent noninnocent passage. The conclusion drawn is that it is permissible to attack submarines that are submerged in the territorial sea. Most submariners would concur that submergence of a submarine in territorial waters for purposes other than avoidance of bad weather or similar reasons of well-being would preclude a designation of the passage as innocent. The crucial point at issue, then, becomes one of devising means of ordering a submerged submarine to vacate the territorial waters. *Id.* at 56-58.

30. Art. 18 (1), printed in Appendix 1.

31. Art. 21, printed in Appendix 1. "The right of innocent passage must . . . be considered as established in the most complete manner to all . . . ships as pass on the seas upon their lawful oceans. It is the natural consequence of the principle of the freedom of the sea." Colombos, *supra* note 2, at 133.

On May 12, 1975, at 3:18 a.m., the United States merchant ship *Mayaguez* was seized some 6½ miles off the Poulo Wai Islands in an area that was claimed by Cambodia as within its territorial waters. President Gerald Ford considered the seizure an "act of piracy" by the Communist government in Cambodia following the collapse of the Lon Nol regime. Sovereignty over the islands was claimed by the states of Cambodia, Vietnam, and Thailand—all three of which asserted a 12-mile territorial sea. Two air attacks and a marine beach assault were subsequently launched by United States forces in recovery strategies. The circumstances here point clearly to the confusion surrounding modern problems in application of the concept of innocent passage.

Does the Cambodian government's claim that prior to the entry of the *Mayaguez* into its territorial water ships surreptitiously operating as fishing vessels from other nations had been engaged in espionage activities, stopped for interrogation, and subsequently released add validity to the *reasonableness* of the Cambodian belief that their coastal security interests might well have been in jeopardy and thus justify their actions relative to the *Mayaguez*? The *Mayaguez* could have proceeded around the area and passed without inconvenience between the Wai and Tang Islands, which were outside the claimed territorial waters.

The interest of the United States in speedy and safe passage for its merchant fleet *en route* to Thailand in no way conflicted with the valid interests Cambodia had in maintaining control of the territorial waters around the Wai Islands and endeavoring to guard against security threats, especially because several convenient alternative routes existed outside waters claimed by Cambodia. Paust, *The Seizure and Recovery of the Mayaguez*, 85 YALE L.J. 774, 795 (1976). See also, Note, *The Constitutional Implications of the Mayaguez Incident*, 3 HASTINGS CONST. L.Q. 301 (1976); Moore, *The Control of Foreign Intervention in Internal Conflict*, 9 VA. J. INT'L L. 205 (1969); Mallsion, *Limited Naval Blockade or Quarantine—Interdiction: National and Collective Defense Claims Valid under International Law*, 312 G.W.L. REV. 335 (1962); M. McDOUGAL & F. FELICIANO, LAW AND MINIMUM WORLD PUBLIC ORDER 242 (1961); McDOUGAL & BURKE, *supra* note 21, at 229. A Government Accounting Office report was highly critical of the precipitant military action taken by the Ford administration in handling the *Mayaguez* affair. The report stressed a greater need for political accommodation here. *Mayaguez Operation Criticized in Report*, New York Times, Oct. 6, 1976, p. 1, col. 5.

For an analysis of a somewhat related action of seizure by a coastal sovereign or, more specifically, the North Korean seizure of the U.S.S. *Pueblo*, on Jan. 23, 1968, for its espionage activities see Butler, *The Pueblo Crisis: Some Critical Reflections*, 1969 PROC. AM. SOC'Y INT'L L. 7.

North Korea has claimed a "military sea boundary" extending 50 miles off its coast. The claimed boundary appears to extend over 5 island groups off the North Korean coast that were assigned to South Korean control by the 1953 armistice; North Korea has disputed this action. The United States has rejected the North Korean claim as a unilateral breach of international law. Int'l Herald Tribune (London), Apr. 4, 1977, p. 3, col. 4.

32. Slonim, *supra* note 7, at 119; Bowett, *supra* note 11, at 418.

33. BROWN, *supra* note 7, at 22.

34. WHITEMAN, *supra* note 25, at 453. See generally, Comment, The Innocent Passage of Warships In Foreign Territorial Sea: A Threatened Freedom, 15 SAN DIEGO L. REV. 573 (1978).

British warships demonstrated force in their passage through the Corfu Channel in order to force Albania to permit passage of their vessels and to desist from any present or future attempts to deny such passage by force. The court appears to have held that the concept of innocent passage is broad enough to include the use or threat of force during passage through the territorial sea to assure recognition of the right of innocent passage by the coastal state. Despite this interpretation, the broader problem raised by the *Corfu Channel* case is whether the concept of innocent passage should be construed to permit the use or threat of force during passage in the territorial sea as part of an effort to affirm other rights derived from international law, which the coastal state seeks to initially deny by the use of force. This question has yet to be answered definitively. See McDougal & Burke, *supra* note 21, at 263; Dean, *supra* note 11, at 621.

The court stated that innocence depends primarily, although not exclusively, on the *manner* rather than the *motive* of the passage. Fitzmaurice, *The Law and Procedure of the International Court of Justice: General Principles and Substantive Law*, 27 Brit. Y.B. Int'l L. 1, 29 (1950).

If the *Corfu Channel* case is interpreted in light of contemporary ideas of what constitutes innocent passage as it applies in general to the territorial sea today, it makes little sense. If the same or similar circumstances occurred today and were interpreted as innocent, the whole concept of innocent passage as presented in the 1958 Territorial Sea Convention would be negated. Yet, when the *Corfu* rule is understood as applying to international straits lying within territorial waters, "it reflects a rational policy of upholding their special legal status in favor of a right of access for international navigation." The right of access upheld thus becomes more than innocent passage as understood today and more akin to a recognition of a high seas right of navigation. Cundrick, *International Straits: The Right of Access*, 5 Ga. J. Int'l Com. L. 107, 121 (1973).

35. Slonim, *supra* note 7 at 119. The proceedings of the Conference show a majority of the delegates did not wish to confer on warships the same rights of innocent passage that they were conferring on other vessels. Brown, *supra* note 7, at 22.

Warships "should not enjoy an absolute legal right to pass through a state's territorial waters any more than an army may cross the land territory." Jessup, Law of Territorial Waters. See also, E. Luard, The Control of the Sea Bed 157 (1974); E. Percy, Maritime Trade in War (1929)

36. Brown, *supra* note 7, at 22. The better view appears to be that during peacetime warships should not be denied the right of innocent passage, when the waters through which innocent passage is allowed "are so placed that passage through them is necessary for international traffic." Colombos, *supra* note 2 at 133. See generally, McDougal, *supra* note 21, at 45.

37. Art. 16 (4) of the convention states there is to be no suspension of the right of innocent passage for foreign ships through straits used for international navigation. See Appendix 1, where the article is printed.

38. Brown, *supra* note 7, at 29.

39. *Id.* at 23.

40. Butler, *Soviet Concepts of Innocent Passage*, 7 Harv. Int'l L.J. 113, 127 (1965); Butler, *The USSR and the Limits to National Jurisdiction over the Sea, 1970-72*, in Limits to National Jurisdiction over the Sea 177, 179, 180 (G. Yates, J. Young, eds. 1974).

Interestingly, the very principle of freedom of the sea is treated in Soviet law and diplomacy as a politico-legal freedom — one that is both characterized and applied in order that the rights of small maritime powers receive maximum protection. Indeed, one of the rather remarkable changes during the present decade relative to the Soviet attitudes concerning the law of the sea has been the effort to balance traditional dispositions to favor the interests of smaller powers with its own enhanced maritime power (cf., *infra* ch 4, n. 14). W.

BUTLER, THE SOVIET UNION AND THE LAW OF THE SEA 19 *passim* (1971).

See Young and Sebek, *Red Seas and Blue Seas: Soviet Uses of Ocean Law*, 22 SURVIVAL 255, 257 (1978), for an informative discussion of the doctrine of regional seas as a Soviet device to promote their national interests in strategically important seas.

41. Farer & Caplovits, *supra* note 13, at 42; Deddish, *The Right of Innocent Passage by Warships through International Straits*, 24 J.A.G.J. 81, 82 (1969).

42. H. SMITH, THE LAW AND CUSTOM OF THE SEA 35 (3d ed. 1959); JESSUP, LAW OF TERRITORIAL WATERS, 122, 144, 145; SCHWARZENBERGER, *supra* note 21, at 105. See also, McDougal, Burke and Vlasic, *Maintenance of Public Order at Sea and Nationality of Ships*, 54 AM. J. INT'L L. 25 (1960).

43. SCHWARZENBERGER, *supra*, note 21, at 105.

44. JESSUP, LAW OF TERRITORIAL WATERS 123.

45. *Id.*

46. McDOUGAL & BURKE, *supra* note 21, at 272-274.

47. Id. at 282.

48. [1876] L.R., 2 Exch. Div. 63.

49. JESSUP, LAW OF TERRITORIAL WATERS 124-130. Although most of the judges and most of the commentators believed the Regina v. Keyne decision was made with respect only to the juridical nature of the territorial sea, they were mistaken. The real problem, seen by several of the judges on the appeal, was reconciling innocent passage with the idea of sovereignty over the territorial sea. O'Connell, *Juridical Nature of the Territorial Sea*. 329-331. See also, Marston, *Crimes on Board Foreign Merchant Ships at Sea: Some Aspects of English Practice*, 88 L.Q. REV. 357 (1972).

50. SMITH, *supra* note 42, at 35. A ship cannot be regarded as a sanctuary for escaped criminals from shore. Local authorities thus have a right to remove any person who is traveling on the ship if that person is wanted for an offense against the laws of the land. *Id.* at 36.

51. 120 U.S. 1, 30 L. ed. 565, 567 (1887).

52. Jessup, Law of Territorial Waters 189.

53. Smith, *supra* note 42, at 37.

54. BUTLER, THE SOVIET UNION AND THE LAW OF THE SEA 176 (1971).

55. Miller, *Indonesia's Archipelago Doctrine and Japan's Jugular*, U.S. NAVAL INSTITUTE PROCEEDINGS 27 (1972). See also, Kusumastmadja, *The Legal Regime of Archipelagoes: Problems and Issues*, in NEEDS AND INTERESTS OF DEVELOPING COUNTRIES 166 (L. Alexander, ed. 1972); G. VON GLAHN, LAW AMONG NATIONS 307 (1965); O'Connell, *Mid-Ocean Archipelagoes in International Law*, 45 BRIT. Y.B. INT'L L. 1 (1971); Amerasinghe, *The Problems of Archipelagoes in the International Law of the Sea*, 23 INT'L & COMP. L.Q. 539 (1974).

Coastal archipelagos are to be found in Finland, Greenland, Iceland, Sweden, and Yugoslavia. Outlying mid-ocean archipelagos are situated in the ocean areas represented by the Fiji Islands, Hawaiian Islands, Indonesia, Japan, Philippines, and Solomon Islands.

Of the earth's total land area, nearly 7% is composed of islands that geographically can be arranged into arcs, quadrangles, triangles, and other quasi-geometric patterns. Of these groups, many are classified as mid-ocean archipelagos and archipelagic states—the latter of which may be, accordingly, defined as groups of 3 or more islands that are united by ties of a geographic, economic, political, or historic nature, which thereby make the islands or portions thereof (not the seas that flow between them) viewable as an entity. Dubner, *A Proposal for Accommodating the Interests of Archipelagic and*

Maritime States, 8 J. INT'L & POLITICS 39 (1975). See also, Burke, *Contemporary Law of the Sea: Transportation, Communication and Flight,* 2 YALE STUDIES IN WORLD PUB. ORDER 184, 193–202 (1976); W. T. BURKE, R. LEGATSKI & W. WOODHEAD, NATIONAL AND INTERNATIONAL LAW ENFORCEMENT IN THE OCEAN 90–93 (1975).

56. VON GLAHN, *supra* note 55; Miller, *supra* note 55.

It has been rather persuasively argued that instead of taking the traditional view that the law of territorial waters should be applied to mid-ocean archipelagos and coastal archipelagic states without distinguishing these two types of archipelagos, an archipelagic state should be permitted to employ a straight baseline method to thereby enclose all of the islands and waters lying between and around them. Thus, rather than serving as a traditional baseline, the resulting line would function as an indicator that would delimit the fishing and mineral rights of the archipelagic state. The advantage of this indicator formula is that it would be identical to the baseline delimitation — determined as such by existing customary and convention law — and hopefully, thus, because of its flexibility, used to forestall "predictable" international conflict. Dubner, *subra* note 55, at 55; BURKE, LEGATSKI & WOODHEAD, *supra* note 55, at 193–202.

On archipelagos see Arts. 49, 52, and 53 of the Informal Composite Negotiating Text printed in Appendix 5.

57. *Information Report on the Law of the Sea: Understanding the Debate on the Law of Ocean Space,* 8 INT'L LAW. 588, 695 (1974).

●

Chapter 3

SHAPING NEW POLICIES FOR THE OCEANS

National and Transnational Vector Forces

The 1945 Truman Proclamation, whereby the United States asserted jurisdiction over its continental shelf resources, appeared—as has been observed—to trigger a wild rush by other nations to lay claim to exclusive control over their continental shelves. Indeed, unilateral claims by nation states for territorial expansion of coastal waters for fisheries jurisdiction, mineral resources, and for a wide variety of other uses have highlighted over maritime policies from the 1960s to the present. Thirty-five states presently claim a territorial sea breadth of three or four miles, sixty-seven other states claim an area of from six to twelve miles, and sixteen states assert jurisdiction over a breadth of over twelve miles.[1] President Lyndon Johnson's caution in 1966 against a "race to grab and to hold the lands under the high seas," has had little effect.[2]

In 1967, Arvid Pardo, the ambassador of Malta to the United Nations, went before the General Assembly and in a lengthy discourse called upon the world community to reserve for *mankind* — not for individual states — seabed wealth beyond "present national jurisdiction." The United Nations Sea Bed Committee was formed as a direct consequence of the discussion generated by the Pardo proposal. The committee was in essence reconstituted in 1970 as a preparatory group with ninety-one members charged with organizing a Third Law of the Sea Conference. A good number of governments must determine which specific interests should be pursued, which interests are therefore preferable, and consequently what sea laws should be favored.[3]

The new epoch in ocean policies has been — in a political sense — initiated as a consequence of technological and scientific advances in multiple aspects of oceanography, new methods of propulsion, new instruments specifically designed for observation and detection, better navigation systems, and improved international communications, together with numerous other devices allowing for exploration of the ocean depths and for exploitation of animate and inanimate sea resources. The vast economic potentialities for new wealth, principally from the seabed resources, have also acted as a vector force in shaping the decision-making process here.[4]

New Nations Mean New Politics

The radical politics of the new nations heighten the interplay of interests in the world community. The impact of cultural traditions is also another force of considerable dimension. Indeed, such traditions may be a part of the definition of the very national interests of the new countries. As these nations more directly participate in the economic and political aspects of international life, they quickly realize that a good number of their legal traditions are inadequate to meet their newly established needs. The net result is a frustration of their level of expectation and, again, a heightened sense of inequality.[5] For the emerging member of the international community, it becomes largely a matter of whether it will seek to compete or to cooperate with its sister states in orchestrating new patterns for the law of the sea. Emerging sea law will reflect "the balance of advantage as seen by important states (or groups of states)," the influence of these states on and in the international legal system, and a degree of national self-restraint.[6]

The United Nations

Within the forum of the United Nations yet another vector of forces is at work shaping, defining, and directing a full range of political interests, as they in turn chart or influence international lawmaking activities. The central role of the United Nations is to execute what may be termed as essential political responsibility: to coordinate the policies of its members toward the achievement of international peace and security.[7]

The vast number of new state members to the United Nations, all of which are equal at least in principle, are most correctly characterized as sovereigns whose territorial bases of power are squeezed and restricted as a consequence of increasing inequality and dependence. Their very existence has strained traditional means of making and remaking law.[8]

Power differentials exist at all levels of United Nations membership—from the composition of the Trusteeship Council to the voting formula in the Security Council. As inequities in bargaining power have arisen with the emergence of new states, efforts have been undertaken to adjust to these situations by structuring elements of organizational stability within the international framework of decision making.[9] The doctrine of equality of states has long been championed by the small states as a safeguard against encroachments by the major powers. Still, in a real sense, conflicts of interest over design for world government have always pitted the great powers against the middle powers. Although the peace of the world is of uppermost concern to all nations, "it is not true that all can make equal contribution to its maintenance."[10]

The majority member states in reality—principles of equality aside—both declare and promote as law what they are precluded from legislating directly. It is they who carefully orchestrate the number of intrusions upon unanimity in areas where a common majority interest is at stake, and they who in rare moments of bold "leadership" also make declarations of "universal" law.[11] An American policy of reliance on and compliance with majority decision making in the United Nations is feasible only as long as such decisions are regarded as just and right from the United States view of its national self-interest. The moral validity of a majority vote may not be enough for the United States today. Already there have been signs from the United States that it is disturbed with voting patterns among the nonaligned states in the United Nations General Assembly, which appear to jeopardize the general patterns of accepted international behavior and of international law.[12]

Vectors of Political Force within the United States

Still other vectors of political force emanate from various national government activities in the United States. Congressional interest and participation in this area are influencing forces. With the passage of the Marine Resources and Engineering Development Act in 1966, the nation had its first mandate not only to improve scientific understanding of ocean resource management and to accelerate its exploration of the field but also to begin drawing upon and developing international marine resources to serve mankind in general.[13] The commercial sector of the United States economy, together with marine labor unions concerned with the shipping and handling of cargo, and an alert segment of the general public, also provide a force of influence in ocean policy development.[14]

The executive branch of the United States government has also been a vector of political force in the development of ocean law. President Richard Nixon enunciated his plan for the oceans on March 23, 1970. It was designed to seek an accommodation, not necessarily a compromise, of the various interests or balance of forces previously discussed. The proposals consisted of three articles and were formally submitted to the United Nations Sea Bed Committee in August, 1971.[15]

International Politics

A number of the vector forces previously discussed could be included in the term, "international politics." The sphere of international politics is all-encompassing and it embraces foreign policy transactions among approximately one hundred fifty sovereign states in their mutual interactions, together with their interactions with the total international system. International politics also encompasses the close associations or dealings of these states with a host of international organizations and social groups other than states, the general overall operation of the international system itself, and the domestic policies of all the states. In contrast, basic or general politics may simply be defined as "the art of creating and maintaining groups and of achieving their politics against the opposition of other groups."[16]

The influence of geography upon the general play of international relations — termed geopolitics — has been an important factor in the development of expansionist claims of maritime jurisdiction by many new Third World states and many Latin American states. It has been often said that international relations is but geography set in motion.[17]

To the extent that a sense of crisis exists in international law today, it may be attributed in large part to accelerating changes within the international political community. Among the factors causing this acceleration are: unchecked inflation, the imbalance of nuclear weapons, the emergence of new states having different cultural backgrounds and levels of economic development, an increase in decolonization, a rise of new ideologies and forms of public order—including militant communism, increasing demands for social reform, the fear of war, rapid technological advances, and a multiplication in both the number and functions of international organizations.[18]

Force

In subscribing to the 1945 Charter of the United Nations, new members agree to avoid the use of force as an instrument of national policy. War is to be outlawed and international peace and security promoted.[19] Regarding the conduct of nations, one central principle stands clear in the charter: "Except in self defense against armed attack, members must refrain from the threat or use of force against other states."[20] The clear and reasonable meaning of this principle enunciated in 1945 is less clear today, and reasonable interpretations and applications of this principle are less certain. While all member nations of the United Nations recognize intervention as unlawful, they are at odds with an agreement on the nature of particular intervention that, in itself, is unlawful. Prohibitions of intervention are properly considered as "part of the quest for an ideal seen as the equal sovereignty and independence of nations."[21]

In the final analysis, what is needed to ensure the observance of international law within the political setting is a decisive stand by the world community as a whole against all unilateral uses of national force. Such a prohibition against the use of such force may rightly be considered as a political norm. Indeed, it is in fact law "with the force of law, designed to control the behavior of nations."[22] If self-restraint were enunciated as a credible policy by leading nations and reenforced by an equally credible policy of effective response for violations thereof, a prohibition of the use of force would thereby become an effective law.[23] At this juncture in time, the outlook for the execution, realization, or implementation of this political norm, however, does not appear to be bright. Whether the process of depolitization of the norm can be achieved is tied to hopeful speculation at best.

Political and Economic Power

The main thrust of international conflict and movements in general has been the pursuit of political or economic power. Economic relations affect political options for decision making just as the development and execution of political goals determine the thrust of economic policy. Within the sphere of international politics, power struggles have often occurred as a consequence of national attempts to strengthen economic positions. These power struggles or economic conflicts are not, as often believed, precipitated by inabilities to increase food sources and other commodities or to raise the standard of living. Rather, an atmosphere for economic conflict is created as a consequence of the proliferation of new, and generally poor, independent states whose customary primary interests are in developing power economies instead of aspiring to transnational ideals of promoting the general welfare of the global community.[24]

Distrustful, nationalistic, and insecure best describe

many members of the world community. For these member states, a strong national economic policy is an important tool for building and maintaining power. Used properly, a policy of this nature not only may acquire but also conserve important raw (e.g., strategic) materials, stimulate local production of goods in order to avoid dependence upon foreign markets, and act as a tool to undermine economic policies of an enemy or strengthen similar policies for an ally. Economic warfare during the 1930s preceded the commencement of military hostilities.[25] Today, members of the Third World are engaged in such warfare against South Africa and Rhodesia. And, of course, some members of the Arab League follow a similar attack on Israel and, of late, threaten economic reprisals against those who trade with her and recognize her sovereignty.

If a marshaling of common interest can be achieved among the major powers (as has been done, for example, in their determination to avoid nuclear war), much can be done by them as a group to promote the observance and strengthening of international law. Ordered cooperation and community interest are, thus, central concepts in any effort of this nature.

Neutrality, Neutralism, or Nonalignment

Jessup determined in 1936 that neutrality as an operable legal principle was not dead; it was merely qualified by Article 16 of the Covenant of the League of Nations. The provisions of this article stated that any member resorting to war violated its obligation to settle disputes peacefully and, thus, was deemed to have acted against *all* other members. The latter were then obligated to cease all trading with and financial support to the aggressor. The covenant was, however, binding only on the members of the League. Nonmember states were free to remain neutral when conflicts arose.[26]

Encroachment by belligerents on the rights of neutral states was recorded early in World War II. During this war, wholesale violations of these rights occurred and were particularly evident on the high seas, where vessels were attacked, sunk, or captured in neutral waters.[27] The now famous *Altmark incident* illustrates the extent to which a belligerent state will, when it believes the occasion warrants it, be contemptous of a duty to abstain from interferring with the movements of enemy forces in neutral waters. In this case, Britain violated Norway's neutrality by seizing within the territorial waters of Norway a German vessel, which had captured British seamen and was trying to return to Germany with them. Britain justified its actions on the grounds that it was acting under a type of international humanitarian duty to rescue its seamen.[28] The lesson of the *Altmark* could easily be repeated today if similar circumstance were to arise.

The Charter of the United Nations does not cause neutrality as a concept to wholly disappear. Article 2, paragraph 5 states:

> *All members shall give the United Nations every assistance in any action it takes in accordance with the present Charter and shall refrain from giving assistance to any state against which the United Nations is taking preventive or enforcement action.*

Paragraph 6 of the same article declares—contrary to previous provisions in the Covenant of the League of Nations:

> *The Organization shall ensure that states which are not members of the United Nations act in accordance with these Principles so far as may be necessary for the maintenance of international peace and security.*

Should the Security Council in fact call upon the member states of the United Nations for military support or general assistance consistent with the provisions of Articles 41, 43, 48, and 49 of the charter, each member would lose its right to remain neutral. Yet, the neutral status of each state would be *lost* only to the extent to which it chose to accept or implement the directions, orders, or suggestions issued by the Security Council.[29]

Only when a war exists sufficiently long enough to make neutrality a meaningful possibility can the concept of neutrality have any relevancy today.[30] Not only does Article 2, paragraphs 3 and 4, of the Charter of the United Nations prohibit the use of force by one state against another, but there would also appear to exist a general consensus amounting to a legal norm that makes an aggressive war unlawful.[31]

Many new states continue to refer to their positions as noncommitment, nonalignment with the policies of the Super World powers, or "neutrality." Quite often what they mean to maintain or assert is, however, more correctly their neutralism. Indeed, the very words, noncommitment and nonalignment, are but synonyms of neutralism.[32]. Instead of developing this political concept of neutralism as a means of positive reenforcement of international law through competition and useful lawmaking, the unaligned states use it as a medium through which they may violate law.[33]

New but economically undeveloped states often view the expansion of their territorial seas as an important factor in strengthening their rights of independence and increasing their sources of wealth. They may seek an extended territorial sea to protect fisheries, preserve mineral exploratory rights to the seabed and subsoil, preserve ecological balance by regulating oil-spill prevention areas, and to guarantee that maritime hostilities among other states will be kept away from their coastlines. Forgotten are the realities of responsibility (i.e., costs of installing and maintaining navigational aids and military considerations), which new territorial acquisitions require.[34]

There is no obvious element of risk implicit in the execution of these new rights. From a military standpoint, if a nonaligned state is successfully to avoid becoming involved in belligerency, it must steadfastly patrol its territorial sea. The wider a territorial sea, the larger the patrol fleet must be. "Minimization of the risk is enlarged."[35] The costs to the state of patrolling an extended territorial sea in order to ensure conformance with requirements of its nonalignment or neutralism would be considerable.

The Exclusive Economic Zone or Concept of Patrimonial Sea

National claims to the sea in excess of twelve miles are to a large extent based upon coastal state desires to obtain jurisdiction over ocean resources, not open to which to control navigation upon the territorial sea. If accommodations could be reached that would allow these claims for resource control to be satisfied, it is believed that the claims for territorial jurisdiction over twelve miles would disappear. Such a compromise or accommodation is found in the concept of a patrimonial sea zone two hundred miles in width, in which coastal states would have exclusive rights (e.g., fishing and mineral exploration) to explore and exploit all the seabed and subsoil resources.[36] The proponents of this compromise note that the central concept of a patrimonial sea was validated in the Santa Domingo Declaration by Colombia, Mexico, and Venezuela on June 9, 1972. They assert that any agreement to set a territorial sea width at twelve miles is *conditioned* solely on the acceptance of an economic zone with a measurable width of no less than two hundred miles from the baselines where the territorial sea is measured. Their marching cry is thus, "There will be no 12 without 200!"[37]

The concept of an exclusive economic zone (EEZ), or functional zone beyond the territorial sea, is in purely jurisdictional terms a valid reflection of contemporary political balance; a balance between the intransigence of the international community in promoting new law for the sea and the spirit of the new postcolonial order seeking to extend territorial boundaries wherever practical.[38] The response of the world community to the concept of the EEZ has historically run the gamut from qualified interest through encouraging support to absolute opposition.[39] It is sufficient to note this as a major, complex problem area and a vector of considerable force, and to show its connection to efforts to limit the territorial sea expansion to twelve miles. In very large part, any investigation of the concept of an exclusive economic zone would involve heavy analysis of seabed resources allocation problems, which is of course beyond the scope of this present undertaking. It may be stated here, however, subject to later amplification, that the acceptance of the concept of a patrimonial sea became the keystone of a compromise solution to territorial sea expansion at the Caracas meeting of the third United Nations Law of the Sea Conference.[40]

NOTES—CHAPTER 3

1. L. HENKIN, LAW FOR THE SEA'S MINERAL RESOURCES 1, ch. 5 (1968): W. FRIEDMANN, THE FUTURE OF THE OCEAN 3 (1971); Knight, *The Third United Nations Law of the Sea Conference: Caracas*, 18 AM. UNIVERSITIES FIELD STAFF REPORTS 1, 2 (No. 2, 1974); Alexander, *Indices of National Interest in the Oceans*, 1 OCEAN DEV. & INT'L L. J. 21, 43 (1973).

For a spirited debate on the extent of the continental shelf under the 1958 convention, see Henkin, *International Law and Interests: The Law of the Seabed*, 63 AM. J. INT'L L. 504 (1969); Finlay, *The Outer Limit of the Continental Shelf: A Rejoinder to Professor Louis Henkin*, 64 AM. J. INT'L L. 42 (1970); Henkin, *A Reply to Mr. Finlay, id.*, 62.

See also, Henkin, *The United Nations and the Rules of Law*, 11 HARV. INT'L L.J. 428, 433 *passim* (1970), for further discussion of the need for redefinition of the width of the contintental shelf and the almost desperate need for new seabed law; Young, *The Legal Regime of the Deep Sea Floor*, 62 AM. J. INT'L L. 641 (1968); Gerstle, "The Politics of United Nation as Voting: A View of the Seabed from the Glass Palace," Law of the Sea Institute, Occasional Paper No. 7, University of Rhode Island (July 1970).

2. HENKIN, LAW FOR THE SEA'S MINERAL RESOURCES 8 (1968). On the same day the Johnson speech was delivered, the President's Scientific Advisory Committee Report, *Effective Uses of the Sea,* was released and heralded (by some) as an innovative guide for ocean policy making. E. WENK, JR., THE POLITICS OF THE OCEAN 258 (1952).

3. HENKIN, LAW FOR THE SEA'S MINERAL RESOURCES 6 (1968); Henkin, *Politics and the Changing Law of the Sea,* 89 POL. SCI. Q. 46, 53 (1974).

The Sea Bed Committee's most notable accomplishment was the preparation of an agenda for the Caracas meeting consisting of 25 items, 61 subitems and 19 sub-subitems. Hollick, "The Third United Nations Conference on the Law of the Sea: Caracas Review," paper presented at Conference, The Law of the Sea: U.S. Interests and Alternatives, American Enterprise Institute for Public Policy Research, Washington, D.C., Feb. 14, 1975, p. 2.

Yet, certain rather important proposals for new rules on innocent passage emerged from various Sea Bed Committee reports and in turn served as bases for draft proposals submitted at Caracas. The most significant reports are: Committee on the Peaceful Uses of the Sea Bed and the Ocean Floor beyond the Limits of National Jurisdiction, *Report,* U.N. GEN. ASS. OFF. REC. 28th Sess. Supp. No. 21 (A/9021) (1973) vol. III, pp. 19-22; *Ecuador, Panama and Peru: Working Paper* containing draft articles for inclusion in a convention on the law of the sea, July 13, 1973 (sec. III), A/AC. 138/SC.II/L.27 and Corr. 1 and 2 at 30-35; *Malta, Preliminary Draft Articles* on the delimitation of coastal state jurisdiction in ocean space and on the rights and obligations of coastal states in the area under their jurisdiction, July 13, 1973, A/AC.138/SC.II/L.28 at 35-70; *China, Working Paper* on the sea area within the limits of national jurisdiction, July 16, 1973, A/AC.138/SC.II/L.34 at 71-74; *Argentina, Draft Articles,* July 16, 1973, A/AC.138/SC.II/L.37 and Corr. 1 at 78-81; *Bulgaria, Draft Articles,* July 16, 1973, on the nature and characteristics of the territorial sea and its breadth, A/AC.138/SC.II/L.51 at 106. Also of particular importance were: *Draft Articles on Navigation through the Territorial Sea Including Straits Used for International Navigation* sponsored by Cyprus, Greece, Indonesia, Malaysia, Morocco, Phillipines, Spain, and Yemen (commonly referred to as the Eighth Power Draft), Mar. 27, 1973, A/AC.138/SC.II/L.18; *Draft Articles Relating to Passage through the Territorial Sea* sponsored by Fiji, July 19, 1973, A/AC.138/SC.II/L42 and Corr. 1 at 91-98. See E. BROWN, PASSAGE THROUGH THE TERRITORIAL SEA: STRAITS USED FOR INTERNATIONAL NAVIGATION AND ARCHIPELAGOS. ch. 4 (1973).

4. E. JONES, LAW OF THE SEA 66-68 (1972); Henkin. *The Once and the Future Law of the Sea,* in TRANSNATIONAL LAW IN A CHANGING SOCIETY 157 (W. Friedmann, L. Henkin, O. Lissitzyn, ed. 1972); W. FRIEDMANN, THE CHANGING STRUCTURE OF INTERNATIONAL LAW 11 (1964); R. ANAND, NEW STATES AND INTERNATIONAL LAW, ch. 4 (1972); J. BHAGWATI, THE ECONOMICS OF UNDERDEVELOPED COUNTRIES (1966); E. BLACK, THE DIPLOMACY OF ECONOMIC DEVELOPMENT (1961).

The United States in essence, already has and is maintaining a 12-mile territorial sea. This country once held exclusive fishing right in a 3- to 12-mile belt, but this area has been expanded to 200 miles as a consequence of new federal legislation. The United States also exercises exclusive rights of exploitation of nonliving resources, together with rights regarding sedentary species of living resources in and beyond the 3- to 12-mile belt, and holds power to establish and enforce rules and regulations regarding fiscal matters, customs, health, and immigration. The only aspect of power the United States does not possess today in the contiguous 9-mile sea area is over navigation, which is of course subject to innocent passage. Interestingly, the 9-mile contiguous zone of high seas was not established until June 15, 1972. Knight, *The 1971 United States Proposals on the Breadth of the Territorial Sea and Passage through International Straits,* 51 OREGON L. REV. 759, 767, 768, (1972), citing the Exclusive Fisheries Zone Act, 80 Stat. 908, 16 U.S.C. §§ 1091-1094 (1970); Convention of the Continental Shelf, 499 U.N.T.S. 311 (1964); Art. 24, 1958 Territorial Seas Convention. The Fishery Conservation and Management Act, 90 Stat. 331, 16 U.S.C. § 1801 (1976), which became effective on Mar. 1, 1977, expanded the United States fishing rights zone to 200 miles.

The 1976 Fishery Conservation and Management Act provides that any eventual law of the sea treaty will supersede the United States law. This 200-mile fishery limit would surely be a part of any acceptable sea treaty, however. The new act does not prohibit foreign fishing within the 200-mile limit, but it does give American fishermen a first right of recovery of the fishing resources and allows foreigners only the excess stock that will not be harvested domestically. Eight regional fishery management councils have been established and given authority to control the fisheries of all the shores of the United States; thus, a totally new concept in American resource management has been introduced. Ristori, *Long-Sought 200 Mile Limit Can Turn Tide,* New York Times, Jan. 14, 1977, § A, p. 18, col. 1. *Coast Guard to Start Patrol Soon on New 200 Mile Fishing Limit, id.,* Feb. 6, 1977, p. 18, cols. 2, 3. East coast fishermen claimed that the new 200-mile fishing limit, but 6 weeks old, would be ineffective unless the federal government agreed to take harsh action against foreign violators. *Fishermen Demand Tougher Action on 200 Mile Violators,* Washington (D.C.) Post, Apr. 10, 1977, § A, p. 12, col. 3. *Soviet Fishing Captain Arraigned: U.S. Seeks Forfeiture of Trawler,* New York Times, Apr. 16, 1977, p. 1, col. 2. This was the first prosecution of a foreign fisherman under the new 200-mile fishing zone law. *A Little Stink About a Lot of Fish,* Time, Apr. 25, 1977, p. 42. *Russian Pleads Guilt to Violating U.S. Fishing: Is Fined $10,000.00,* New York Times, May 3, 1977, § C, p. 20, col. 4.

It has been estimated that this year 800 foreign vessels will fish within the 200-mile nautical limits and pay permit fees to the U.S. Treasury totaling $11,000,000. The following countries have vessels within the 200-mile nautical limits: Bulgaria, South Korea, Italy, Spain, Taiwan, Cuba, Japan, The Soviet Union, Mexico, and Poland. So far, the Soviets have paid $3,500,000 in permit fees to obtain the right to land 494,000 metric tons of fish — usually pollack, a cod-like fish. *Washington Post,* Mar. 26, 1978 (Magazine) p. 14.

See Schoenbaum & McDonald, *State Management of Marine Fisheries after the Fishery Conservation and Management Act of 1976 and Douglas v. Seacoast, Products, Inc.* 19 W & M. L. REV. 17 (1977). See also, Shabecoff, *Officials in Dispute over 200 Mile Ocean Jurisdiction Agree to Seek a Single U.S. Policy,* New York Times, Jan. 8, 1978, p. 20, col. 1.

The absence of clearly defined sea boundaries between the United States and Canada was compounded by the extension of offshore economic zones from 12-to 200-miles by both countries over 2 years ago. Tensions rose to such a state that when Canada imposed a ban on United States fishing in its territorial waters, the United States in turn closed its waters to Canadian fishermen. Negotiations continue for a long-term agreement, however, of the matter. Doder, *Canada, U.S. Bar Each Other's Fishermen,* Washington Post, June 3, 1978, § A, p. 16, col. 1. Only where very limited overlapping territorial waters are chartered is reciprocal fishing allowed today between the two parties. Deliberatins continue for a consolidated Maritime Boundaries and Fisheries Compact. Relative to the East coast boundaries, it appears that after 18 months of negotiations a third party arbitrator may be needed to break the deadlock here. A fisheries compact, however, seems a more realistic possibility. There is a mild degree of hope, however, that a boundaries and fisheries agreement concerning the West Coast area may be reached soon. Telephone conversation between author and Thomas Boehm, of the Canadian Embassy, Jan. 22. 1979, Washington, D.C.

Interestingly, on Feb. 14, 1979, it was announced that Canada and the United States had reached agreement, for sharing fishing catches in disputed Atlantic areas — with the boundary dispute, itself, to be submitted to third party arbitration. Talks continued over disputed areas on the Pacific coast and in the Arctic. Giniger, *U.S. and Canada Set Pact to Share Fish*, New York Times, Feb. 15, 1979, §A, p. 22, col. 1.

See generally, Hollick, *The Roots of U.S. Fisheries Policy*, 5 Ocean Develop. & Int'l. L. J. 61 (1978).

5. Lissitzyn, *The Less Developed Nations*, in 2 The Strategy of World Order: International Law 245, 263 (R. Falk, S. Mendlovitz, eds. 1966).

6. Henkin *The Once and Future Law of the Sea*, in Transnational Law in A Changing Society 162, (W. Friedmann, L. Henkin, O. Lissitzyn, eds. 1972); L. Henkin, How Nations Behave, ch. 9 (1968). See also, McDougal, *The Impact of International Law upon National Laws: A Policy-Oriented Perspective*, 4 S.D.L. Rev. 25 (1969).

7. E. Lefever, Ethics and United States Foreign Policy 100 (1957).

Professor Eugene Rostow has stated that the main function of the United Nations is to develop and express a public opinion that may be viewed as the ultimate source of governmental policy in a free society and the indispensable condition of public order. The United Nations is one means of registering and expressing the prevailing balance of power; it is not an independent power. E. Rostow, Power and the Pursuit of Peace 5, 6 (1968).

See also, Gutteridge, *The U.N. and the Law of the Sea*, in 3 New Directions in the Law of the Sea 313 (R. Churchill, K. Simmonds, J. Welch, eds. 1973); D. Kay, The United Nations Political System, ch. 3 (1967); Stang, *The 25th General Assembly and the Law of the Sea*, in The Fate of the Oceans 13 (J. Logue, ed. 1972); Friedham & Kadane, *Ocean Science in the U.N. Political Arena*, 3 J. Maritime L. & Comm. 473 (1972); Henkin, *The United Nations and the Rule of Law*, 11 Harv. Int'l. L. J. 428 (1970); G. Schwarzenberger, International Law and Order 79 (1971) discusses the concept of positive and negative sovereignty in the United Nations.

8. Henkin, *Force, Intervention and Neutrality in Contemporary International Law*, in 2 The Strategy of World Order: International Law 430 (R. Falk, S. Mendlovitz, eds. 1966); Lissitzyn, *The Less Developed Nations*, in *id.* at 245 *passim*. See also, Fatourous, *Participation of the "New" States in the International Legal Order of the Future*, in 1 The Future of the International Legal Order, ch. 7 (R. Falk, C. Black, eds. 1969); Bergsten, *The Threat from the Third World*, 11 Foreign Policy 102 (1973).

9. P. Jessup, Modern Law of Nations 30 (1948).

The National Oceanic and Atmospheric Administration of the United States Department of Commerce has promulgated rules that will inhibit highly automated foreign "factory ships" from roaming freely in the 200-mile zone. Foreign processing ships would have to obtain permits from the Commerce Department to bid for that part of the total catch reserved by the 1976 Fishery Conservation and Management Act (see *supra* note 4) and to operate in the zone. 43 Fed. Reg. 539B (Feb. 8, 1978, No. 27). Under the present law — at least in theory — Americans are allowed to take all the fish they can get in the

200-mile zone, within government conservation guidelines. Foreigners are allowed to take what is left under specific quotas established by the United States Department of State. Foreign interests may retain access to resources in the zone by buying-up segments of the United States fishing fleet or by forming joint ventures with American fishermen to buy the United States catch at sea; but only the catch, not the processing or destination of the product, counts against the quotas allocated to foreign countries. See, J. Landauer, *U.S. Fish Processors May Get Monopoly on Seafood Caught Inside 200 Mile Zone*, Wall Street Journal, Feb. 2, 1978, p. 15 cols. 2 and 3. See also, McDougal, *International Law, Power and Policy: A Contemporary Conception*, 82 RECUEIL DES COURS 137 (1953).

10. P. JESSUP, MODERN LAW OF NATIONS 31 (1948); N. HILL, INTERNATIONAL RELATIONS 248 (1950). See generally, P. JESSUP, A. LANDE, O. LISSITZYN, INTERNATIONAL REGULATION OF ECONOMIC AND SOCIAL QUESTIONS (1955).

11. Henkin, *Force, Intervention and Neutrality in Contemporary International Law*, in 2 THE STRATEGY OF WORLD ORDER: INTERNATIONAL LAW 431 (R. Falk, S. Mendlovitz, eds. 1966). See also, Ketsching, *The United Nations as an Instrument of Economic and Social Development*, in THE GLOBAL PARTNERSHIP 16 (R. Gardner, M. Milliken, eds. 1968).

12. On Dec. 6, 1974, in New York City, the then United States representative to the United Nations, John Scali, addressed a plenary session of the General Assembly and agonized over the growing tendency of the United Nations to "adopt one-sided, unrealistic resolutions that cannot be implemented." Such actions were, he noted, in arbitrary disregard of the rules of the United Nations and of its Charter. He further noted that "the United Nations, and this Assembly in particular, can walk one of two paths. The Assembly can seek to represent the views of the numerical majority of the day, or it can try to act as a spokesman of a more global opinion."

Scali continued by observing that every time the Assembly adopted resolutions which it knew would not be implemented it damaged the credibility of the United Nations. "Each time that this Assembly makes a decision which a significant minority of members regard as unfair or one-sided, it further erodes vital support for the United Nations among that minority. But the minority which is so offended may in fact be a practical majority, in terms of its capacity to support this Organization and implement its decisions. Unenforceable, one-sided resolutions destroy the authority of the United Nations . . . they encourage disrespect for the Charter . . . ."

The former ambassador also commented on the "great investment" made by the United States in the United Nations. He continued by noting that the financial loyalty and good faith shown by the citizens of America is shaken when "the rule of the majority becomes the tyranny of the majority," which has happened at the United Nations. "Every majority must recognize that its authority does not extend beyond the point where the minority becomes so outraged that it is no longer willing to maintain the covenant which binds them."

In remarks at the swearing-in ceremonies for Scali's successor, Daniel P. Moynihan, June 30, 1975, President Gerald Ford reaffirmed the Scali message of Dec. 6 and pledged firmly to resist efforts of the Third World countries to "exploit the machinery of the United Nations for narrow political interests." Moynihan had, in an earlier statement that year, proclaimed it was time for the United States to start "raising hell" in the United Nations. Naughton, *Ford Says U.S. Rejects Manipulation of U.N.*, International Herald Tribune (London), July 1, 1975, p. 1, col. 5.

Former Secretary of State Henry Kissinger echoed the Scali-Moynihan theme in remarks he made in Milwaukee, Wisconsin, where he expressed fear that the United Nations might not survive in reckless Third World pressures continue. Beeston, *U.N. is at Risk Says Kissinger*, Daily Telegraph (London), July 16, 1975, p. 14, col. 4.

An editorial in the Daily Telegraph criticized more than 80 new, unaligned members of the United Nations for disrupting the processes of peaceful accommodation and designated such actions a form of irresponsibility verging on imbecility. The editorial favored Kissinger's position. Editorial, *Kissinger's Warning*, Daily Telegraph, July 16, 1975, p. 14, col. 1.

New attitudes of conciliation, cooperation, and basic understanding among Third World nations have been forthcoming, however, under President Carter's Ambassador to the United Nations, Andrew Young, Time Dec. 27, 1976, p. 10; Lelyveld, *Our New Voice at the U.N.*, New York Times, Feb. 6, 1977 (Magazine), p. 17; Teltsch, *Young in U.N. Post a Year, Is Quieter but Still an Activist*, id., Mar. 4, 1978, §, p. 2, col. 1.

See generally, McDougal, *The Role of Law in World Politics*, 20 MISS. L. J. 253 (1949); McDougal & Burke, *Crisis in the Law of the Sea: Community Perspectives versus National Egoism*, 67 YALE L. J. 539 (1958).

13. E. WENK, JR., THE POLITICS OF THE OCEAN 31, 33 (1972).

The author identified the following as involved in ocean resource decision making to one degree or another: 29 bureaus and 11 departments and agencies within the executive branch; 33 subcommittee of the two houses of Congress. He also identified as participants or forces in fostering ocean policy development: 30 states bordering the United States seacoasts and great lakes — especially the legislatures of these states; 63 universities engaged in marine science teaching and research.

British ocean policy has been termed a patchwork — "the product of many different ministeries and offices, each with its own inherited interests and specialized pressure groups." Young, *Britain Gains Valuable Time on Sea Law*, Daily Telegraph, July 21, 1975, p. 10, col. 1.

For expressions of congressional intent, see, for example, STAFF OF SENATE COMMITTEE ON COMMERCE, 93RD CONG., 2D SESS., THE ECONOMIC VALUE OF OCEAN RESOURCES TO THE UNITED STATES (Comm. Print 1974); House Committee on Foreign Affairs, *Law of the Sea Treaty: Alternative Approaches to Provisional Application* (prepared for Subcommittee on International Organizations and Movements), H.R. REP. No. 29-211, 93rd Cong., 2d Sess. (1974); *Hearings on S. Res. 82 before the Subcommittee on Oceans and International Environment of the Senate Committee on Foreign Relations*, S. REP. NO. 93-296, 93rd Cong., 1st Sess., June 19, 1973.

14. Chemical, mineral, oil, fishing, shipping, shipbuilding, dredging, and construction industries are included here. Wenk, *supra* note 13, at 31, 45. See generally, G. J. MANGONE, MARINE POLICY FOR AMERICA (1977); PROBLEMS OF SEA POWER AS WE APPROACH THE TWENTY-FIRST CENTURY (J. George, ed., 1977).

15. Stevenson, *Who Is to Control the Oceans: U.S. Policy and the 1973 Law of the Sea Conference*, 6 INT'L LAW. 465, 468-469 (1972). See Finlay, *The Position of the APA on the Law of the Sea*, 8 CASE W. RES. J. INT'L L. 84 (1976).

DRAFT ARTICLES ON THE BREADTH OF THE TERRITORIAL SEA, STRAITS, AND FISHERIES SUBMITTED BY THE UNITED STATES

Article I

1. *Each State shall have the right, subject to the provisions of Article II, to establish the breadth of its territorial sea within limits of no more than 12 nautical miles, ensured in accordance with the provisions of the 1958 Geneva Convention of the Territorial Sea and Contiguous Zone.*

2. *In instances where the breadth of the territorial sea of a State is less than 12 nautical miles, such State may establish a fisheries zone contiguous to its territorial sea provided, however, that the total breadth of the territorial sea and fisheries zone shall not exceed 12 nautical miles. Such State may exercise within such a zone the same rights in respect to fisheries as it has in its territorial sea.*

Article II

1. *In straits used for international navigation between one part of the high seas and another part of the high seas or the territorial sea of a foreign State, all ships and aircraft in transit shall enjoy the same freedom of navigation and overflight, for the purpose of transit through and over such straits, as they have on the high seas. Coastal States may designate corridors suitable for transit by all ships and aircraft through and over such straits. In the case of straits where particular channels of navigation are customarily employed by ships in transit, the corridors, so far as ships are concerned, shall include such channels.*

2. *The provisions of this Article shall not affect conventions or other international agreements already in force specifically relating to particular straits. United Nations Doc. A/AC.138/SC.II/L4 (3 August 1971).*

(In the interests of brevity and conciseness, Article III is not printed here because of its sole relevance to fisheries, which are not a point of investigation in this analysis.)

The United States Draft Article on transit through straits recognized the legitimate safety and pollution concerns of strait states. It was, thus, then proposed that surface ships transiting straits observe the traffic separation schemes of the *Inter-Governmental Maritime Consultative Organization* (IMCO) and that state aircraft normally comply with the regulations of the International Civil Aviation Organization (ICAO). It was also proposed that strict liability apply for damage caused by deviations from such IMCO or ICAO regulations.

The objective of the United States proposals here was to find a balance between the reasonable concerns of strait states and the need of the international community for guarantees of meaningful uses of the high seas. The United States proposal on straits was not limited to military vessels and aircraft; it was equally concerned with unimpeded transit for commercial vessels particularly since the energy dilemma has brought widespread attention to the fact that a nation's well-being may be intimately linked to an adequate and secure supply of petroleum and other basic imports. Bureau of Public Affairs, Office of Media Services, U.S. DEPARTMENT OF STATE, 1 *Special Report* (rev.), *U.N. Law of the Sea Conference, 1975.* This report is quite comprehensive and is based upon statements made by Ambassador John R. Stevenson and Deputy Special Representative John Norton Moore before the Senate Foreign Relations Committee and the House Committee on the Judiciary.

16. Q. WRIGHT, CONTEMPORARY INTERNATIONAL LAW: A BALANCE SHEET 56 (1955).

The politics of any state must necessarily be tied to elements of common understanding, which means to a considerable degree it must involve "the language of the past, for who understands and who can demonstrate the unknowable future?" A. BERLE, JR., TIDES OF CRISIS 18 (1957).
A political culture is said to consist of traits, techniques, and institutions that are shared by the members of a social system. Such a culture defines the processes through which the members of the social system compete and cooperate for influence and other social values; it exists only when a set of patterns and institutions is developed and accepted by the members of the system. As a concept it is fluid, not static. The development of international political cultures is generally inhibited because of various feelings among states that they have few common cultural patterns and beliefs. While there may be a basis for sharing a common political culture, the existing one is inadequate to meet the needs of the members of the total system. W. COPLIN, THE FUNCTION OF INTERNATIONAL LAW 186, 187, 191 (1966). See McDougal, *The Role of Law in World Politics,* 20 MISS. L.J. 253 (1949).

17. C. HODGES, THE BACKGROUND OF INTERNATIONAL RELATIONS 88 (1931). See also, P. RENOUVIN & J. DUROSELLE, INTRODUCTION TO THE HISTORY OF INTERNATIONAL RELATIONS, ch. 1 (1968).

18. O. LISSITZYN, INTERNATIONAL LAW TODAY AND TOMORROW 102 (1965); Schwarzenberger, *Civitas Maxima?* 29 Y.B. WORLD AFFAIRS 337, 362 (1975).

19. Henkin, *Force, Intervention and Neutrality in Contemporary International Law,* in 2 THE STRATEGY OF WORLD ORDER: INTERNATIONAL LAW 335 (Falk, S. Mendlovitz, eds. 1966). See also, HENKIN, HOW NATIONS BEHAVE 127 *passim* (1968). The concept and use of anticipatory self-defense is ably discussed *id.,* pp. 233-236. See also, P. CORBETT, THE GROWTH OF WORLD LAW, ch. 6 (1971).

20. Henkin, *Force, Intervention and Neutrality in Contemporary International Law,* in 2 THE STRATEGY OF WORLD ORDER: INTERNATIONAL LAW 336 (R. Falk, S. Mendlovitz, eds. 1966).

21. *Id.,* 335, 342, 344. See also, Henkin, *International Law and the Behavior of Nations,* 114 RECUEIL DES COURS 171, 276 (1965); Henkin, *Review,* 9 J. PUB. L. 229, 237 (1960). See generally, L. HENKIN, ARMS CONTROL AND INSPECTION IN AMERICAN LAW (1958).
The ultimate form of power politics is war, which is but a continuation of politics by other means. N. HILL, INTERNATIONAL RELATIONS 299 (1960). See also, McDougal, *Law and Power,* 46 AM. J. INT'L L. 102 (1952).
Unless there is popular assurance and support, governments will not declare war. Root, *The Need of Popular Understanding of International Law,* in ELIHU ROOT: ADDRESSES ON INTERNATIONAL SUBJECTS 3 (R. Bacon, J. Scott, eds. 1916).

22. HENKIN, HOW NATIONS BEHAVE 249 (1968).
The progress of civilization, when viewed through the relationships of nations, may be recorded as "movement from force to diplomacy, from diplomacy to law. The hope of civilized men has long been that nations would cease to pursue their interests by force, and attempt instead to negotiate in question of peace." *Id.* at 3. See also, McDougal, *Law and Power,* 46 AM. J. INT'L L. 102 (1952); Falk, *The Role of Law in World Society: Present Crisis and Future Prospects,* in TOWARD WORLD ORDER AND HUMAN DIGNITY: ESSAYS IN HONOR OF MYRES S. MCDOUGAL. ch. 5 (W. M. Reisman, B. H. Weston, eds. 1976).

23. See references, *supra* note 22.

24. W. FRIEDMANN, AN INTRODUCTION TO WORLD POLITICS 4 (4th ed. 1960);

Morse, *Crisis Diplomacy, Interdependence and the Politics of International Economic Relations*, 23 WORLD POLITICS 123, 124 (1972); N. HILL, INTERNATIONAL RELATIONS 248 (1959); A. LALL, MODERN INTERNATIONAL NEGOTIATION, Ch. 15 (1966).

See also, H. LASWELL, WORLD POLITICS FACES ECONOMICS (1945); G. HUGO, APPEARANCE AND REALITY IN INTERNATIONAL RELATIONS (1970); W. BACCHUS, FOREIGN POLICY AND THE BUREAUCRATIC PROCESS (1974). See generally, P. JESSUP, A. LANDE & O. LISSITZYN, INTERNATIONAL REGULATION OF ECONOMIC AND SOCIAL QUESTIONS (1955).

25. See references, *supra* note 24. See generally, L. JAFFEE, JUDICIAL ASPECTS OF FOREIGN POLICY (1933).

26. P. JESSUP, 4 NEUTRALITY: ITS HISTORY, ECONOMICS AND LAW 86 (1936).

The concept of neutrality may be traced back to 1478 in France. Sometime between the 1620s and 1630s it became generally recognized in Europe, and neutral rights began to be formed and recognized. P. JESSUP & F. DEAK, 1 NEUTRALITY: ITS HISTORY, ECONOMICS AND LAW 20, 157 (1935). The first neutrality law in the United States was passed by Congress in 1794 for a 3-year duration. JESSUP, *supra* at 211.

"The whole history of the fight for neutral rights is a history of failures. The power which is politically the freest and most liberal in the world has by its practice tenaciously prevented an enlargement of neutral rights." N. ANGELL, THE WORLD HIGHWAY, ch. 6 (1915).

See Trimble, *Violations of Maritme Law by the Allied Powers during the World War*, 24 AM. J. INT'L L. 79 (1930).

Neutrality, it has been maintained, means noninvolvement in war. Neutralism concerns noninvolvement in the Cold War and is thus accordingly defined as a state of continuous preparation for war or a continuous war alert. *The* Cold War is one where, presently, the principals are the United States and Russia. P. LYON, NEUTRALISM 17, 20, (1963). See also, JESSUP, *supra* at 211. One could question the validity of the term, "Cold War," today since *detente* is the current approach the two major world powers are pursuing.

See also, Henkin, *Force, Intervention, and Neutrality in Contemporary International Law*, 57 AM. SOC. INT'L LAW PROC. 147, 159-162 (1963), for a discussion of neutrality and neutralism, and C. COLOMBOS, THE INTERNATIONAL LAW OF THE SEA 748 *passim* (6th rev. ed. 1967); H. SMITH, THE LAW AND CUSTOM OF THE SEA, ch. 14, (3d ed. 1959).

Henkin has asserted that neutrality, as an often proclaimed element in war between nations, is largely academic today. Its relevancy can only be recognized when war exists long enough to make it meaningful as a possibility. Neutralism, however, is a different matter; it is a political term, not a legal one. If it promoted competition and agreement for the development of international law, it would be positive in its reenforcement. All too often, however, neutralism affords a type of immunity to censure, with small nations being tempted to violate law under its guise. Henkin, *Force, Intervention and Neutrality in Contemporary International Law*, in 2 THE STRATEGY OF WORLD ORDER: INTERNATIONAL LAW 335, 349, 350 (R. Falk, S. Mendlovitz, eds. 1966).

27. G. VON GLAHN, LAW AMONG NATIONS 627, 629 (2d ed. 1970).

28. Waldock, *The Release of the Altmark's Prisoners*, 26 BRIT. Y. B. INT'L L. 216, 220 (1947). See also, MacChesney, *The Altmark Incident and Modern Warfare: "Innocent Passage" in Wartime and the Rights of Belligerents to Use Force to Redress Neutrality Violations*, 52 NW. U. L. REV. 320 (1957). See generally, McDougal & Feliciano, *International Coercion and World Public Order: The General Principles of the Law of War*, 67 YALE L. J. 771 (1958).

The *Altmark* was a German supply ship, but since it was included in the official German Naval List, for all practical purposes it was regarded as a warship. After engaging in combat in the Atlantic Ocean and capturing approximately 300 British merchant seamen, the ship sought to return to Germany. This aspect of her voyage was, thus, military as to its origin. The English Channel was barred to her as a direct return route so the *Altmark* proceeded north in an effort to avoid being captured by the British navy. She entered Norwegian territorial waters on Feb. 14, 1940, and proceeded through these waters for some 400 miles until on Feb. 16 she was stopped by British destroyers that forcibly removed the 300 prisoners. The British justified their actions on the grounds that the *Altmark*'s actions were an operation of war and therefore unlawful. If such actions were consummated, it would be a serious breach of international law, which would materially prejudice British interests.

Norway contended that since the *Altmark* was in reality a German warship, it was immune from search. Thus, Norway only possessed the right to verify the *Altmark*'s identity and status; this was done on Feb. 14 by a Norwegian torpedo boat. Since international law did not prohibit the conveyance of prisoners of war by a belligerent through neutral waters, the *Altmark*'s passage was in fact legal. The maneuvers of the *Altmark* did not bring it into any Norwegian port—they were but activities of passage. Consequently, no obligation existed or could be imposed on the *Altmark* to leave the territorial waters of Norway. Moreover, the laws of neutrality did not impose any obligations of the nature claimed by Britain upon Norway. Britain, therefore, had acted maliciously in its violation of Norway's neutrality by invading her territorial waters. Waldock, *supra*.

29. VON GLAHN, *supra*, note 27, at 631.

30. Henkin, *Force, Intervention, and Neutrality in Contemporary International Law*, 57 AM. SOC. INT'L LAW PROC 147, 195-162 (1963).

31. O. LISSITZYN, INTERNATIONAL LAW TODAY AND TOMORROW 30, 31 (1965).

32. Schwarzenberger, *The Scope of Neutralism*, 15 Y.B. WORLD AFFAIRS 233, 234, 235 (1961).

33. Henkin, *Force, Intervention, and Neutrality in Contemporary International Law*, 57 AM. SOC. INT'L LAW PROC. 147, 159-162 (1963).

34. LISSITZYN, INTERNATIONAL LAW TODAY AND TOMORROW 86, 87 (1965). Franklin, *The Law of the Seas: Some Recent Developments*, 53 NAVAL WAR COLLEGE INT'L STUDIES 121, 123 (1961). See generally, Lawrence, *Military-Legal Considerations in the Extension of the Territorial Sea*, 29 MILITARY L. REV. 47 (1965); Moore, *The Legal Tradition and the Management of National Security*, in TOWARD WORLD ORDER AND HUMAN DIGNITY: ESSAYS IN HONOR OF MYRES S. McDOUGAL, ch. 10 (W. M. Reisman, B. H. Weston, Eds. 1976).

35. Knight, *The 1971 United States Proposals on the Breadth of the Territorial Sea and Passage through International Straits*, 51 OREGON L. REV. 759, 766 (1972). As to the law of the sea, economic rather than ideological lines separate Latin American countries. Zacklin, *Latin America and the Development of the Law of the Sea: An Overview*, in THE CHANGING LAW OF THE SEA 59, 73 (R. Zacklin, ed. 1974). See also, Garcia-Amador, *The Latin American Contribution to the Development of the Law of the Sea*, 68, AM. J. INT'L L. 33 (1974).

36. Knight, *supra* note 35, at 767.

For more detail on the United States-Latin American compromise, see Farer & Caplovitz, *Towards a New Law for the Seas: The Evolution of United States Policy*, in THE CHANGING LAW OF THE SEA 49-51 (R. Zacklin, ed. 1974). Since the United States jurisdiction over its present 12-mile maritime belt is complete, it has submitted that it already has a defacto 12-mile territorial sea regime. *Id.*

From a very practical stance, the economic zone is but an attempt to solve the classical dilemma of choice when a consideration of *mare clausum* and *mare liberum* is made; for the very force and application of the economic zone theory is tied to designing and applying modified *mare clausum* and *mare liberum* solutions to different problems within the same area. In contradistinction to the contiguous zone, the economic zone is not to be considered a "buffer" where jurisdiction is linked to a violation of law either in the territory or, for that matter, in the coastal state's territorial sea. Furthermore, unlike the continental shelf doctrine, the economic zone concept applies in major ways to multiple uses of the water column. Some activities listed in the Revised Standard Negotiating Text may be conducted within the economic zone only by first obtaining the pertinent coastal states' consent. Unfettered discretion is, however, not conferred upon any state in its administration of its economic zone. The precise nature and extent of residual rights remains a contentious problem regarding the legal status of the economic zone. Oxman, *The Third United Nations Conference on the Law of the Sea: The 1976 New York Session,* 71 Am. J. Int'l L. 247, *et seq.* (1977).

The basic debate over the status of the economic zone should not be viewed as relating strictly in a legal sense to the preservation of navigational and other communications freedoms or to the preservation of what might be considered as classic high seas laws in the zone itself. There is an implication that high sea freedoms and high sea laws are not preserved in the economic zone. Yet, a close reading of the Revised Standard Negotiating Text clearly contradicts this implication. From a strictly juridical viewpoint, the economic zone is to be more properly regarded as but an overlay on the high seas. Interestingly, it generally eliminates freedom of fishing and, to a more certain degree, some other freedoms (e.g., with respect to some scientific research and installations), yet goes on to establish a degree of concurrent rights or jurisdiction with respect to others (e.g., some scientific research and some vessel-source pollution). It does not, however, eliminate the traditional role of the flag state. Oxman, *supra.*

The core issue here is, then, determining the scope of national jurisdiction in the economic zone. While one group of nations contend the *totality* of national jurisdiction within the zone, other maritime states, which use and engage in flight over the seas quite extensively, argue that coastal state jurisdiction should be limited to a right to exploit both the living and non-living resources in the zone itself. Following their argument, the territorial sea would be limited to 12 miles, and the remainder of the 200-mile zone would, in turn, be defined as part of the high seas subject only to a certain economic rights of the coastal state. Charney, *Law of the Sea: Breaking the Deadlock,* 55 Foreign Affairs 598, 600 (1977).

It has been suggested that perhaps the best way to achieve balance and, hence, stability in this problem area is to adopt that approach set forth in the 1958 Territorial Sea, Continental Shelf, and High Seas conventions; namely, the establishment of clear coastal state rights beyond the territorial sea and the reassertion of the areas beyond the territorial sea as high seas.

Given the present uncertainty surrounding the economic zone, it seems very possible that only a fishing zone — instead of an economic zone as set out in the Revised Standard Negotiating Text — will ultimately be absorbed into generally recognized customary law in the near future. Some states will, to be sure, continue to claim a total economic zone. The content of the fishing zone is likely (in the ultimate sense) to resemble that described in the Revised Standard Negotiating Text. Oxman, *supra*.

37. Aguilar, *The Patrimonial Sea or Economic Zone Concept,* 11 SAN DIEGO L. REV. 558, 596 (1974). See also, Hollick, *Sea Beds Make Strange Politics,* 9 FOREIGN POLICY 148, 170 (1972).

The very first outline of a regional position in Latin America with respect to the sea emerged in Santiago on Aug. 18, 1952, when Chile, Ecuador, and Peru signed a Declaration on the Maritime Zone proclaiming their exclusive sovereignty and jurisdiction over their coastal waters to a distance of 200 miles. It is important to note that the declaration was concerned with a maritime zone rather than with the territorial sea. Subsequent conferences of the Caribbean States were held in Montevideo in 1970, in Lima in 1970, and finally in Santa Domingo in 1972 to consider problems of maritime sovereignty and control of ocean resources. Zacklin, *supra* note 35 at 62–66.

38. Brown, *Maritime Zones: A Survey of Claims,* in NEW DIRECTIONS IN THE LAW OF THE SEA 157, 167 (R. Churchill, K. Simmonds, J. Welch, eds. 1973).

39. *Id.* at 74. The major criticisms of the concept are stated *id.,* beginning at 172. See also, Amerashinghe, *The Third United Nations Conference on the Law of the Sea,* 6 UNITAR NEWS 2, 3 (No. 1, 1974).

The 200-mile claim is not a unified Latin American position. Indeed, contemporary legislation and practice may be conveniently grouped into 3 main categories:

1. Claims to a territorial sea not exceeding 12 miles: Barbados, Colombia, Cuba, Guyana, Jamaica, Dominican Republic, Haiti, Guatemala, Honduras, Mexico, Trinidad, Tobago, and Venezuela.

2. Claims to a 200-mile maritime zone of limited sovereignty: Costa Rica, Chile, Argentina, Uruguay, El Salvador, and Nicaragua.

3. Claims to a strict 200-mile territorial sea: Brazil, Ecuador, Panama, and Peru. Zacklin, *supra* note 35, at 64.

Centrifugal forces of political, economic, and cultural diversity have frustrated all efforts to establish a cohesive Latin American posture with respect to the law of the sea.

Vietnam, interestingly, announced the extension of its sea rights and thereby posed a potential problem with China. While maintaining a territorial sea of 12 miles, Vietnam announced the extension of an exclusive economic zone 200 miles from its shores. The zone would thus include the Paracel Islands, occupied by China after the Vietnamese were driven off them in 1974. New York Times, May 22, 1977, p. 5, col. 1.

Australia considered legislation in 1978 which will establish a 200-mile fishing zone. Walshington Post, Feb. 7, 1977, § A, p. 9, col. 1. In late August of 1978, in fact, implementing legislation was passed structuring an extension of the fisheries zone to 200 nautical miles. Fisheries Amendment Act of 1978, No. 99.

40. Stevenson & Oxman, *The Third United Nations Conference on the Law of the Sea: The 1974 Caracas Session,* 69 AM. J. INT'L L. 1, 13 (1975).

Chapter 4
THE POLITICS OF NEGOTIATION

Free Transit: Historical Recapitulation

Free transit, right of free transit, or free passage are phrases used interchangeably to delineate a right of free navigation on the seas. The concept of such a right is an expression of the very principle of freedom of the seas. Free transit should be viewed more properly as separate from any statements concerning the territorial seas and their breadth. The functional character of the right of free transit should remain 'operationally secure regardless of a new width of the territorial sea or resource zones agreed upon."[1] Current practice does not, however, always make this needed separation.

The right of free transit developed through the practice of customary international law. States were long believed obligated to act in fulfillment of their responsibilities as members of the international community to all who wished passage over or across their territory. Grotius, in his *De jure belli ac pacis* observed that "lands, rivers and any part of the sea that has become subject to ownership of a people ought to be open to those who, for legitimate reasons, have need to cross over them."[2] A more recent commentator stressed that the strength of claims to transit across foreign territory depended upon the nature and importance of the particular channel of communication to the transit state.[3]

It is generally regarded necessary for those states claiming a right of free transit to establish a basis of necessity or convenience and further to agree that no harm or prejudice will come to that transit state as a consequence of its exercise of the right. The transit state may exercise its discretion and refuse passage on the grounds of self-defense or general public policy.[4] When a coastal state, in manifesting its sovereignty in such a way exceeds the necessities of protecting valid interests and interferes with the legitimate interests of other states, this is regarded as an *abuse of rights.*[5]

The right of free transit as an international right has been recognized in many international conventions. As observed, the right of free passage by warships through international straits in peacetime was recognized by the International Court of Justice in its decision in the *Corfu Channel* case as a rule of customary international law. The Montreux Convention of July 20, 1936, stipulated a complete freedom of transit and navigation for merchant ships regarding access to the Black Sea. Other similar conventions have granted free transit through other international straits.[6] Finally, the 1958 Territorial Sea Convention recognized passage rights through straits.

In the interest of the principle of innocent passage, both as it emerged in maritime history and as it eventually was codified in the Territorial Sea Convention, the international community has attempted to strike an equitable

balance between the need to allow a free flow of commerce through international straits and at the same time
to protect the valid interests of many states. Today many
states believe this balance is inadequate.[7]

A Strategy for Diplomatic Negotiations: Tradeoffs

The strategic theory that prompted Nixon's 1970 seabed proposal was simple and direct: encourage other
members in the world community to seriously consider, if
not adopt, the policy of promoting a narrow continental
shelf. The Department of Defense hoped a side effect of
this proposal would be the inducement of a favorable
climate for the separate negotiations then under way concerning the breadth of the territorial sea, transit through
international straits, and fisheries.

As a consequence of subsequent negotiations that took
place through 1971 with allies of the United States—principally at the United Nations—an official negotiating
package was formed consisting of territorial seas, straits,
and fisheries. The decision to promote consideraton of
these three areas as a unit, separate and apart from questions involving the continental shelf and seabed, was
based as much on bureaucratic factors as on tactical
negotiating factors. The issues had been previously
handled as separate matters within the governmental
agencies participating in ocean policy making. This
bureaucratic division had been reenforced by an additional preference among government officials for developing well-packaged *tradeoffs*: freedom of transit
through and over international straits in exchange for a
twelve-mile territorial sea, with preferential littoral state
fishing rights in the area beyond; or a narrow continental
shelf for a generous seabed regime. Development and
preservation of resource interests were always given secon-
dary consideration over strategic military considerations
in both packages.[8]

Under the United States proposal before the Third United Nations Law of the Sea Conference, the coastal state would be given a right to establish its territorial sea breadth at a maximum distance of twelve nautical miles from the baseline. Thus, states wishing to set varying breadths — three, four, or six nautical miles — would be allowed to do. The second pertinent provision of the Draft Proposal structures a system of free transit through international straits, which is now largely agreed to informally. Not only would the existing regime of passage be changed from "innocent passage" to "free transit," but submerged and overflight passage would be allowed in this new right of free transit. By the use of the phrase, "all ships," this proposal would also guarantee to warships the right of free transit through international straits.[9]

Broad general agreement has been recorded for a twelve-mile maximum limit for the territorial sea. Many states, however, make the formalization of this agreement contingent upon a satisfactory resolution of other treaty issues, especially those regarding straits and coastal resources. Indeed, "while the international area beyond coastal state jurisdiction has received more attention than any other area, the heart of negotiations in terms of achieving a generally acceptable agreement, is the extent and nature of coastal jurisdiction in the coastal area."[10]

If agreement were reached on a territorial sea of twelve miles, between one hundred sixteen and one hundred twenty-one international straits of considerable importance not only to commerce but also to strategic naval interests would be brought into the regime of the territorial sea and thus be made subject to the right of innocent passage. Fearful of these impediments to maritime commerce, and more especially to military preparedness, the United States has linked its proposal for a twelve-mile territorial sea to a provision of free rather than innocent passage through and over international straits. The United States had deemed it advisable to link these two

provisions to avoid improper exercises of coastal state discretion in determining whether the purpose of a vessel's
use of the waters is innocent or noninnocent. Opposition
to free transit is built upon the argument made by certain
strait states "that the innocent passage should apply to all
parts of the territorial sea, including the territorial sea
overlapping straits."[11]

The Department of Defense
and Military Preparedness

National security is, perhaps, the controlling interest in
United States foreign policy, and therefore it is but natural to assume that American defense strategies will be developed around effective use and control of the seas,
which constitute seventy percent of the earth's surface.
Any efforts that would jeopardize this policy and abridge
ocean freedoms by restricting naval operation are regarded as intolerable. Naval force — and all other forms
of military power — may be ultimately viewed as a form of
"coercive diplomacy" whenever the occasion arises.[12]

Experts from inside and outside the federal government are concerned that the Department of Defense is
uncompromisingly committed to this rigid position on
free transit through straits to the extent that it threatens
to disrupt any type of negotiated compromise effort aimed at establishing a "minimal international order essential
to America's broader ocean interests," undertaken at the
Law of the Sea Conference. Yet, given the increasing
threats to petroleum and other commercial transit
brought on by conflicts in the Middle East and the very
real prospect of "subjective" constructions of innocent
passage, the official negotiating posture has understand-
ably become unyielding on the issue of free transit
through straits.[13]

The Soviet Union has aligned itself with the policies of
the leading Western maritime powers on the issue of free

transit through international straits. Russia in fact controls the world's largest submarine fleet, and its sea-based defense posture dictates the same uncompromising position on the straits issue as that of the United States.[14]

The United States capacity for nuclear deterrence through the use of its nuclear-powered submarines with nuclear missiles (SSBNs) would be made more difficult if a twelve-mile territorial sea boundary were set and no right of free transit through international straits guaranteed, but this capability would not be destroyed, since there are really only three or four international straits of particular strategic value to the United States. Greater destruction would befall the state of American military preparedness if more coastal nations assert their control over straits, claim up to two-hundred-mile territorial sea boundaries, demand that innocent passage be abridged through restrictions, and otherwise delimit the use of ocean space. Confrontations would seem almost certain under situations of this nature.[15]

One leading authority maintains that military power—its use or threatened use—to accommodate political purposes of the state in future law of the sea problems is not to be expected.[16] Yet, if strategic military straits were closed, for example, to United States warships, which in order to accomplish the fulfillment of a goal of national governmental importance required passage through them, it is doubtful that a small coastal state restriction on or hastily maintained defense thereof would be respected. When a secretary of state can note with alarming candor that the United States government will not allow itself to be strangled economically by Middle East oil restrictions and will use whatever force necessary to avert such an occurrence, it is but natural to presume that such an exercise of military power will be aserted if vital national security goals are threatened by restrictive policies concerning the use of international straits.[17]

NOTES—CHAPTER 4

1. Cundrick, *International Straits: The Right of Access,* 5 GA. J. INT'L & COMP. L. 107, 111 (1975): J. MERRYMAN & E. ACKERMAN, INTERNATIONAL LAW: DEVELOPMENT OF THE TRANSIT TRADE OF LANDLOCKED STATES — THE CASE FOR BOLIVIA 21 (1969).

2. Lauterpacht, *Freedom of Transit in International Law,* 44 GROTIUS SOC. TRANSACTIONS 313, (1958-59).

3. C. HYDE, 1 INTERNATIONAL LAW 628 (2d rev. ed. 1945).

4. Lauterpacht, *supra* note 2, at 332, 340, 345.

5. D. BOWETT, THE LAW OF THE SEA 44, 50 (1967).

6. Convention Regarding the Regime of the Straits, 173 U.N.T.S. 213 (1936).

Although the Strait of Gibraltar is within the Spanish territorial sea, right of overflight and freedom of passage of warships is granted liberally by the Spanish government. F. KRUGER-SPRENGEL, THE ROLE OF NATO IN THE USE OF THE SEA AND SEABED 28 (1972).

The Barcelona Convention of Freedom of Transit of 1921 allows "transit in accordance with customary conditions" across the territorial waters of the contracting parties.

The Straits of Magellan are governed by a treaty of 1881 between Chile and Argentina, under which freedom of passage is assured for ships of *all* nations. Passage through the Panama Canal is governed by the Hay-Pauncefote Treaty of 1901, supplemented by the Hay-Varilla Treaty of 1903. The Constantinople Convention of 1888 established rights of passage through the Suez Canal. Exclusion of Israeli ships therefrom cannot be justified under the convention. H. SMITH, THE LAW AND CUSTOM OF THE SEA 33, 34 (3d ed. 1959).

The Panama Canal posed an interesting problem. Panama expressed a strong desire to exercise full rights of sovereignty over the waterway. The Varilla treaty signed by the United States with the Republic of Panama on Nov. 18, 1903, not only granted to the federal government the right to build an Isthmian canal but also granted in perpetuity — according to Art. 2 — "the use, occupation and control" of the 10-mile wide Canal Zone to the United States government. Art. 3 authorized the United States to exercise power and authority as if it were the sovereign of the territory.

See, *Panama Presses for Commitment by Carter on Canal Negotiations,* New York Times, Jan. 14, 1977, p. 1, col. 6; *The Canal: Time to Go,* Newsweek, Aug. 22, 1977, p. 28; Editorial, *The Panama Compromise,* Wall Street Journal, Feb. 3, 1978, p. 6, col. 1; *On Voting Yes or No on the Panama Treaties — Reagan v. Buckley,* National Review, Feb. 17, 1978, p. 210; Johnson, *Senate Approves Canal Treaty 68-32, Drama Pervades Historic Call,* The Washington Post, Mar. 17, 1978, p. 1, col. 1; Clymer, *Senate Votes to Give Up Panama Canal; Carter Foresees "Beginning of a New Era,"* New York Times, Apr. 19, 1978, p. 1, col. 6.

The two Panama Canal treaties may be found in 72 AM. J. INT'L L. 225 *et seq.* (1978).

See generally, *Symposium on the Panama Canal,* 9 N. Y. UNIV. J. INT'L L. & POLITICS 1 (1976); Smit, *The Panama Canal: A National or International Waterway,* 75 COLUM L. REV. 965 (1976); G. A. MELLANDER, THE U.S. IN PANAMANIAN POLITICS (1971); L. O. EALY, YANQUI POLITICS AND THE ISTHMIAN CANAL (1971); S. B. LISS, THE CANAL (1967).

7. Knight, *The United States Proposals on the Breadth of the Territorial Sea and Passage through International Straits,* 51 OREGON L. REV. 770 (1972).

8. A. Hollick & R. Osgood, New Era of Ocean Politics 40 (1974). See also, Hollick, *The Law of the Sea and U.S. Policy Initiatives*, 15 Orbis 670, 685 (1971); Allison & Halperin, *Bureaucratic Politics: A Paradigm and Some Policy Implications*, 24 World Politics (450 Supp. 1972); Hollick, *United States Oceans Politics*, 10 San Diego L. Rev. 467, 487 (1973); R. Falk, The Status of Law in International Society 33 (1970), where the author analyzes bureaucratic as opposed to crisis decision making. See generally, Halperin, *Why Bureaucrats Play Games*, 2 Foreign Policy 70 (1971); Lake, *Laying Around Washington*, 2 *id.* at 106 (1971); Hull, *The Political Ocean*, 45 Foreign Affairs 492 (1967); Young, *To Guard the Sea*, 50 *id.* at 136 (1971); M. Halperin, Bureaucratic Politics and Foreign Affairs (1974); I. Destler, Presidents, Bureaucrats and Foreign Policy (1972).

9. *Information Report on the Law of the Sea: Understanding the Debate on the Law of Ocean Space*, 8 Int'l Law. 688, 692 (1974); Knight, *supra* note 7 at 773.

Art. 24 of the 1958 Convention on the Territorial Sea and the Contiguous Zone, which sets a 12-mile maximum breadth for a special contiguous zone, would be rendered inoperable if a 12-mile territorial sea were established. Art. 24 would, however remain relevant for those states claiming less than a 12-mile territorial sea.

10. Stevenson & Oxman, *The Third United Nations Conference on the Law of the Sea: The 1974 Caracas Session*, 69 Am. J. Int'l L. 8, 9 (1975). See also, Knight, *Issues Before the Third United Nations Conference on the Law of the Sea*, 34 La. L. Rev. 155, 184 (1974); Knight, *United States Ocean Policy: Perspective 1974*, 49 Notre Dame Law. 241, 261 (1973).

11. Stevenson & Oxman, *supra* note 10, at 11. See also, Kildow, *The Law of the Sea: Alliances and Divisive Issues in International Ocean Negotiation*, 11 San Diego L. Rev. 558, 570 (1974); Nolta, *Passage through International Straits: Free or Innocent? The Interests at Stake*, 11 *id.* at 815 (1974).

One rather simple solution to resolving the straits problem would have simply been to exclude straits from provisions that sought to extend the territorial sea — at least where such proposed extensions failed to leave an acceptable navigation and overflight corridor on and through the high seas. This was not pursued because it was believed the corridor might have been difficult to establish in some cases and because, to pursue such a solution would possibly have imposed broader restrictions on coastal state rights than necessary to protect transit. Stevenson & Oxman, *supra* note 10, at 8, 9.

Regarding the issue of straits and their status in international law, see: R. Baxter & J. Tuska, The Law of Waterways (1964); H. Crocker, The Extent of the Marginal Sea (1919); P. Graves, The Question of Straits (1931); J. Shotwell & F. Deak, Turkey at the Straits (1940); C. Phillipson & N. Buston, The Question of the Bosphorus and Dardanells (1917); L. Bouchez, The Regime of Bays in International Law (1964).

12. Franklin, *The Law of the Seas: Some Recent Developments*, 53 Naval War College Int'l Studies 121 (1961); E. Luttwak, The Political Uses of Sea Power (1974).

The basic military use of the sea received new dimension after the launching of the first nuclear-powered submarine, the U.S.S. Nautilus, in 1957. Yet in the early 1960s, seapower still meant dominating the seas' surface and controlling its use as channels of supply. Today the strategic use of submarines is directed toward controlling the seas in order to dominate a possible enemy's land areas. Kruger-Sprengel, *supra* note 6.

Foreign policy should, at a minimum, seek to promote nonviolent means of resolving conflict, enlarge the scope of universally shared policy values, and both promote and guarantee the preservation of individual freedom. E. HAAS, TANGLE OF HOPES 236 (1969).

For foreign policy, perhaps the most important legal mechanism is the international agreement, and the most important principle of international law is *pacta sunt servanda*: agreements shall be observed. This principle makes international relations possible. L. HENKIN, HOW NATIONS BEHAVE 19 (1968).

See also, Kissinger, *Reflections on American Diplomacy*, in FIFTY YEARS OF FOREIGN AFFAIRS 257 (H. Armstrong, ed. 1972); H. MORGENTHAU, IN DEFENSE OF NATIONAL INTEREST 33, 34 (1951). Moore, *The Legal Tradition and the Management of National Security*, in TOWARD WORLD ORDER AND HUMAN DIGNITY: ESSAYS IN HONOR OF MYRES S. McDOUGAL, ch. 10 (W. M. Reisman, B. H. Weston, eds. 1976).

13. HOLLICK & OSGOOD, *supra* note 8, at 76. The advantage of free transit over innocent passage has been defined almost exclusively in terms of maintaining American strategic nuclear capabilities, guaranteed as such by the unannounced underwater passage of nuclear-powered submarines with nuclear missiles (SSBNs). Three additional security interests are also promoted by a strong United States position on free passage through international straits: "the limitation of territorial boundaries, (which might be expanded from twelve to two hundred miles by virtue of Latin American boundary claims, the assertion of anti-pollution zones — as by Canada — and the process of 'creeping jurisdiction' that would extend the assertion of anti-pollution and resource exploitation zones to claims of territorial sovereignty); the right of military overflight (to which not even innocent passage applies) over key international straits; and the right to emplace anti-submarine listening devices on the continental shelf." HOLLICK & OSGOOD, *supra* note 8, at 78, 79.

Of particular strategic importance is the fact that the United States Department of Defense regime would allow use by all states of "other" seabed activities — which is construed as including the right to deploy antisubmarine warfare tracking and detection devices. Knight, *Special Domestic Interests and United States Ocean Policy*, in INTERNATIONAL RELATIONS AND THE FUTURE OF THE OCEANS 24 (R. Wirsing, ed. 1974). See also, LUTTWAK, *supra* note 12; W. BUTLER, THE LAW OF SOVIET TERRITORIAL WATERS (1967).

14. Butler, *The USSR and the Limits to National Jurisdiction over the Sea 1970–72*, in LIMITS TO NATIONAL JURISDICTION OVER THE SEA 177, 206 (G. Yates, J. Young, eds. 1974); Sub Committee II, U.N. Sea Bed Committee, Summary Records, 1971, A/AC/138/SC II, SR6, at 27.

To be precise, the Soviet Union calls for "equal freedom of transit and overflight through international straits," whereas the United Staters has promoted "free transit through international straits." Janis, *The Soviet Navy and Ocean Law*, 26 NAVAL WAR COLLEGE REV. 52, 55 (1974).

See Jessup, *Ends and Means of American Foreign Policy*, in INTERNATIONAL STABILITY AND PROGRESS 11, 18-20 (The Am. Assembly, ed. 1957).

The purpose of American foreign policy, as that of other great powers, is to establish and sustain a world order that guarantees its national security; to encourage among other nations (particularly the smaller ones) a need for the stable development of their own social, political, and economic institutions in harmony with American values; and to endeavor to minimize the possibility of armed aggression. Kristol, *American Intellectuals and Foreign Policy*, in FIFTY YEARS OF FOREIGN AFFAIRS 368 (H. Armstrong, ed. 1972).

A definite *political* content has marked many of the maritime incidents over the last 10 years. The Arab-Israeli conflict over the Straits of Tiran, the Cuban crisis, the Gulf of Tonkin and *Pueblo* incidents, the Jordian guerrillas insurgencies in Sept. 1970, and the 1971 East Pakistan-India fighting are all conflicts of national rights which, in one way or another, involved the seas in either an offensive or defensive position. What are the boundaries of territorial waters? What is free passage through certain straits: Is it an international right? When is such passage considered a privilege conferred by the nation that claims a legal right to control access? To what extent will the seas be used to provide defensive "moral" support to land insurgencies in other countries? Controversies of this nature are not new. Their real importance is to be found in their potential use for *political purposes* — as a trigger for military action. Owen, *Western Naval Strategy for the Eighties*, 28 Y.B. WORLD AFFAIRS 43, 47 (1974).

Since 1945, a history of the 14 Mediterranean littoral states and 2 island states, Malta and Cyprus, reveals that almost all of these states has been involved in some form of conflict with another. Territorial disputes, ethnic rivalries, and religious and ideological tensions have all contributed to the factors promoting varieties of political unrest. Owen, *supra* at 53.

15. HOLLICK & OSGOOD, *supra* note 8, at 92, 93, 95, 101.

There are, in addition to problems of detection, other operational difficulties associated with surfacing nuclear submarines in straits. Because of their huge size and inability to maneuver with ease on the surface, such submarines present fewer safety problems not only to surface shipping but also to themselves when under water. If a submarine gives prior notice to a littoral state of its approaching transit, the submarine loses its opportunity for a secret "strategic" passage. HOLLICK & OSGOOD, *supra* note 8, at 102, 103. See also, O'Connell, *International Law and Contemporary Naval Operations*, 44 BRIT. Y. B. INT'L LAW 19 (1970).

Of the approximately 120 international straits not within the high sea waters (which become territorial waters when the breadth of the territorial sea is expanded to 12 miles) 16 of the straits would be regarded as reasonably strategic, but 9 of these would not be essential to the strategic capability of the United States. Of the 9, the 5 Caribbean straits would be of little value to a Polaris/Poseidon patrol, since the Caribbean is not regarded as an essential attack-launching area. Of the remaining 4, only Gibraltar and 2 Indonesian straits, Ombai-Wetar and Lombok, would be, for strategic military purposes, important ones. United States nuclear-powered submarines carrying nuclear missiles may presently enjoy submerged passage through 3 straits. Yet, the United States continued use of the straits might well be dramatically curtailed if a territorial sea boundary of 12 miles were to be established. See KRUGER-SPRENGEL, *supra* note 6, at 22-28.

Current negotiations relative to free transit through international straits have been influenced to a considerable degree by the present situation regarding the Straits of Tiran. These straits have a total width of but 3 miles. They actually consist of 2 navigable channels: one 900 yards in width and the other 1,300 yards wide. These channels are the only access from the Red Sea to the Gulf of Aqaba and to the Israeli port of Elath. The only port in Israel accessible to ships inbound from the Indian Ocean is Elath. The Suez has, in the past, been closed to vessels *en route* to Israel. If a 3-mile territorial sea limit is applied, the Gulf of Aqaba will be part of the high seas, but if a 12-mile limit is applied, the gulf will be in territorial waters. Egypt and Saudi Arabia made claims to the 12-mile territorial sea in 1958 in order that these waters could be closed to Israeli shipping. The prevalent view today is that the Straits of Tiran and the Gulf of Aqaba constitute an international strait. McNees, *Freedom of*

Transit through International Straits, 6 J. MARITIME L. & COMM. 175, 195 (1975).

The Suez Canal was reopened on June 5, 1975. See Lapidoth, *The Reopened Suez Canal in International Law*, 4 SYRACUSE J. INT'L L. & COMM. 1 (1976); R. BOWIE, INTERNATIONAL CRISES AND THE ROLE OF LAW: SUEZ, 1956 (1974).

See also, Mackie, *Egypt's Suez Reconstruction: A Major Test of Capability*, 20 MIDDLE EAST ECON. DIG. 11 (July 16, 1976); Arndt, *Suez: The Re-opening*, 26 ARAMCO WORLD MAG. 10 (Sept./Oct. 1975); Klinghoffer, *Soviet Oil Politics and the Suez Canal*, 31 *World Today* 397 (Oct. 1975); *Egypt: A Threatened Shoot-out over a Rich Oil Field* (Israeli insistence on rights to eastern half of the Gulf of Suez to which Armco Int'l Oil Co. had a concession from Egypt), Bus. Week, Oct. 4, 1976, p. 40 *et seq.; Lippman Israeli Ships A Problem for Arab Djibouti*, Washington Post, June 29, 1977, p. 14, col. 1, where the issue of freedom of navigation (for Israeli ships) and the coordinate issue of economic development through the mouth of the Red Sea by the narrow Bab el Mandeb strait between Djibouti and South Yemen are discussed.

Lapidoth argues that the Straits of Bab el Mandeb and Tiran and the Suez Canal are by treaty open to the traffic of all nations, and disputes Egypt's claimed right to close the canal to Israel. She also postures that the Panama and Kiel canals — as well as the Suez — are not subject to closure because such acts would be contrary to both positive and customary international law. R. LAPIDOTH, FREEDOM OF NAVIGATION, WITH SPECIAL REFERENCE TO INTERNATIONAL WATERWAYS IN THE MIDDLE EAST (1975).

16. Henkin, *Old Politics and New Directions*, in 3 NEW DIRECTIONS IN THE LAW OF THE SEA 3, 4, 5 (R. Churchill, K. Simmonds, J. Welch, eds. 1973). Henkin maintains that major powers refrain from using military power against smaller countries because such action would be not only impolitic but also a use of force now regarded as illegal. See also, Ratiner, *United States Oceans Policy: An Analysis*, 2 J. MARITIME L. & COMM. 225, 232 (1971); THE LAW OF THE SEA: U.S. INTERESTS AND ALTERNATIVES 11-31 (R. C. Amacher, R. J. Sweeney, eds. 1976). See generally, Ratiner, *National Security Interests in Ocean Space*, 4 NATURAL RESOURCES LAW. 582 (1971).

All indications point to the fact that the Soviet Union is attempting to exercise greater control of the Baltic and the Black seas. The obvious purpose of the Soviet strategies is to establish itself as a dominant influence in the Mediterranean sea and their approaches to it and thereby to become a recognized power in the Turkish straits through which its warships must pass from the Black Sea into the Aegean and the Mediterranean.

The problem of the Turkish straits and of the Middle East as a whole should be viewed in a historical and yet in a contemporary perspective. The United States has had long-standing and wide-ranging interests in the area since the beginning of the 19th century; its political-strategic interests in the area began during World War II. American policy in the area has been tied to a recognition of Turkey as a key to the northern tier of the Middle East and the Eastern Mediterranean. Although United States interest in the Turkish straits down to the post-World War II years was essentially of a commercial character, it expressed political-strategic interest in the straits when the Soviet's threatened Turkey in the immediate postwar years. Yet, since the beginning of the 19th century, the United States has maintained a consistent policy of free commercial passage in this area and has encouraged the open character of the Black Sea.

The Middle East, in its traditional role as a line of communication, may well be a wasting asset to the West, but since the Soviet Union has taken on an increasing interest in Turkey and the straits as key points in its military strategy, the United States has been forced to maintain a self-protecting interest in the area, regardless of the military costs. H. HOWARD, TURKEY, THE STRAITS AND U.S. POLICY (1974). See Knight, *The Kiev and The Turkish Straits,* 71 AM. J. INT'L L. 125 (1977).

The Soviet Union continues to assert itself militarily in an effort to expand air and naval activities in other areas as well. In the strategically important Persian Gulf-Indian Ocean area, dramatic Soviet expansion has been noted. To be specific, while the American presence in the Indian Ocean is limited to 2 destroyers and a command ship, the Soviets have developed a permanent fleet in that area varying from 8 to 12 ships. Middleton, *Soviets Said to Expand Air and Naval Activities in Persian Gulf area,* New York Times, Mar. 8, 1975, p. 2, col. 2. See also, Middleton, *Soviet Site in Portugal would Peril Sea Links, id.,* Feb. 1, 1975, § C, p. 3, col. 1.

17. *Kissinger on Oil, Food and Trade,* Bus. Week, Jan. 13, 1975, pp. 66, 69; HOLLICK & OSGOOD, *supra* note 8, at 120, 121. See also, F. DEROCHER, FREEDOM OF PASSAGE THROUGH INTERNATIONAL STRAITS: COMMUNITY INTEREST AMID PRESENT CONTROVERSY 128, 129 (1972).

Chapter 5

DEVELOPING NEW MARITIME LAW

Only three avenues for developing a new ocean consti-
tution exist: 1) through the customary process of lawmaking wherein change is accomplished primarily through
the practice of unilateral claims that are either accepted
or acquiesced in over the course of time by other states; 2)
through the use of multilateral treaty procedures of international conferences; and 3) through the creation of new
international organizations that are given authority both
to enact and enforce binding ocean legislation. It is difficult to achieve a "functional accommodation of interests" through unilateral customary lawmaking. This
form of lawmaking promotes the use of a blunt instrument of design—namely, territorial sea extensions—
instead of developing an adjustment or accommodation
of functional needs. Although in some rather limited
areas the creation of an international organization with

defined areas of rule making and a balanced decision-making procedure may be helpful, the international community is not yet ready to reorder the total national state system by creating such an organization with broad all-inclusive powers both to enact and enforce substantive rules. A comprehensive multilateral treaty appears to be the best solution to effective ocean lawmaking.[1]

While the 1958 Law of the Sea Conference was essentially concerned with codifying existing law, the present Conference attempts not only to modernize codified law in order to accommodate it to changing world circumstances — and thereby to fill in gaps relative to the breadth of the territorial sea — but also to "provide progressive development of entirely new law in areas such as the deep seabeds and the protection of the environment."[2]

Caracas and Geneva: Seeking to Resolve Confusion?

Caracas

During the summer of 1974 in Caracas, from June 20 to August 29, 1974, the first substantive session of the Third United Nations Law of the Sea Conference was held. March 17, 1975, marked the beginning of the second substantive session, which was held in Geneva and which concluded early in May 1975. The official goal of the Conference is to draft a single, comprehensive treaty that would be widely accepted.[3]

By the conclusion of the Caracas session of the Conference, little more had been achieved than a sharpening of different perspectives and the preparation of alternate treaty texts called "Main Trends."[4] It has been maintained that perhaps one reason for the impasse at this Conference could be attributed to the fact that many of the conferees — and especially those from the Third World — do not understand the alternatives to conference decision making, if the law of the sea negotiations do not succeed.

The states in attendance at the Conference espouse a variety of interests. They may be classified according to their interests as: technologically developed and developing states—especially with regard to their ability to exploit and use ocean resources; military powers and nonmilitary powers; maritime and nonmaritime powers; coastal states, landlocked states, and shelflocked states; states with long coastlines and those with resource-poor offshore areas; archipelagic states; states situated astride straits used for international navigation; states possessing a substantial merchant marine or which are heavily dependent on ocean commerce; and states with strong coastal fishing industries and those with distant-water fishing capabilities.[5] With such a wide scope of interests present at the Conference negotiations, agreement will not be easy. The various levels of economic development, regional cohesion, and geographic and resource situations combine with ideological differences to produce these interest groupings. It is but natural, when the world community is presented not only with lengthy but also with heterogeneous lists of issues to be negotiated at a Conference of this nature, that interest and subinterest groups should emerge. Recognizing points of coincidence between national self-interest and supranational ideals in seeking a balancing point "is one of the highest tasks of statemanship."[6] Another clear impediment to the success not only of the various sessions of the Conference but also of the entire procedural format of the Conference, itself, has been the delay in and obstruction of consensus voting.[7] In sum, then, it may well be that the task of negotiating durable international regimes for each of the various complex ocean issues on the agenda in a single text is beyond the capacity of a political forum of the nature the Conference presents.[8]

Given the state of confusion and disagreement over the

procedural as well as the substantive matters before the Conference, some have even speculated that it may be well to avoid a law of the sea treaty at this time. The result of this strategy would be to promote a needed flexibility for resolution of future ocean problems as they develop on an *ad hoc* basis by individual states. Yet, the absence of a treaty could lead to farther and farther coastal state expansion. Instead of developing through international agreement, the law of the sea would evolve from all the inherent weaknesses of the customary international processes that are fraught with the potential for conflict. And, furthermore, if no international agreement on the law of the sea is negotiated soon, the Congress of the United States may be expected to act and pass legislation regulating deep-seabed mining. The United States would then join the many other members of the world community in acting unilaterally on matters of the sea.[9]

Nevertheless, in spite of numerous and varying negotiating positions and disagreements regarding, among other issues, the territorial sea — particularly its breadth — and free passage through international straits, the keystone of a possible compromise solution was discovered at Caracas. A majority of states seeking broad coastal state resource management jurisdiction concluded that the breadth of the territorial sea should be set at twelve miles *if* an exclusive economic zone beyond the territorial sea, up to a maximum distance of two hundred miles, would be guaranteed. The major maritime powers made the acceptance of this idea as a compromise solution dependent upon a satisfactory solution being reached (i.e., a *guarantee*) on the equally important issue of free passage through international straits.[10] As will be seen, at the Geneva session of the Conference, this particular compromise was included in the Informal Negotiating Text, which was the work product of the Geneva session. Should an ultimate treaty be formulated that solely follows the dictates of the major maritime powers, the likely outcome would be that many of those states with borders on international straits will remain non-signatories.[11]

Geneva

The president of the Third United Nations Law of the Sea Conference, Hamilton S. Amerasinghe of Sri Lanka, in assessing the work of the Conference at its Geneva session, declared it not a success because it was unable to produce an agreement; yet he declared it not a failure, since "it did not break up." He announced that a third session of the Conference would be held for eight weeks in New York City during the spring of 1976. A subsequent meeting at a later time in 1976 was also planned.[12]

At its meeting on April 18, 1975, the Conference adopted a proposal that allowed the chairmen of the three main committees to prepare a single text covering the subjects under the committees' jurisdiction as well as all formal and informal discussions and proposals to date.[13] The chairmen acted quickly to accomplish this during the closing days of the Geneva meeting. This strategy was followed because had a single unified text been presented at the commencement of the Conference, endless debate over its content would have been generated with no negotiating document of any nature being produced.[14] Debate, general discussion, and criticism of the Informal Negotiating Text, which emerged from this session, came in the spring of 1976 in New York City.

The Preface to the Informal Negotiating Text clearly states that it serves as a "procedural device and only provides a basis for negotiation." Further qualification is made by stating that the text is not to be in any way "regarded as affecting either the status of proposals already made by delegations, *or the right of delegations to submit amendments or new proposals.*"[15] These qualifications were taken at face value and were on occasion used rather carelessly and imprudently by some states at the New York meeting. Although more than 3,700 interventions were made to the Informal Negotiating Text, a surprisingly compact Revised Single Negotiating Text finally emerged.[16]

Interestingly, the United Kingdom's Draft Articles on the Territorial Sea and Straits Convention on the Law of the Sea have played a most important role in both the Caracas and Geneva meetings and — finally — in the New York meetings. In Caracas, these Draft Articles served to create the dominant theme of the Main Trends Document that was pertinent to the work of the Second Committee. The Geneva Negotiating Document mirrors the same imprint of these Draft Articles, with the section on archipelagos bearing the imprint of the Fijian proposals.[17] The New York Revised Single Negotiating Text carries through with the initial focus of the original Draft Articles.

The Geneva Negotiating Document

The 1974 Law of the Sea Conference, termed a reenactment of the 1958 Conference, was made necessary because of the rapid emergence of new states since 1958.[18] The expansion of coastal state sovereignty, initially begun in 1945 with the Truman Proclamation and carried forward in the 1958 Geneva Convention on the High Seas and its companion Territorial Seas Convention, continues with the present Conference. Under the Geneva Negotiating Document of the spring of 1975, officially designated as the Informal Negotiating Text, a state may choose to establish a twelve-mile territorial sea, a twenty-four-mile contiguous zone, and a two-hundred-mile exclusive economic zone. Thus, a considerable part of the seas will be under coastal state sovereignty to one degree or another. Innocent passage through territorial waters has been reaffirmed, and objective standards have been structured for aiding in determining when passage is prejudicial to coastal state interests and, thus, noninnocent. Coastal states are, under the Negotiating Document, as they are in the 1958 Territorial Sea Convention, told that they "should not" exercise their civil and/or criminal jurisdiction when foreign ships are passing through their territorial waters. For submarines and other underwater vehicles to be accorded innocent passage, they must—as in the past—navigate on the surface and show their flag. Yet, submarines may in a submerged state enjoy free or transit passage through international straits. Warships have been given the same right of free transit through straits as have aircraft. There are provisions in the Negotiating Document that also impose liability upon the flag state for loss or damage that may occur during negligent passage.[19]

With the vast increase in oil tankers and nuclear-powered vessels using the seas, coastal state concern for safety when passage occurs in territorial waters is a natural consideration. Rather than allow the coastal state power to write special rules concerning ship building—which it was believed would inhibit the ship-building business and commerce in general—provisions in the Negotiating Document sought to guarantee safety by allowing the coastal state to design safety schemes using designated sealanes for passage by vessels. The Intergovernmental Maritime Consultative Organization (IMCO) has already begun to assist in developing such schemes rather successfully in the Irish Sea.[20]

Some believe that the "right balance" has been attained between coastal state needs and those of the international community for freedom of navigation on the seas in the Geneva Negotiating Document.[21] This "balance" appears to be weighted, however, in favor of coastal state needs, and it was retained as such in the Revised Single Negotiating Text. As two commentators have observed, the coastal states get more and the international community less. Under contemporary standards this is a fact of life.[22]

New York—The Fifth Session

As the fifth session of the Third United Nations Law of the Sea Conference opened on August 2, 1976, a series that had begun in December 1973, most of the delegates were resigned to the belief that their efforts would be rendered inconclusive. And, when the session concluded its work on September 17, 1976, it could indeed be said that inconclusiveness was the hallmark of its meetings.[23] The fourth session, which lasted from March 15, 1976, to May 7, 1976, and was held in New York City, made marginal progress, but was successful in at least developing or engendering a more distinct spirit for treaty making in this area. A Revised Single Negotiating Text was the session's work product.[24]

Whereas four-fifths of the four hundred and seven proposed articles of the proposed treaty were generally acceptable, the remaining articles—and principally those dealing with deep-seabed mining, an exclusive economic zone, the nature and extent of the rights of some fifty-three landlocked and geographically deprived states (LLGDS), and other issues—remained vexatious and unresolved.[25] Since the Conference normally functions by consensus, however, it has not voted on or approved a single article.[26]

It is precisely because of the protracted negotiations and the uncertainty of their future course here, coupled with unilateral actions taken by individual countries in asserting jurisdictional claims to coastal waters up to two hundred miles offshore, that the United States Congress acted in passing the Fishery Conservation and Management Act of 1976, which became effective on March 1, 1977.[27] Under this legislation, the United States established a two-hundred-mile fishing zone. Interestingly, the boundaries of this zone come into direct conflict with a similar zone that Canada has previously set. Additionally, some thirty nations whose fishing fleets have traditionally operated within the two-hundred-mile limit must be "reeducated" to these new boundaries.[28]

The Revised Single Negotiating Text produced by this session followed the guidelines regarding innocent passage and free transit through international straits as structured by the Single Negotiating Text which emerged from the Geneva session of the Conference.[29]

During the fifth session of the Conference, the Second Committee — whose work parallels to a large extent a part of the modern focus of the final work product of the Conference itself — held no formal meetings. They merely selected some questions calling for priority consideration and thereby attempted to begin a serious negotiating process in connection with these questions.[30]

The chairman of the Second Committee, Andrés Aguilar, reported that the committee broke down into five negotiating groups to discuss, among other items, the legal status of the exclusive economic zone and the rights and duties of states with respect to the living resources of the exclusive economic zone, the use of straits for international navigation, and the delimitation of the territorial sea. Chapter 2 of the Revised Single Negotiating Text concerning straits for international navigation and the delimination of the territorial sea appeared to provide an acceptable negotiating basis for the great majority of the delegates. Some states bordering straits noted that their acceptance of the text would, however, in the final analysis, be contingent upon incorporation into it of certain changes designed to achieve a better balance between their interests and the interests of users of straits. These changes were not specified by Aguilar in his report and are, therefore, thought to be rather insignificant. The straits articles provide for the regime of transit passage, which is an essential element in the adoption of a twelve-mile maximum breadth of the territorial sea.

Regrettably, the chairman concluded that "no concrete results were achieved at this session regarding any of the questions considered by the various Negotiating Groups."[31]

In summarizing the work of the fifth session of the Conference, former Secretary of State Henry A. Kissinger sounded a most positive note by observing that a basis for agreement did in fact exist. But, if success is not forthcoming, "it will not be the result of unabridgeable substantive gaps between states or groups of states. Rather, it will result from a failure of collective will."[32] He had previously cautioned that if rapid progress was not achieved at the Conference, the world community would face the distinct possibility that domestic pressures within various member groups of the world community could well set in motion unilateral national moves that could gravely impair chances of ever obtaining a treaty.[33] The effect of this admonition has already been realized in the unilateral actions taken by some countries in their establishment of two-hundred-mile fishing zones.

The Sixth Session and Beyond

"Severally and collectively unacceptable" were the words used by Elliott L. Richardson, the United States ambassador to the Law of the Sea Conference, in describing a major part of the "work product" of the sixth session of the Conference as it concluded on July 20, 1977.[34] He specifically applied these words to those parts of the new Informal Composite Negotiating Text, which concerned the system of exploitation and governance of the deep-seabed area and which emerged from the First Committee under the initial leadership of Minister Jens Evensen of Norway and, later, that of Paul Engo of the Cameroons as chairman. The compromise Evansen Text gave way to the version by Engo, which was submitted to the president of the Conference and then released. The Evensen Text would have provided a useful basis for further negotiation, the Engo Text—produced in private and never actually discussed by a representative group of member nations—has proven to be most vexatious.[35] Tragically, the near paralysis of the sixth session may clearly be traced to the work of the First Committee and the rejection by the Group of 77 (which now includes over one hundred developing countries embracing, as such, a wide spectrum of economic, social, and political interests) of the provisions of the Revised Single Negotiating Text concerning the recognition and administration of a deep-ocean mining regime.[36]

Political realities shape, as has been seen, negotiating postures. Whether industrialized states will yield to the militant demands of the Third World nations with respect to deep-seabed mining of manganese nodule resources is a matter of speculation. The basic challenge made by the Group of 77 is that the oceans are the common heritage of mankind and must therefore be exploited for mankind's benefit. But who is to do the exploitation and how is it to be undertaken? The developed-world nations argue that such activities be undertaken by the member states of the world community and specially licensed private parties. The Group of 77 argues, to the contrary, that all exploitation be under an "Authority" having jurisdiction over all deep-seabed mineral development, and furthermore that the Authority, representing as it will *all* mankind, decide on an individual basis to what extent states are private parties to be associated with it.[37] While the developed countries, led by the United States, have accepted in principle the concept of Authority jurisdiction, efforts have been undertaken to develop ways by which the authority's discretion can be exercised under a set of detailed conditions.[38]

The sixth session of the Conference was not a total failure, however, for new provisions were negotiated to clarify the legal status of the proposed two-hundred-mile economic zone. These provisions seek to safeguard traditional freedoms of the high seas within the zone, itself, except for specific resource-related coastal state rights protected by the convention. Additionally, these provisions are regarded as a means of preventing the eventual erosion of high-sea freedoms by coastal states that are attempting to extend their bases of sovereignty over the oceans.[39]

The Informal Composite Negotiating Text of the sixth session introduces four new elements into the proposed convention—none of which are strikingly different from those regimes of internal waters, the territorial sea, and the contiguous zone as set forth originally in the 1958 Territorial Sea Convention. Twelve nautical miles is established by the text as the maximum permissible breadth of the territorial sea, whereas the maximum breadth of the contiguous zone for customs, fiscal, immigration, or sanitary purposes is extended from twelve to twenty-four miles from the baseline. International navigation through straits is treated as a separate matter and is thus not regarded as identical to the innocent passage regime except for specified types of straits. The elaboration in greater detail of the meaning of innocent passage together with the regulatory rights of the coastal state, the duties of the flag state regarding innocent passage, and the specific control and prevention of pollution is achieved in the Informal Negotiating Text.[40]

The status of international access routes, as studied in relationship to their application in straits and archipelagic states, reveals that the Conference continues to reaffirm the rejection of innocent passage restrictions on such routes.[41] Although efforts have been made to achieve a type of universal status of recognition for archipelagic states and at the same time to structure the limits of its application, the central problem here is the recognition of a two-hundred-mile economic zone. The recognition of such a zone for continental as well as insular territory would most likely mean that the zone, itself, would be applicable to all those waters within the islands of archipelagic states and within the waters of those states merely pretending to possess status as an archipelago. To be remembered is that the 1958 Law of the Sea Conference did not accept the archipelagic concept.

The Informal Composite Negotiating Text attempts to define carefully what is an archipelagic state, denominate the waters around such states as archipelagic waters, and confer upon ships and aircraft a right of archipelagic passage — separate and distinct from innocent passage — for purposes of traversing the archipelago. The application or execution of the right is set up to twenty-five miles to either side of an axis in accordance with a set of detailed procedures.[42] Interestingly, the wording of the regimes of "transit passage" of straits and "archipelagic sealanes passage" are almost identical, with only slight inconsequential differences. In the absence of an acceptance of the Negotiating Text, it is uncertain whether the community of states would be willing to recognize the archipelagic concept.[43]

Even though Ambassador Richardson recommended to President James Carter that the United States seriously consider withdrawing from further treaty deliberations, the United States participated in the seventh session of the Conference, which began on March 28, 1978, in Geneva.[44] The ambassador cautioned that the odds were against the emergence of an accord at this session.[45] A former ambassador to the Law of the Sea Conference, John Norton Moore, suggested — on a more positive note — that spring, 1979 might be a considerably more realistic date for concluding the Conference.[46]

The Seventh Session

Geneva was the setting of the seventh session of the Third United Nations Law of the Sea Conference. To forestall any verdict on the final outcome of the entire conference, yet another session was set for four weeks beginning on August 21, 1978, in New York City. The United States delegation maintained significant reservations about the likelihood of the success of the session prior to its opening, but the Geneva session concluded with a public sense of "cautious optimism" for the eighth session.[47]

The meetings in Geneva were termed "difficult, demanding and frustrating—but not boring" and were recognized as yielding a tightly orchestrated scenario for a showdown at the New York session. The three major hard-core issues-—from which subsets derive and from which must come an eventual two-thirds acceptance of resolution for there to be a recorded consensus on the document, itself—are: 1) consideration of the system of exploration and exploitation of deep-seabed mining resources, 2) the financial arrangements for an International Seabed Authority and 3) the composition and voting authority of the Council of the Authority.[48]

At the conclusion of the sixth session of the Conference, after the issuance of the Informal Composite Negotiating Text, the United States and other industrialized countries rejected Part XI (Deep Seabed Mining) of the text and the method by which it was produced. The seventh session witnessed the establishment of seven negotiating groups—three of which were concerned with problems associated with Part XI of the Informal Composite Negotiating Text.[49]

The practical use of the various texts emerging from the negotiating groups presented an initial difficulty. The number of articles being considered did not appear to call for the issuance of an entirely new informal text of the treaty as a whole. Yet, the Group of 77 and others concluded that all future negotiations on deep-seabed mining would be based on the new texts produced in the first negotiating group. This same attitude existed in the Conference with respect to most of the other next texts. Thus it would appear that relevant provisions of the Informal Composite Negotiating Text are for all practical purposes replaced by the new texts emerging from the negotiations. Interestingly, the very implication of the new procedural requirements for revision of the Composite Text caused a number of delegations to refrain from taking formal steps in Plenary to confirm this understanding.[50]

Concerning the revision of the Composite Text, the Plenary established the following rule:

> Any modifications or revisions to be made in the Informal Composite Negotiating Text should emerge from the negotiations themselves and should not be introduced on the initiative of any single person, whether it be the President or a Chairman of a Committee, unless presented to the Plenary and found, from the widespread and substantial support prevailing in Plenary, to offer a substantially improved prospect of a consensus.[51]

The actual route to revision of the Composite Text proved so difficult that revisions were not produced at the session, although a number of new texts met the standards of inclusion. Variously termed, Revised Suggested Compromise Formula or Compromise Suggestions, they derived from the Composite Text, itself, and were designed to promote compromise solutions by consensus; in some situations, the texts covering those hard-core issues of the Conference were so sufficiently improved over the Composite Text that they offered a substantially enhanced prospect of eventual consensus.

The most significant achievement of the seventh session was, perhaps, its negotiation of access rights for landlocked and geographically disadvantaged states to those living resources found within the two-hundred-mile ex-

clusive economic zone.[52] Progress was also recorded on
the issue of shaping a formula that would define the outer
limit of national jurisdiction over the continental shelf
and toward reaching a compromise on the extent of
revenue sharing in the proceeds of exploitation of the
resources of the continental margin beyond two hundred
miles. As to the related issue of dispute settlement over
living resources of the economic zone, negotiations pro-
gressed from initially rejecting such settlements of
fisheries questions to insisting on compulsory adjudication
to a more equitable middle point of compulsory conciliation of claims that the coastal state has abused its power.

The negotiations on maritime pollution—its prevention, reduction, and control of from ships—brought forth
new texts that expanded the world community's obligation to protect endangered species and fragile ecosystems
from pollution. Furthermore, these negotiations produced agreement on a widening of jurisdictional bases to
establish ship-routing systems in order to protect the environment, clarify the coastal state's rights to obtain a
prompt notice of events that might result in pollution off
its coast—thereby affording it time within which to act—
and to remove restraints on coastal state powers both to
establish and to enforce discharge standards stricter than
international standards for ships in innocent passage in
the territorial sea.

Various texts—some of which were definite improvements over the Composite Text, as previously noted—
dealing with the seabeds and the deep mining thereof
emerged. A good number of the developing countries
continue to be most suspicious of the scope and commitment of the developed countries to the parallel scheme
of exploration and exploitation of the deep-seabed
resources. These apprehensions find cutting relevance in
a number of the revised texts, particularly on the issue of
transfer technology. Wisely, transfer of technology is,
under one of the new texts, no longer a precondition for

obtaining a contract to mine. A contractor must undertake, under the new text, to transfer such technology at
any time after the contract is approved only if requested
both on fair and reasonable commercial terms. Yet, in
certain limited cases, the text still requires a transfer of
technology to developing countries.

The composition and voting privileges of the Council of
the Authority remain vexatious issues. The developing
countries stress that the Council should operate under a
principle of equitable geographic distribution or of one-
nation-one-vote. The position of the United States is that
the Council should, in addition to reflecting a geographic
balance among members, endeavor to assure sufficient
protection of the major economic interests of the miners,
consumers, and land-based producers affected by a deep-
seabed mining treaty. Unless such protection is given, investments required to commence the seabed mining
operations will not be forthcoming.

In the final analysis, the test of an effective treaty is the
extent to which United States interests are protected and
guaranteed. These interests in international maritime
navigation and the protection of national security interests are achieved in the presently proposed draft treaty;
but the maintenance of security interests would be less-
ened if no treaty emerges from the United Nations Conference. A negotiated law of the sea treaty must be
equitable and embody in it a fair compromise of competing interests.[53]

Geneva and the Spring of 1979

Secretary-General of the United Nations Kurt Wald-
heim, in his message of April 9, 1979, to the Law of the
Sea Conference, warned that if a comprehensive law of
the sea convention is not completed, "we risk being over-
taken by events that will make it more difficult, if not
impossible, to reach an agreement at a later stage on a

new legal order for the oceans. . . . . we have come to the moment of decision and we cannot afford to fail." In 1973, the General Assembly of the United Nations instructed the Law of the Sea Conference, "to adopt a convention dealing with all matters relating to the law of the sea." Since December of that year — for nearly sixty weeks of intermittent sessions — the Conference has endeavored to fulfill this mandate by attempting to find consensus, cohesion, and certainty in an area never before marked by such degrees of unity or agreement.

Geneva is a place where, it is said, the dreamer meditates, acts, and achieves. Regrettably, in attendance at the eighth session of the Conference were a number of confused and contentious dreamers who were still unable to awake from their somnambulistic state and to take action to realize their dreams and the hope of the world community for stability.

Although Ambassador Elliott L. Richardson of the United States commented after the Geneva meetings that "a generally acceptable convention is closer," he also stated that a large number of difficulties still impede progress toward the achievement of consensus on a universal treaty for a new legal order for the seas. Agreement was reached, however, on the need to issue a new Revised Negotiating Text for the continuance of the eighth session.[54]

It was, as such, a revision of the Informal Composite Negotiating Text, but it was not regarded as a negotiated text. The revision included new compromise proposals that emerged at the Geneva meetings this spring concerning: the exploration and exploitation of the international seabed area; delimitations of the outer margin of the continental shelf and revenue sharing in the zone beyond two hundred miles from the shore; the access of developing-landlocked states and states with special geographic characteristics to the living resources of the exclusive economic zones of states in the same region or subregions;

the settlement of disputes concerning the exercise of sovereign rights of coastal states in the economic zones; the protection and preservation of the marine environment and the development and transfer of marine technology; and, finally, the delimitation of the territorial sea between adjacent or opposite states. As in the past, these are the "hard-core" issues confronting the Conference. Reaching a consensus on them will be quite difficult.

On a slightly more positive note, the Geneva session witnessed the completion of negotiations on a legal code for the prevention of marine pollution and the protection of the ocean environment. A text was also accepted regarding the development and transfer of marine technology, but serious work remains to be done on formulating rules to govern marine scientific research in the conomic zones and on the continental shelves of foreign states.

New York and the Summer of 1979

The second part of the eighth session of the Conference was held at the United Nations Headquarters in New York City from July 19 through August 24, 1979. This session, much as the previous ones since work commenced in 1975 on a basic treaty text, did a considerable part of its work in informal meetings—closed to the public and without official records. No doubt the most decisive step taken at this session was the formulation—for the first time—of a "definite deadline," August 1980, for the adoption of a law of the sea convention. To be remembered, however, is that in the record of its deliberative actions, the United Nations has never shown itself to be constrained to honor deadlines. The Conference was unable to produce a second revised negotiating text at the close of this session. Because of time restraints, President H. Shirley Amerasinghe ruled such a revision "would be impossible to effect." This task will be undertaken during the end of the first part of the 1980 session.[55]

As the session concluded, various chairmen of the three main committees, the seven negotiating groups established in April 1978 to deal with the "hard-core" issues preventing agreement on a convention—together with the Working Group of 21 on seabed matters (established in April 1979 in Geneva), the Group of Legal Experts on Seabed Disputes, and the Group of Experts on Final Clauses— joined forces in seeking to report out agreement on a number of compromise proposals aimed at achieving consensus on outstanding issues. Nevertheless, no consensus was reached on such critically important issues as: validating a system for exploiting the deep seabed beyond national jurisdiction; defining the outer limits of the continental shelf and structuring criteria for delimiting overlapping maritime boundaries. On this last issue, strong efforts were made to draft procedures for the settlement of delimitation disputes. Compulsory resort to a conciliation commission was sought as the only feasible way in which compromise could be achieved. Yet here—as in so many other areas—there was no consensus on the matter and, thus, it remains subject to further negotiations.[56]

If the United States Congress should act and pass seabed-mining legislation before the Conference concludes its debate and drafts a convention, what effect would this have on the work of the Conference, itself? Ambassador Richardson has commented that for the participants of the Conference an awareness that seabed-mining legislation is inevitable—either through reciprocal national legislation or by universal convention—has served to reinforce a tone of urgency to their deliberations. The ambassador noted further that the pending congressional legislation is designed to be complementary to the general approach of the Informal

Composite Negotiating Text in that provision is made for setting aside payments by the mining companies and thereby recognizing the legitimacy of the claims of other countries to share in the proceeds thereto. Any treaty to which the United States would become a signatory, upon ratification by the Senate, would of course supersede any national legislation passed by the Congress. Owing to the additional fact that seabed mining cannot feasibly be undertaken on a commercial scale before 1985 at the very earliest, this would enable a treaty to be negotiated easily before that date.[57]

Ambassador Elliott Richardson continued to express "hope" that the work of the Conference will end on a successful note; yet he "cannot confidently predict it."[58] Even before the eighth session commenced in Geneva during the spring of 1979, he noted several important areas where substantial consensus had been reached. Regarding the territorial sea, agreement has been achieved recognizing its extension to twelve miles. Overlapping straits will be dealt with by a new regime of transit passage which, in effect, preserve the principal legal aspects of the high-seas passage that in turn exists where there remains a high-seas lane between the three-mile territorial seas on each side of the straits. The issues of freedom of navigation and overflight in the two-hundred-mile economic zone is, again, according to the ambassador's view, resolved basically by a provision in the text allowing that these two freedoms apply within the two-hundred-mile economic zone and are the very *same* freedoms of navigation and overflight applicable to the high seas beyond the two-hundred-mile economic zone.[59]

For those countries comprising a group of islands such as the Philippines and Indonesia surrounded as such by "archipelagic waters," a consensus has been reached which in effect acknowledges the waters embraced by these islands as equivalent to territorial seas yet agrees to chart lands for navigation that would be open to free navigation and overflight. The lanes would be established as well as defined by courses and distances from point to point through the archipelagic waters — with a permitted deviation of a certain number of miles on each side of the axis being recognized.[60]

Ambassador Richardson, while able to cite these three examples of substantial consensus reached by the Conference as evidence of a balance being struck between the preservation and enforcement of the coastal states rights against the broader maritime interests of unimpeded navigation, of course realizes that the ultimate success of the Conference hinges in very large measure upon whether complex vectors of force coalesce into a spirit or ethic of international cooperation.

NOTES—CHAPTER FIVE

1. Stevenson, *Lawmaking for the Seas*, 61 A.B.A.J. 186, 187 (1975). See generally, G. SCHWARZENBERGER, 1 INTERNATIONAL LAW, ch. 20 (3d ed. 1957); Schwarzenberger, *The Fundamental Principles of International Law*, 87 RECUEIL DES COURS 195, 358 *passim* (1956).

Sterling Professor Emeritus Myres S. McDougal of the Yale University Law School has expressed his belief that no treaty will in fact emerge from the present Law of the Sea Conference sessions. He predicts that customary law will be left to evolve and expand, and thus will gain as the controlling point in resolving law of the sea questions. Interview, Nov. 12, 1976, Yale Law School, New Haven, Conn.

See Raman, *Toward a General Theory of International Customary Law*, in TOWARD WORLD ORDER AND HUMAN DIGNITY: ESSAYS IN HONOR OF MYRES S. MCDOUGAL, ch. 11 (W. M. Reisman, B. H. Weston, eds. 1976).

2. Stevenson, *supra* note 1, at 185, 188.

3. Hollick, *What to Expect from a Sea Treaty*, 18 FOREIGN POLICY 68 (1975) [hereinafter cited as Hollick, *What to Expect from a Sea Treaty*]. See generally, Gelb, *Sea-Law Talks Resume Today in Geneva with U.S. Hopeful*, New York Times, Mar. 17, 1975, § L, p. 10; Editorial, *The Sharks at Geneva*, id., § L, p. 28.

The very first session of the Conference was a procedural, planning meeting held in New York City, Dec. 3-15, 1973. The official numbering of the successive sessions follows consecutively from this meeting. The principal commentator for the *American Journal of International Law*, Professor Bernard Oxman, while correctly referring to the first *substantive* meeting of the Conference as being held in Caracas, somewhat deceptively in his writings (to which reference is made throughout this chapter) refers to the first session as though it started in Caracas. He then proceeds to number his references to successive sessions from the Caracas meeting. Care should be taken, thus, not to confuse proper references to subsequent meetings. The complete chronology is as follows:

1st procedural, nonsubstantive session, New York, Dec. 3-15, 1973
2d session (first substantive meeting), Caracas, June 20-Aug. 29, 1974
3d session, Geneva, Mar. 17-May 9, 1975
4th session, New York, Mar. 15-May 7, 1976
5th session, New York, Aug. 2-Sept. 17, 1976
6th session, New York, May 23-July 15, 1977
7th session, Geneva, May 28-May 19, 1978
        New York, Aug. 21-Sept. 15, 1978
8th session, Geneva, Mar. 19-April 27, 1979
        New York, July 19-Aug. 24, 1979

4. A 127-page document entitled, "Main Trends," was issued by the Second Committee. Its purpose was "to reflect in generally acceptable formulations the main trends which emerged" from the conference. See A/CONF. 62/C.2/WP. 1/Corr. 1 (27 Nov. 1974). See also SENATE COMMERCE COMMITTEE, 94TH CONG., 1ST SESS., THIRD U. N. LAW OF THE SEA CONFERENCE, Feb. 5, 1975, (Comm. Print 1975).

The substantive work of the Caracas meeting was carried out by three committees recognized as committees of the whole. The First Committee was there, as at Geneva, primarily responsible for considering a resolution to the problems of seabed mining beyond limits of national jurisdiction. The Second Committee of the Conference was assigned 15 items dealing with such matters as the territorial sea, economic resources zone, continental shelf, fishing, and navigation. Finally, the Third Committee considered the problem areas of marine environment, preservation, scientific research, and technology transfer. Hollick, "The Third United Nations Conference on the Law of the Sea: Caracas Review," paper presented at *Conference on the Law of the Sea: U. S. Interests and Alternatives,* American Enterprise Institute for Public Policy Research, Washington, D.C., Feb. 14, 1975, pp. 3-5.

The mere prospect or threat of force may be sufficient to moderate the process of resolving conflicts of national interest. "Short of armed force, the practices of American security interests in the ocean will depend on four factors: (1) the configuration of political interests and military power among states in a position to affect vital American military and resource interests; (2) the balance of U. S.-Soviet interests and influences as it affects the actions of these states; (3) the perceived and actual disposition of the U. S. to back its ocean interests with force and only in this total context; (4) the process of asserting, contesting, accommodating, and negotiating the modalities of the rights of navigation through and over offshore waters and international straits." HOLLICK & OSGOOD, NEW ERA OF OCEAN POLITICS 123 (1974).

It does appear, however, that the United States government is determined to achieve the objectives of its ocean security within the context of a foreign policy characterized as "selective retrenchment" (i.e., the reduction of the extent of United States foreign support and involvement) without political disengagement (i.e., the abandonment of existing commitments) in which the first concern is the orchestration of what might be called a global *modus vivendi* with the Soviet Union fortified by an overall strategic parity. While reaffirming its pledge to shield allies and other states of vital interest from direct agression by nuclear states, the United States has virtually ruled out direct participation in insurgent wars. Osgood, "U.S. Security Interests and the Law of the Sea," paper presented at *Conference on the Law of the Sea: U.S. Interests and Alternatives,* American Enterprise Institute for Public Policy Research, Washington, D.C., Feb. 14, 1975, p. 3. See also Etzold, *Sea Power: Our Tarnished Treasure,* Washington Post, Sept. 18, 1978, § A, p. 23, col. 3.

A fine analytical classification of some proposals relating to the Law of the Sea Conference may be found in 6 UNITAR NEWS (No. 1, 1974). The proposals, which are an outgrowth of some 250 submitted to Sub Committee II of the United Nations Sea Bed Committee, are grouped and presented accordingly in 6 tables: archipelagos, territorial sea, straits used for international navigation, continental shelf, economic zones, and fisheries.

5. Friedheim, A Law of the Sea Conference— Who Needs It, in INTERNA- TIONAL RELATIONS AND THE FUTURE OF OCEAN SPACE 44, 64 (R. Wirsing, ed. 1974).

6. R. OSGOOD, IDEALS AND SELF INTEREST IN AMERICAN FOREIGN RELATIONS 23 (1953); Knight, Issues before the Third United Nations Conference on the Law of the Sea, 34 LA. L. REV. 155, 164 (1974); Ratiner, United States Ocean Policy: An Analysis, 2 J. MARITIME L. & COMM. 255, 240 (1971). See also, E. M. BORGESE & D. KRIEGER, eds., THE TIDES OF CHANGE (1975).

Law and diplomacy complement one another. Their relationship is at two levels: the settlement of disputes and the maintenance of a system of ordered relations among nations. Dillard, Some Aspects of Law and Diplomacy, 91 RECUEIL DES COURS 449, 548 (1957).

"The greater part of what passes for diplomatic history is little more than the record of what one clerk said to another." P. JESSUP, THE BIRTH OF NATIONS 337 (1974).

The Conference inherited 6 regional groups from the United Nations: African, Asian, Eastern European, Latin American, Western European, and others. The inheritance also spread to include the so-called "Group of 77" com- posed principally of the developing countries of Africa, Asia, and Latin America, which actually number well over 100. Alignments, or at least subregional meetings, occurred among such interest groups as the Arab states and members of the European Economic Community. Landlocked and other geographically disadvantaged states consulted with one another. Stevenson & Oxman, The Third United Nations Conference on the Law of the Sea: The 1974 Caracas Session, 69 AM. J. INT'L. 1, 5, 6 (1975).

7. OSGOOD, IDEALS AND SELF INTEREST IN AMERICAN FOREIGN RELATIONS 74 (1953). Stavropoulos, Procedural Problems of the Third Conference on the Law of Sea, 6 UNITAR NEWS 16 (No. 1, 1974).

The central issues at the Conference are so contentious that if put to a premature vote before at least a near consensus is achieved, the Conference will fail totally. The requirement of near consensus "puts a premium on intran- sigence, leads to least common denominator solutions and makes negotiations tedious and laborious." When a consensus is in fact needed, the most intran- sigent participant is likely to be found at a distinct negotiating advantage if he can hold out for as long as possible. Although he may not achieve fulfillment of all his needs, his practical utility is increased by refusing compromise. Friedheim, supra note 5, at 55. See also, Hollick, What to Expect from a Sea Treaty, 68, 71 n. 4; Vignes, Will the Third Conference on the Law of the Sea Work According to the Consensus Rule?, 69 AM. J. INT'L L. 119 (1975); Broder, Editorial, Laws of the Sea: A Search for Consensus, Washington Post, Mar. 19, 1978, ⁸ C, p. 7, col. 5.

8. See Hollick, Seabeds Make Strange Politics, 9 FOREIGN POLICY 148, 170 (72-73); Hollick, What to Expect from a Sea Treaty, 68, 78. See also, Sohn, U.S. Policy toward the Settlement of Law of Sea Disputes, 17 VA. J. INT'L L. 9 (1976); ADEDE, Law of the Sea: The Integration of the System of Settlement of Disputes under the Draft Convention as a Whole, 72 AM. J. INT'L L. 84 (1978); Barkenbus, How to Make Peace on the Seabed, 25 FOREIGN POLICY 211 (76-77).

9. Knight, *The Third United Nations Law of the Sea Conference: Caracas,* 18 AM. UNIVERSITIES FIELD STAFF REPORTS 1, 9, 10 (No. 2, 1974). See also, Frank, *The Law at Sea,* New York Times, May 18, 1975, Magazine, p. 14. See generally, Caminos, *The Law of the Sea at the Caracas Session: A Brief Evaluation,* 14 COLUM. J. TRANSNAT'L L. 80 (1975).

There were other points that the conferees agreed to accept if a compromise solution of some type could be structured regarding the continental shelf's outmost limit, the retention of the concept of a continental shelf, and some type of realized aspirations for the landlocked countries and other countries, which for various reasons viewed themselves as disadvantaged as a consequence of geographic placement. Regarding the economic zone, there was a consensus that freedom of navigation and overflight would be allowed within it, and that rights both to lay and maintain pipelines and submarine cables in this zone would be recognized. Stevenson & Oxman, *supra* note 6.

Of course, the United States has already passed legislation expanding its fishing jurisdiction to 200 miles. See discussion in note 4, ch. 3, *supra; cf.* note 27, ch. 5, *infra.*

10. Stevenson & Oxman, *supra* note 6, at 3, 9, 15, 16. See also, Miles, "An Interpretation of the Caracas Proceedings," paper presented at *Ninth Annual Law of the Sea Meeting,* Law of the Sea Institute, Miami, Fla., Jan. 6-9, 1975, p. 58 *passim.*

Appendix 2 sets out various major views regarding these issues, which were raised by delegate states at the Caracas meeting.

11. Hollick, *What to Expect from a Sea Treaty* 68, 76.

12. *Nations Urged to Hold Back on Sea Exploration,* New York Times, May 10, 1975, § L, p. 4, col. 3.

13. A/CONF.62./WP.8/Part II, 7 May 1975, at 1, 2. See also, Stevenson & Oxman, *The Third United Nations Conference on the Law of the Sea: The 1975 Geneva Session,* 69 AM. J. INT'L L. 763 (1975); Rosenne, *The Third United Nations Conference on the Law of the Sea,* 11 ISRAEL L. REV. 1 (1976).

14. Interview with Prof. R. Y. Jennings, Jesus College, Cambridge University, Cambridge, England, May 31, 1975; Interview with David H. Anderson, Esq., British Foreign Office, London, England, July 2, 1975.

15. Italics supplied by author. Stavropoulos observes the General Assembly's decision to adopt a "gentleman's agreement" requirement in structuring the Law of the Sea Conference procedures to the effect that the Conference should proceed by consensus on substantive matters and that, until all efforts at consensus failed, there should be no voting on such matters, was a central impediment to the real success of the Caracas Conference. Consensus voting is essentially a way of proceeding without formal obligation. He notes that in the history of the United Nations, consensus procedure has been used principally with regard to declarations. In relation to treaty-making activities, states may be less willing in some cases to facilitate adoption without a vote on the statement of legal rules. Failure to sign and ratify a treaty because important parts of it are not supported by various states could obviously have a serious effect on the authority of a convention. Stavropoulos, *supra* note 7, at 19.

16. See Appendix 4, where the provisions pertinent to the present discussion are printed.

17. A/CONF. 62/C.2/L.3, 3 July 1974; Anderson Interview, *supra* note 14. See Appendix 2.

18. Anderson Interview, *supra* note 14.

19. This brief analysis is expanded in Appendix 3, where specific regulating provisions of the Geneva Negotiating Text are analyzed.

20. Anderson Interview, *supra* note 14. See also, Appendix 3; 1970 IMCO SHIP'S ROUTING AND TRAFFIC SEPARATION SCHEMES; Stevens & Perles, *Tanker Safety Incentive: A Legislative Proposal,* 19 W. & M. L. REV. 99 (1977).

21. Anderson Interview, *supra* note 14.

22. Interview with Prof. Georg Schwarzenberger, University of London, University College of Law, London, England, June 30, 1975. Schwarzenberger has stated that the historical evolution of international customary law on the high seas has been marked by good faith and common sense. See his article, *Equity in International Law,* 26 Y.B. WORLD AFFAIRS 346 (1972). See also, Anderson Interview, *supra* note 14.

23. Hoffman, *Law-of-Sea Talks Resuming at U.N.,* New York Times, Aug. 1, 1976, p. 19, col. 1. *Background papers,* The Law of the Sea, Third United Nations Conference on the Law of the Sea, The Fourth Session, New York, 15 Mar.-May, 1976, OPI/559, Mar. 1976. See Appendix 4, where pertinent sections of the Revised Single Negotiating Text are printed.

24. Hoffman, *supra* note 23; *Background Papers, supra* note 23. Teltsch, *U.N. Talks Seeking a Sea-Law Accord Close with Differences Unresolved,* New York Times, May 8, 19976, p. 2, col. 4.

25. One delegate said that the conferees were engaging in "too much nit-picking." Teltsch, *Delegates Doodle as Procedural Details Slow Down Progress at the U.N.'s Law of the Sea Conference,* New York Times, Mar. 28, 1976, p. 13, col. 1.

26. Oxman, *The Third United Nation's Conference on the Law of the Sea: The 1976 New York Session,* 71 AM. J. INT'L L. 247, 248 (1977).

27. 90 Stat. 331 (1976), 16 U.S.C. § 1801 (1976).

28. New York Times, Nov. 14, 1976, § 4, p. 2, col. 5. Former Secretary of State Kissinger warned the Law of the Sea conferees that if these negotiations completely deadlocked, there would be a much greater danger of the United States acting unilaterally than changing its foreign policy and deviating from a path that would jeopardize its permanent interests and values. Remarks of Henry A. Kissinger, Press Release, USUN-97 (76), Sept. 1, 1976, U.S. Mission to the United Nations.

29. A/CONF. 62/WP. 8/Rev. 1/Part II, 6 May 1976. See Appendix 4. See also Appendix 3 for an analysis of the parent Geneva text.

30. A/CONF. 62/L.17, 16 September 1976.

31. *Id.* See also, Unclassified U.S. Delegation Report, Third United Nations Conference on the Law of the Sea, Aug. 2–Sept. 17, 1976; Teltsch, *U.N. Law of the Sea Meeting Recesses, Still Deadlocked on Mineral Riches,* New York Times, Sept. 18, 1976, § p. 2, col. 3; Butson & Rollins, *Still No Law of the Sea, id.,* Sept. 19, 1976, § E, p. 3, col. 2.

32. Kissinger Press Release, *supra* note 28.

33. Remarks of Henry A. Kissinger, Press Release, USUN-87 (76), Aug. 4, 1976, U.S. Mission to the United Nations.

34. Statement by Ambassador Richardson, Press Release USUN-57 (77), July 20, 1977, United States Mission to the United Nations. See also, 67 DEPT. STATE BULL. 389 (Sept. 19, 1977).

See letter to author from Prof. Daniel S. Cheever, Graduate School of Public and International Affairs, University of Pittsburgh, Aug. 2, 1977. Dr. Cheever attended the Conference and attests, in this letter, to the inconclusiveness of the session.

35. Richardson Press Release, *supra* note 34; Unclassified U.S. Delegation Report, Third United Nations Conference on the Law of the Sea, May 23–July 15, 1977.

36. It has been suggested, furthermore, that two additional issues deadlock this Conference: the legal status of the agreed-upon 200-mile economic zone and the rights of landlocked and geographically disadvantaged states. The author predicts total failure of the Conference if these conflicting issues are not resolved. Charney, *Law of the Sea: Breaking the Deadlock,* 55 FOREIGN AFFAIRS 598, 617 (1977).

Pertinent sections of the Informal Composite Negotiating Text, A/CONF. 62/WP.10, 15 July 1977, are printed in Appendix 5. The entire document is reprinted in 16 ILM 1108 (1977).

37. Haight, *Law of the Sea Conference—Why Paralysis,* 8 J. MARITIME L. & COMM. 281, 187 (1977).

38. Moore, *Salvaging UNCLOS III from the Rocks of the Deep Seabed,* 17 VA. J. INT'L L. 1, 4, 7 (1976).

Many countries assert that deep-seabed and mineral exploitation is of less concern here than the future role of multinational corporations in the development of both national land and offshore resources. Thus, some believe a deep-seabeds regime cannot be achieved until there is a broader North-South settlement. Oxman, *The Third U.N. Conference on the Law of the Sea: The 1976 New York Session,* 71 AM. J. INTL'L L. 247, 253 (1977).

The Congress of the United States is presently considering a unilateral extension of United States jurisdiction to ensure environmental protecton and to continue the serious study of the need for developing deep-seabed mining legislation. Current legislative proposals would authorize and encourage United States mining companies to unilaterally begin to mine trillions of dollars of cobalt, nickel, manganese, and copper on the oceans bottoms. Indeed, it would have been a "negotiating dream" if ocean mining legislation from the Congress had reached President Carter's desk in the middle of the 7th session of the Conference. Such a situation would have provided real political leverage for the United States negotiating team in pushing the conference toward decisive action. See Deep Seabed Minerals Act, S. 713, 94th Cong., 2nd Sess. (1976); Deep Seabed Hard Minerals Act, H.R. 11879, 94th Cong. 2nd Sess. (1976). The House International Relations Committee completed hearings on H.R. 3350, 95th Cong., 1st Sess., which would—if it had subsequently passed—authorized United States mining companies to move forward in the area of deep-seabed mining.

Four House committees have laid jurisdictional claims to the issue of deep-seabed mining. A House Rules Committee version of a bill recently reported out-scuttles a provision favorable to potential United States deep-sea mining companies, which would have given them a government guarantee against losses that they might well incur from a limitation on private production if a law of the sea treaty is passed. Yet, a form of guarantee remained alive in a companion bill (S. 2053), 95th Cong., 1st Sess., approved by the Senate Energy Committee. This companion bill then went to the Senate Committee on Commerce, Science, and Transportation and next to the Committee on Foreign Relations, where it was reported out favorably by the committee and placed on the calendar. In the haste of the closing days of the 2d session of the 95th Congress, no deep-seabed mining legislation came to the floor, however.

An intent of Congress section of the House Rules Committee version of the mining bill stated that any future treaty should provide "assured and nondiscriminatory access" to seabed minerals by United States companies. It also stated that a subsequent treaty should not "materially impair the value of investments" made by United States companies that may be mining nodules at the time the treaty would become effective. Large, *Deep-Sea Mining Bill,*

Closely Watched Abroad, Clears House Rules Committee, Wall Street Journal, June 9, 1978, p. 14, col. 1. See also Clairborne, *Long Running U.N. Conference—U.S. Seeks Seabed Mining Showdown,* Washington Post, Feb. 13, 1978, p. 1, col. 3.

Richard G. Darman, vice-chairman of the United States delegation to the 1977 session of the Law of the Sea Conference, has called for a limited "mine treaty" among mining states should the Conference fail. Such a "treaty" could conform with the United States view of an optional regime through which the United States, itself, could seek not only to develop seabed resources to its advantage and that of all mankind but also to include a licensing regime with a framework for environmental regulation, not a complex bureaucracy along the lines of an "Enterprise." Darman, *The Law of the Sea: Rethinking U. S. Interests,* 56 FOREIGN AFFAIRS 373, 393, 394 (1978). See also, Whitney, *Environmental Regulation of United States Deep Seabed Mining,* 19 W. & M. L. REV. 777 (1977).

Interestingly, on Feb. 26, 1979, S. 493, 96th Cong., 1st Sess., was introduced into the Senate. This bill embodies the basic provisions and philosophy of the previously introduced legislation (S. 2053), 95th Cong., 1st Sess.,) relative to deep-seabed mining. On December 14, 1979, the Senate passed S. 493 and sent it to the House, 125 CONG. REC. S18554 (Dec. 14, 1979). The companion bills in the House are H.R. 2759 and H.R. 3268.

39. Unclassified U. S. Delegation Report, Third United Nations Conference on the Law of the Sea, May 23-July 15, 1977 at 13.

The Revised Single Negotiating Text, which served as the basis for discussion at the 6th session, states unequivocally that the economic zone is *not* high seas. The constituent elements of the economic zone have not been changed significantly by the Informal Composite Text. The quality and quantity of rights executed in the zone are clarified. See Appendixes 3, 4, and 5. See also, Oxman, *The Third United Nations Conference on the Law of the Sea,* 72 AM. J. INT'L L. 57, 67 (1978).

40. For the articles of the Informal Composite Negotiating Text on the breadth of the territorial sea, see Appendix 5, Art. 3; on the breadth of the contiguous zone, see *id.,* Art. 33; on international navigation through straits, see *id.,* Pt. III (consisting of Arts. 34-35), Arts. 7-32; on innocent passage and duties and rights of coastal states, see *id.,* Art. 19, 21-24, 211, 212, 217, 218, 221, 224-228, 230-233, 235-237.

As to pollution enforcement and vessel-building requirements to ensure the prevention of pollution, the Inter-Governmental Maritime Consultative Organization would undoubtedly assume a more important role.

41. Oxman, *supra* note 39, at 65, n. 27.

42. For the articles of the Informal Composite Negotiating Text on archipelagos, see Appendix 5, Arts. 46, 47, 49, 53.

43. Oxman, *supra* note 39 at 66. The critical analysis of the sections of the Informal Composite Negotiating Text in this chapter is largely drawn from Oxman's article, *supra.*

44. Clairborne, *High Stakes Seabed Fight Begins,* Washington Post, Aug. 14, 1977, *8* A, p. 11, col. 1.

45. Wall Street Journal, Jan. 24, 1978, p. 1, col. 3. The chances of success at the 7th session of the Conference were rated as 1 in 3 by Ambassador Richardson. See also, Clairborne, *Long Running U.N. Conference—U.S. Seeks Seabed Mining Showdown,* Washington Post, Feb. 13, 1978, p. 1, col. 3; Flalka, *Richardson Issues Warning in Seeking Sea Compromise,* Washington Star, Mar. 12, 1978, §*A,* p. 6, col. 1.

46. Moore, *supra* note 38.

47. Address by Hon. Elliot L. Richardson, ambassador and special representative of the president to the United Natins Law of the Sea Conference, The Doherty Lecture in Ocean Policy, University of Virginia Law School, Nat'l Academy of Sciences Bldg., Washington, D.C., May 31, 1978. See also, *Sea Conference Ending after Little Progress,* New York Times, May 20, 1978, *8* C, p. 5, col. 2.

48. The principal subsets derived from the hard-core issues are 1) the extent of coastal state jurisdiction over the economic zone and continental shelf versus that of the landlocked and geographically disadvantaged states attending the Conference (composing an easy third of the entire membership of the Conference), 2) the nature of dispute settlements concerning fisheries, 3) the methodology of drawing the boundaries of the economic zone, and 4) ways to delimit the continental margin. Richardson Address, *supra* note 47. See also, Unclassified Delegaton Report, Third United Nations Conference on the Law of the Sea, Mar. 28-May 19, 1978.

49. Unclassified Delegation Report, *supra*, note 48.

50. Id.

51. *Id.* at 8.

52. The remaining analysis of the 7th session in this paragraph and the following three paragraphs is drawn not only from the Richardson Address, *supra* note 47, and the Unclassified Delegation Report, *supra* note 48, but also from The Report of the Committees and Negotiating Groups on Negotiations at the Seventh Session Contained in a Single Document both for the Purposes of Record and for the Convenience of Delegations, 19 May 1978 GE. 78-85880, and the Statement by Elliot L. Richardson, Ambassador at Large, May 22, 1978.

53. Richardson Address, *supra,* note 47. For additional detailed analysis of the work of the 7th session, see Oxman, *The Third United Nations Conference on the Law of the Sea: The Seventh Session 1978,* 73 Am. J. Int'l L. 1 (1979).

See generally, Synopsis, Recent Development in the Law of the Sea 1977-78, 16 San Diego L. Rev. 705 (1979).

54. See Appendix 6, *infra.*

55. United Nations Press Release SEA/375, 24 Aug. 1979.

All treaty-writing efforts of the Conference have been based on a succession of "negotiating texts" — the first of which was prepared in 1975. The present text before the Conference is a first revision of the Informal Composite Negotiating Text (ICNT). This text was issued in 1977 and the first revision of it was authored in May 1979, following the first part of the eighth session of the Conference in Geneva.

56. *Id.*

57. Richardson, *Law of the Sea,* 32 Naval War College Rev. 3, 10 (1979). See also, McCloskey & Losch, *The United Nations Law of the Sea Conference and the United States Congress: Will Pending United States Unilateral Action on Deep Seabed Mining Destroy Hope for a Treaty?* 1 Nw. J. Int'l L. & Bus. 240 (1979).

58. Richardson, *supra.*

59. *Id.,* at 7.

60. *Id.*

CONCLUSION

Nations behave, they negotiate, and they undertake lawmaking directed by a vector of competing forces and interests. Indeed, the process of world politics has been declared to be "a race between the forces which tend to fragment the world and those which work toward harmony."[1] While nations are obviously drawn together in association by common fears, values, and interests, they are— similarly—parted by suspicion, nationalism, acquisitiveness, fear, pride, aggression, and ignorance of each other's motives. Mutual trust and selfinterest can be used as building blocks for enlargement of international confidence and respect. Yet, the most basic factor in determining a nation's observance of international law is its rather pragmatic determination of the cost and advantage of applying such law.

Understanding, amelioration, adjustment, agreement, compromise, and settlement are all words of art in modern international negotiation. Confrontation yields little but conflict. Negotiation and compromise promote a form of ordered stability. Crucial to any effort at negotiation is an agreement on the objectives to be served by the negotiation. At the current sessions of the United Nations Law of the Sea Conference, there appears to be little more than a common agreement regarding its *raison d'être*: namely, to create a new legal and political order for ocean development. Beyond this, however, there appears to be little common acceptance of what must be done in order to build and maintain that order.[2]

An effective or politically viable ocean policy for the United States is one which, while protecting the national interests of America, nonetheless accommodates to a substantial degree the needs of all other countries. This balancing point is difficult to discover and more difficult to maintain over time. Any treaty that is developed at the Law of the Sea Conference which does not protect important national interests of the United States will never be ratified. There will be no treaty in the first instance if the interests of some seventy countries are not adequately protected.[3]

The edge of the apocalypse will not be within imminent view if the Conference should end its working sessions without a popularly subscribed treaty. How much time will be left to reach a clear and comprehensive global ocean regime is, however, debatable. Surely decisive action should be taken before the end of the century. Conflicts of interest which may arise can, as in the past, be temporarily resolved through bilateral and limited-multilateral agreements. Although such actions would not of course be the most desirable strategy to pursue, they would, nevertheless, be better than doing nothing at all or allowing marine law to be determined by a crazy-quilt pattern of custom.[4]

One conference surely cannot be expected to produce one treaty that will structure a new order for the oceans and comprehensively deal with the social, economic, technological, ideological, and political spheres of emerging influences. This is an undertaking that will probably continue for the remainder of the century. Whether world interests can be harmonized in an age of political militancy where new, equally militant and frustrated ideals are advanced by small, emerging nations is debatable. Changing circumstances dictate the level of response law takes in order to be reflective of the social order. This response, however, does not guarantee harmony. This is especially the situation when it is realized that the new law of the sea will, to a very significant degree, be shaped by patterns and strategies of group solidarity found among the unaligned, underdeveloped members of the world community who wish to promote, build, and develop a new law that is basic to their own egoistic interests.[5]

NOTES—CONCLUSION

1. R. Osgood, Ideals and Self Interest in American Foreign Relations 23 (1953); O. Lissitzyn, International Law Today and Tomorrow 9, 10 (1965).

No movement for revision of sea law or its recodification can take place, at least through international agreements, unless the states in the world community are willing to view their own interests in the larger context of the interests of international society. This is the essence of the compromise that will be needed to secure general acceptance of a rule of any controversial issue. Bowett, The Second United Nations Law of the Sea Conference, 9 Int'l & Comp. L. Q. 415, 435 (1960).

2. A. Lall, Modern International Negotiation 4 (1966); F. Ikle, How Nations Negotiate 26 passim (1967).

3. Ratiner, United States Ocean Policy: An Analysis, 2 J. Maritime L. & Comm. 225, 242 (1971); Swing, Who Will Own the Oceans? 54 Foreign Affairs 527 (1976). See also, Sohn, U.S. Policy toward the Settlement of the Law of the Sea Dispute, 17 Va. J. Int'l L. 9 (1976).

4. Brown & Fabian, Diplomats at Sea, 52 Foreign Affairs 301, 315 (1974).

If the involved parties are unwilling to make political and economic compromises for a unified treaty, it has been suggested tht it might be feasible to separate the subjects being negotiated, thereby allowing the subjects that have been agreed upon to be organized as a convention and come into force, while allowing for the negotiation of the remaining issues. Yet, such an approach has been regarded as infeasible principally because the "quid pro quos," given in order to obtain the present understandings and postures, "have so intertwined the negotiations that any attempt to isolate the deadlocking issues might cause the whole Revised Negotiating Text to unravel, leaving only the most unimportant subjects for codification." Charney, Law of the Sea: Breaking the Deadlock 55 Foreign Affairs 626 (1977).

On the issue of unilateral action in the event the conference fails, see Darman, *The Law of the Sea: Rethinking U.S. Interests,* 56 *id.,* 393 (1978). See also, Alexander, Cameron & Nixon, *The Costs of Failure at the Third Law of the Sea Conference,* 9 J. MARITIME L. & COMM. 1 (1977).

5. Henkin, *The Once and Future Law of the Sea,* in TRANSNATIONAL LAW IN A CHANGING SOCIETY 155 (W. Friedmann, L. Henkin, O. Lissitzyn, eds. 1972.) See also, McDougal & Burke, *Crisis in the Law of the Sea: Community Perspectives versus National Egoism,* 67 YALE L. J. 539 (1958); W. DOUGLAS, INTERNATIONAL DISSENT: SIX STEPS TOWARD WORLD PEACE 154 (1971).

APPENDIX 1

The Pertinent Provisions of the 1958 Geneva Convention on the Territorial Sea and the Contiguous Zone Regarding Innocent Passage

ARTICLE 14

(1) Subject to the provisions of these articles, ships of all States, whether coastal or not, shall enjoy the right of innocent passage through the territorial sea.

(2) Passage means navigation through the territorial sea for the purpose either of traversing that sea without entering internal waters, or of proceeding to internal waters, or of making for the high seas from internal waters.

(3) Passage includes stopping and anchoring, but only insofar as the same are incidental to ordinary navigation or are rendered necessary by *force majeure* or by distress.

(4) Passage is innocent so long as it is not prejudicial to the peace, good order or security of the coastal State. . . .

(5) Passage of foreign fishing vessels shall not be considered innocent if they do not observe such laws and regulations as the coastal State may make.

(6) Submarines are required to navigate on the surface and to show their flag.

ARTICLE 15

(1) The coastal State must not hamper innocent passage through the territorial sea.

(2) The coastal State is required to give appropriate publicity to any dangers to navigation, of which it has knowledge, within its territorial sea.

ARTICLE 16

(1) The coastal State may take the necessary steps in its territorial sea to prevent passage which is not innocent. . . .

(3) Subject to the provisions of paragraph 4, the coastal State may, without discrimination amongst foreign ships, suspend temporarily in specified areas of its territorial sea the innocent passage of foreign ships if such suspension is essential for the protection of its security. Such suspension shall take effect only after having been duly published.

(4) There shall be no suspension of the innocent passage of foreign ships through straits which are used for international navigation between one part of the high seas and another part of the high seas or the territorial sea of a foreign State.

ARTICLE 17

Foreign ships exercising the right of innocent passage shall comply with the laws and regulations enacted by the coastal State in conformity with these articles. . . .

ARTICLE 18

(1) No charge may be levied upon foreign ships by reason only of their passage through the territorial sea . . . .

ARTICLE 19

(1) The criminal jurisdiction of the coastal State should not be exercised on board of foreign ships passing through the territorial sea to arrest any person or to conduct any investigation in connection with any crime . . . .

ARTICLE 20

(1) The coastal State should not stop or divert a foreign ship passing through the territorial sea for the purpose of exercising civil jurisdiction in relation to a person on board the ship.

ARTICLE 21

The rules contained in sub-sections A and B shall also apply to government ships operated for commercial purposes.

ARTICLE 22

(1) The rule contained in sub-section A and in article 18 shall apply to government ships operated for non-commercial purposes . . . .

ARTICLE 23

If any warship does not comply with the regulations of the coastal State concerning passage through the territorial sea and disregards any request for compliance which is made to it, the coastal State may require the warship to leave the territorial sea.

APPENDIX 2

Selected National Viewpoints on Issues of the
Territorial Sea, International Straits, and Navigation
Emerging from the Law of the Sea Caracas Meetings,
Summer 1974, and the United Nations Seabed
Committee Deliberations

The citations listed herein are to official United Nations
documents that were presented at the Caracas Confer-
ence. Selected Sea Bed Committee reports are also cited.
In addition to relying upon a survey of pertinent United
Nations documentation, the author substantially relied
upon a paper, Positions on Law of the Sea of Selected
Countries, prepared by Dr. Ann L. Hollick, of the Johns
Hopkins School of Advanced International Studies,
Washington, D.C., December 1974.

BELGIUM:
   A/CONF.62/C.2/L.33 (Austria, Belgium, Bolivia,
Botswana, Byelorussian Soviet Socialist Republic,

Czechoslovakia, Federal Republic of Germany, Finland, Hungary, Laos, Lesothe, Luxembourg, Mongolia, Netherlands, Paraguay, Singapore, Swaziland, Sweden, Switzerland, Uganda, Upper Volta, Zambia subscribing). Each coastal state shall have the right to establish the breadth of its territorial sea, up to a limit not exceeding twelve nautical miles from the baselines. This right shall not be exercised in a manner which would cut off the territorial sea of another state from the high seas. Normal provision for the baseline is to be the low water line along the coast. Low tide elevations are not used unless permanent installations have been built on them. Straight baselines are used where coasts are deeply indented or there is a fringe of islands. They must not depart to any appreciable extent from the general direction of the coast, and if they enclose as internal waters areas previously considered territorial sea, a right of innocent passage shall exist.

BRAZIL:

A/AC.138/SC.II/L.25. The breadth of the territorial sea shall in no case exceed two hundred nautical miles measured from the baseline. States that do not face the open ocean shall consult with the other states of the region to determine a mutually agreed maximum breadth of the territorial sea. Innocent passage is construed so as to allow free transit in the territorial sea, provided the pertinent activities connected therewith remain limited to passage and not to broader navigational rights.

COLOMBIA:

A/AC.138/SC.II/L.21. (Colombia, Mexico, Venezuela). The territorial sea shall not exceed twelve nautical miles from applicable baselines. The right of innocent passage shall apply to ships of all states through the territorial sea. In the patrimonial sea, ships and aircraft of all states shall enjoy the right of freedom of navigation and

overflight, and the laying of submarine cables and pipelines shall exist in the high seas.

DENMARK:

A/CONF.62/C.21/L. 15. Transit passage is the exercise of freedom of navigation and overflight solely for the
purpose of continuous and expeditious transit of a strait
that 1) is more than six miles wide between the baselines,
2) is used for international navigation, and 3) connects
two parts of the high seas. Transit passage shall apply in a
strait only to the extent that an equally suitable high seas
route does not exist through the strait or, if the strait if
formed by an island, an equally suitable high seas passage
does not exist seaward of the island.

PHILIPPINES, INDONESIA:

A/CONF.62/C.2/L.49 (Fiji, Mauritius subscribing).
An archipelagic state may draw straight baselines connecting the outermost points of its outermost island and
drying reefs from which the territorial sea, economic
zone, and other special jurisdictions are to be measured.
In the enclosed archipelagic waters, the archipelagic state
enjoys sovereignty and the rights to the waters, seabed,
subsoil, and airspace. Baselines may not be drawn from
low-tide elevations unless there is an above-water installa-
tion or unless they fall within the distance of the territorial sea from an island. Ships enjoy rights of innocent
passage through archipelagic waters. The archipelagic
state may designate suitable sealanes and traffic separation schemes and substitute new sealanes after due publicity. The state may make laws relating to passage
through the archipelagic waters with respect to traffic
safety and regulation, use of navigational aids, submarine
cables and pipelines, sanitary regulations, etc. Foreign
warships may have passage suspended and be required to
leave the waters if they do not comply with the laws and
regulations of the archipelagos. Otherwise, an archi-

pelagic state may not suspend innocent passage through sealanes designated by it except when essential for its security and after substituting other sealanes for those where passage is suspended.

A/CONF.62/C.2/L.69 (Phillipines, Indonesia, Fiji and Mauritius). "High seas" means all parts of the sea not included in the territorial sea, internal or archipelagic waters.

UNITED KINGDOM:

A/CONF.62/C.2/L.3. The territorial sea may not exceed twelve miles from the baseline. Passage is innocent as long as it is not prejudicial to the peace, good order, or security of the coastal state. Prohibitions are placed on the use of force in violation of the United Nations Charter; practice with weapons; and the launching of taking on board aircraft, any military device, or any person or cargo contrary to the customs, fiscal, immigration, or military laws of the coastal state. Temporary suspension without discrimination, after appropriate publicity, is allowed when essential for security. During passage through territorial seas, ships may not carry out any marine research or survey activities. Submarines are required to navigate on the surface. Charges may be levied on ships in passage only as payment for specific services rendered. Rights of transit passage are to be enjoyed in straits or other stretches of water that 1) are used for international navigation, and 2) that connect two parts of the high seas, only to the extent that an equally suitable high seas route does not exist through the strait and if the strait is joined by an offshore island and equally suitable high seas passage does not exist seaward. Straits states may designate sealanes and prescribe traffic separation schemes to promote safe passage. Innocent passage is nonsuspendable in straits connecting the territorial sea of a foreign state to the high seas.

UNITED STATES:

A/AC.138/SC.II/L.4. The territorial sea shall be no more than twelve miles. The method of delimiting it shall be the same as used in the 1958 Territorial Sea Convention. In straits used for international navigation, all ships and aircraft shall enjoy nondiscriminatory rights of unimpeded transit. Coastal states may designate corridors suitable for transit but must include those customarily employed. Some straits may possible be excepted from free transit, if there are alternate routes.

U.S.S.R.:

A/CONF.62/C.2/L.26 (Bulgaria, Poland subscribing). Each state has the right to determine the breadth of its territorial sea within a maximum limit of twelve miles. Innocent passage in the territorial sea excludes fishing and research without prior authorization.

A/CONF.62/C.2/L.11. In straits used for international navigation between two parts of the high seas, all ships shall enjoy the equal freedom of navigation for the purpose of transit passage through such straits. In the case of narrow straits or straits where it is necessary to ensure safety, the coastal states may designate corridors; where particular channels of navigation are customarily employed, the corridors shall include such channels. The coastal state is required to give advance notice of any change in the corridor. Free navigation for purposes of transit passage is subject to rules that guarantee the security of straits states, comply with international rules to prevent collisions between ships (in heavily transited straits, the coastal state may designate traffic separation schemes based on IMCO recommendations), and follow precautionary measures to avoid pollution, etc. Innocent passage applies to straits leading from the high seas to the territorial seas. Free, unimpeded passage of all vessels through straits in archipelagos is provided. These rights would apply only to those archipelagic straits that provide the shortest route from one part of the high seas to another or which are traditionally used for navigation.

APPENDIX 3

An Analysis of Select Provisions of the Informal Single Negotiating Text, Geneva, Spring 1975

The following is an analysis of certain provisions of the Informal Single Negotiating Text that emerged from the spring 1975 meeting of the Law of the Sea Conference in Geneva. The analysis is only of those parts of the Negotiating Text that pertain to the investigation of the present topic as presented to the Second Committee. The importance of this document cannot be overestimated because it formed the bulwark of the Single Negotiating Text that emerged from the New York session of the Conference during the spring of 1976. The complete text from which this analysis of the Single Negotiating Text is taken is found in A/CONF.62/WP.8/PART II, 7 May 1975.

The limit of coastal state sovereignty in its territorial sea is allowed to a limit of twelve nautical miles measured by normal baselines. (Arts. 2, 4).

Ships of all states are accorded the right of innocent passage through the territorial seas (Art. 14). Passage is defined as traversing the territorial seas "without entering internal waters," calling at roadstead or port facilities outside internal waters, or proceeding to or from internal waters or a call at a roadstead or port facility (Art. 15). In order to be classified as *innocent,* the passage must be "continuous and expeditious." Stopping and anchoring is allowed, but only if they "are incidental to ordinary navigation or are rendered necessary by *force majeure* or by distress or for the purposes of rendering assistance to persons, ships or aircraft in danger or distress" (Art. 15 [2]).

Coastal state interests are safeguarded by providing that passage must not only conform with the articles set forth in the negotiating text but also "with other rules of international law." When passage prejudices the "peace, good order or security of the coastal state," it is no longer of an innocent nature (Art. 16 [2]). In order to make this standard more objective than it had been under the 1958 Territorial Sea Convention, certain specific acts are, accordingly, listed as prejudicial to coastal state interests: 1) threats or uses of force "against the territorial integrity or *political independence* of the coastal state or in any other manner" violative of the United Nations Charter (italics added by author); 2) any weapons exercise or practice; 3) acts designed to collect information that would prejudice the defense or the security of a coastal state or disseminate propaganda with the same intent or purpose; 4) the launching, landing, or taking on board of any aircraft or of any military device; 5) acts of embarkation or disembarkation of either commodities, currencies, or people that would be violative of coastal state sanitary regulations, customs, or fiscal integrity; 6) acts of willful pollution; 7) research or survey activities of any kind; 8) acts that would interfere with coastal communication networks or other facilities or installations; and 9) any other activity *not* having a direct bearing on passage (Art. 16

[2]. If *prior authorization* is given by a coastal state for passage of a vessel or if *force majeure*, distress, or samaritan assistance is being given to persons, ships, or aircraft, none of the previously described restrictions are applicable. The coastal state is to be notified promptly when circumstances of this nature arise (Art. 16 [3].

Provision is made that the coastal state neither will interrupt nor hamper innocent passage of foreign ships through its territorial sea by imposing regulations that deny or prejudice the right of innocent passage or discriminate against ships carrying cargoes from other states (Art. 21). No charge may in fact be levied by the coastal state upon foreign ships for passage through the territorial waters. Charges for services rendered are allowed (Art 24).

The coastal state is permitted to make laws and regulations — consistent with the Negotiating Text provisions on innocent passage — in eight areas: 1) navigational safety, which includes designating sealanes and establishing traffic separation schemes; 2) navigational aids and facilities and facilities used for exploration and exploitation of marine resources; 3) cable and pipeline protection; 4) conservation of living resources of the seas; 5) fisheries regulations; 6) environmental preservation; 7) marine environment research and hydrographic surveys; and 8) the prevention of infringement of customs, fiscal, immigration, quarantine, or sanitary regulations. Unless specific authorization is made by current international rules, coastal state laws and regulations are inapplicable to the design, construction, manning, or equipment of foreign ships. In making laws and promulgating regulations, the coastal state is required in every case to give "due publicity" to them (Art. 18 [3].

With the immense delegation of power given to the coastal states under the Negotiating Text to make laws and regulations in key maritime area, care must be taken to assure that these acts do not burden vessels to the extent that they hamper their passage. This cautionary note is all the more important when the all-encompassing scope of actions said to prejudice the "peace, good order or security of the coastal state," is carefully considered. The imposition of coastal state liability in Article 23 for improper obstruction of innocent passage is a needed safeguard to what could well become reckless application of provisions in the Negotiating Text.

The coastal state may, under the provisions of the Negotiating Text, *temporarily suspend* foreign ships from its territorial sea if the suspension is deemed essential for its security. Such suspension is only effective after notice of it has been published. A coastal state may take whatever steps are necessary to prevent noninnocent passage (Art 22).

A ship not complying with coastal state laws and regulations is liable for any damage caused to the coastal state *or* any ships flying its flag (Art. 23). Similarly, if a coastal state acts inconsistently with and contrary to its own laws and regulations pertinent to innocent passage, thus causing loss or damage to foreign ships, then that coastal state is liable to the owners of the ship for the loss or damage thereto (Art. 23).

Aircraft are given *no* right of innocent passage but are accorded a right of transit passage through straits used for international passage (Art. 38).

A differentiation is made regarding types of sea-going vessels. Passage by foreign fishing vessels will be considered innocent if they observe coastal state laws and regulations designed to prevent them *from fishing* in the territorial sea (Art. 16). For *submarines* and other underwater vehicles to be accorded innocent passage, they must navigate on the surface and show their flag unless otherwise authorized by the coastal state (Art. 17). Foreign ships must comply with international regulations relating to the prevention of collisions at sea when exercising innocent passage (Art. 18). Tankers and ships carrying nuclear or inherently dangerous or noxious substances may be required to confine their passage to *sealanes* or follow traffic separation schemes designated by the coastal state (Arts. 19 and 20). *Government ships other than warships* (Art. 26) and those operated for noncommercial purposes (Art. 28) are accorded the right of innocent passage as long as they meet the normal requirements set out for passage in Articles 15 and 16.

Warships are defined as: ships "belonging to the armed forces of a State bearing the external marks distinguishing such ships of its nationality, under the command of an officer duly commissioned by the government of the State and whose name appears in the appropriate Service list or its equivalent, and manned by a crew who are under regular armed forces discipline" (Art. 29). Passage is allowed for warships consistent with the requirements imposed on other vessels in Articles 15 and 16. If, however, a warship chooses not to comply with coastal state laws and regulations relating to passage and disregards a request for compliance, it may be required to leave the territorial seas of the coastal state (Art. 30). The immunities warships enjoy under other rules of international law are in no way affected by these provisions concerning their innocent passage. (Art. 31) Should any warship or other government ship operated for noncommercial purposes fail to comply with coastal state laws and regulations and thereby cause damage to the coastal state *or* to any ships flying its flag, liability will be *fixed on the flag state* of the ship which causes the damage (Art. 32).

Criminal and Civil Jurisdiction

Coastal state criminal jurisdiction "should not" be exercised as foreign ships pass through the territorial sea either to arrest or conduct investigations into crimes committed on board the ship unless: 1) the "consequences of the crime extend to the coastal State;" 2) the crime disturbs the country's peace or the good order of the territorial seas; 3) the ship's captain or consular officer of the country whose flag the ship flies requests assistance; or 4) the coastal state's interference is necessary to suppress illicit narcotic trade and "psychotropic substances" (Art. 25 [1]. Yet, the right of the coastal state to act under the purposes of its laws either to make an arrest on board a foreign ship or to investigate on board a ship *after* it leaves the state's internal waters is preserved (Art. 25 [2]). For any crime committed on board such a foreign ship *before it enters* a state's territorial sea or is in the process of passing through that sea without entering internal waters, the coastal state "may not" board the vessel to make an arrest or conduct an investigation in connection with a crime committed (Art. 25 [5]).

On the issue of *civil jurisdiction,* again, the Negotiating Text declares a coastal state "should not" exercise its civil jurisdiction over a person on board by stopping or diverting a foreign ship passing through its territorial sea (Art. 26 [1]). Furthermore, the coastal state "may not" arrest a ship unless its obligations of liabilities are "assumed or incurred" either during the course or for the purpose of its voyage through coastal state waters (Art. 26 [2]). For foreign ships lying in the territorial sea or passing through the territorial sea *after* leaving internal waters, the coastal state — consistent with its laws on the subject — may levy execution against or arrest such ships for any civil proceeding (Art. 26 [3]).

Straits

The Geneva Negotiating Text established a "regime of passage through straits for international navigation," (Art. 34 [1]) "between one area of the high sea or an exclusive economic zone and another area of the high seas or an exclusive economic zone" (Art. 37). If a route of passage through the high seas or exclusive economic zone of similar convenience exists, then the right of unimpeded transit passage that is accordingly conferred on ships and aircraft is *not* applicable (Arts. 37, 38 [1]). Transit passage may be exercised for purposes of transit to or from another strait, subject to conditions of entry which may be imposed (Art. 38 [3]). The need for the transit passage to be "continuous and expeditious" is stressed. Indeed, the very concept of transit passage is defined as the exercise of freedom of navigation *and* overflight for purposes of "continuous and expeditious" transit through straits (Art. 38 [2 AND 3]).

Ships (which presumably includes *submerged submarines and warships* and aircraft are required, when exercising this right, to refrain from activities that involve force or the threat thereof against the "the territorial integrity or political independence of a strait State." Ships, specifically, are directed to comply with international regulations concerning safety at sea and the prevention and control of pollution. Aircrafts are directed to observe the Rules of the Air set by the International Civil Aviation Organization (ICAO) for civil aircraft and other pertinent safety measures (Art. 39). If either a ship or aircraft violates strait state laws and regulations, with resultant loss or damage to a strait state or *other* state in the vicinity of the strait, "the flag state shall be responsible for that loss or damage" (Art. 41 [5]).

A state bordering a strait or "strait State" is allowed, in the interests of promoting ship safety, to designate sealanes and prescribe traffic separation schemes for navigation in straits. But before acting in this respect, the strait state "shall refer" its proposals to "the competent international organization with a view to their adoption." Interestingly, the Inter-Governmental Maritime Consultative Organization (IMCO)—is only allowed to adopt those sealanes and schemes for separation "as may be agreed with the strait State" (Art. 40). A strait state is not allowed, in its effort to make laws and regulations pertinent to transit passage, to design them so that the *practical effect* of them is to deny, hamper, or impair the right of transit (Art. 41 [2]). The specific areas of permissible law-making concern: safety navigation and marine traffic regulation; pollution prevention with particular regard to oil discharges; fishing vessels and the prevention of fishing; and customs, fiscal, immigration, or sanitary regulations (Art. 41 [1]).

Article 44 provides that the régime of innocent passage in straits used for international navigation shall include: "(a) one area of the high seas or an exclusive zone and another area of the high seas or an exclusive economic zone, other than those straits in which the regime of transit passage applies . . . ; or (b) one area of the high seas or an exclusive economic zone and the territorial sea of a foreign State." Provision is made that there "shall be no suspension of innocent passage through such straits." Article 44 was designed to make innocent passage applicable and nonsuspendible in straits of international importance such as the Straits of Tiran. Presently, Article 16 (4) of the Territorial Sea Convention provides basically the same thing.

Exclusive Economic Zone

The "position" adopted at the Caracas meeting regarding an exclusive economic zone yielded a total of 35 provisions with some 72 alternative formulae for resolving conflicts. (The "Main Trends" document drafted by the Second Committee contains these provisions. See A/CONF. 62/C.2/WP.1/Corr. 1, 17 Nov. 1974) The basic tone of these various provisions was to acknowledge the existence of such a zone and to chart the parameters of its functional use, as well as to establish rights and obligations of those who both possessed and traversed it.

Article 45 of the Geneva Informal Negotiating Text establishes an "area beyond and adjacent to the territorial sea" designated as an exclusive economic zone and confers on the coastal state various rights and duties for its operation therein. Exclusive jurisdiction is conferred upon the coastal states in their exploration, exploitation, and management of natural resources in the zone to an extent of *200 miles* from the baseline from which the breadth of the territorial sea is measured (Art. 46).

The coastal state is to determine the "allowable catch of the living resources in the exclusive economic zone" (Art. 50 [1]). A factor in this determination will be the recognition of the need to maintain proper conservation measures of these resources so as to avoid their exploitation. When a coastal state has determined that it does not have sufficient capacity to harvest its predetermined allowable catch of living resources, it "shall" allow other states an opportunity to harvest the surplus (Art. 51 [2]). Among considerations to be evaluatd by a coastal state in allowing other states access to the exclusive economic zone are "the requirements of developing countries in harvesting part of the surplus and the need to minimize economic dislocation in States whose nationals have habitually fished in the zone or which have made substantial efforts in research and identification of stocks" (Art. 52 [3]). Among the eleven areas in which coastal state regulations may be developed in relation to the use of an exclusive economic zone are size and type of fishing vessel, quotas of catch, and determination of which species (their age, size) may be caught (Art. 52 [4]).

Article 33 of the Negotiating Text provides for the establishment of a *contiguous zone* not to "extend beyond 24 miles from the baseline from which the breadth of the territorial sea is measured."

Article 123 allows all ships *innocent passage* through *archipelagic waters.* An archipelagic state "may" designate sealanes and air routes suitable for safe, continuous, and expeditious passage of ships and aircraft through its waters (Art. 124). Archipelagic states are allowed to draw straight baselines in determining their territorial seas. The baselines are not to exceed 80 nautical miles. However, the total number of baselines enclosing any arch may exceed that length up to a maximum length of 125 nautical miles (Art. 118). The archipelagic state may make laws and require compliance with international laws regarding ships and planes comparable to—in almost verbatim terms—with those rights given strait states.

APPENDIX 4

Remarks and Selected Provisions of the
Revised Single Negotiating Text: Part Two
Text Presented by the Chairman of the
Second Committee
6 May 1976
A/CONF. 62/WP. 8/REV. 1/PART II

[Only those sections of the chairman's introductory
note and those sections of the text considered germane to
a full understanding of the problem areas considered in
this book, and which thus show the evolutionary change
in Conference diplomacy, have been printed here.]

Introductory Note

1. The Conference, at its 55th meeting on 18 April
1975, decided that the chairmen of the three main committees should each prepare a single negotiating text covering the subjects entrusted to his committee. In compli-

ance with this decision, Ambassador Galindo Pohl, the previous Chairman of the Second Committee, submitted a text contained in Part II of document A/CONF.62/ WP.8.

2. At its 57th meeting on 15 March 1975, the Conference established guidelines for the work during its fourth session. In accordance with these guidelines, the Second Committee decided, at its 49th meeting on 16 March 1976, to study the informal single negotiating text, article by article, to determine, through a process of collective discussion, to what extent the text served the purpose for which it was intended. Upon the conclusion of this process, I was to produce a revised text, reflecting the results in the most appropriate manner.

3. The present text was prepared in compliance with that decision of the Committee.

4. I began my task following consideration of the text by the Committee in the course of 52 informal meetings, during which more than 3700 interventions were made. The participation in these meetings, was very large. As a rule, over 120 of the 149 delegations accredited to this session were represented. My first conclusion upon analyzing that discussion was that the text served well as a basis for negotiations in the Committee . . . .

5. The guiding principle in revising the single text was to make such changes as would make the text conform more to the views of delegations, as expressed during discussion in the Committee. In my opinion, very few of the over one thousand amendments proposed during the session would achieve the purpose of making the text a more adequate instrument for the fulfillment of the final objectives of the Conference.

11. On the question of the rights of land-locked States and certain developing coastal States in the exploitation of the resources of the exclusive economic zone, I made no major changes. Despite the fact that a great amount of effort was devoted in the special interest group and in

other informal groups dealing with the issue, I was offered no clear guidance on possible changes. No single proposal commanded significant support. I consider that any major change in the relevant provisions could jeopardize any further negotiations which might take place.

12. On the issue of delimitation of the exclusive economic zone and the continental shelf between adjacent or opposite States an extensive exchange of views took place. A close study of the discussion ... revealed broad support for the thrust of the article in the single negotiating text. However, paragraph 3 of former articles 61 and 70 posed a problem. Since the Conference may not adopt a compulsory jurisdictional procedure for the settlement of delimitation disputes, I felt that the reference to the median or equidistant line as an interim solution might not have the intended effect of encouraging agreements. In fact such reference might defeat the main purport of the article as set out in paragraph 1. Nonetheless, the need for an interim solution was evident. The solution was, in my opinion, to propose wording in paragraph 3 which linked it more closely to the principles in paragraph 1 . . . .

14. The matter on which the Committee was perhaps the most divided was whether or not the exclusive economic zone should be included in the definition of the high seas. I felt initially that I should at least point the way to a compromise solution, giving tangible recognition in the same manner to my opinion that an accommodation could be found.

15. However, upon more closely analyzing the discussion, I decided that to change the text now might be counterproductive, in the sense that it could upset the balance implicit in the single negotiating text.

16. It was perhaps unfortunate that the issue was addressed in terms of the definition of the high seas in article 75. There could be little debate as to which of the provisions in the chaper on the high seas apply in the exclu-

sive economic zone, whether included in the definition of high seas or not.

17. Nor is there any doubt that the exclusive economic zone is neither the high seas nor the territorial sea. It is a zone *sui generis*.

18. As has often been pointed out, the matter should be addressed in terms of the "residual rights." In simple terms, the rights as to resources belong to the coastal State and, insofar as such rights are not infringed, all other States enjoy the freedoms of navigation and communication. In fact, this is specified in general terms in article 46, when read in conjunction with articles 44 and 47. Many had thought that these provisions dealt adequately with the matter. My original intention to point the way to a compromise solution would have related closely to those provisions. And, I would encourage a reorientation of the discussion around these articles.

19. As a result, while the article on the definition of the high seas has not been changed, I hope it is clear from these comments that I have given this controversial issue careful consideration.

21. On the issue of enclosed or semi-enclosed seas, I have responded to expressions of dissatisfaction with the provisions in the single negotiating text by making less mandatory the co-ordination of activities in such seas. Consequently, I decided not to make the definition of such seas more restrictive.

24. The revised text and the process which preceded and conditioned its preparation must be seen as an important stage in the work of the Conference towards the fulfillment of its mandate. The discussion in the Committee was in every respect complete. All items were given the same status and opportunities were afforded for the expression of all views.

Andrés Aguilar M.
Chairman, Second Committee

Chapter I: The territorial sea and the contiguous zone

SECTION 1. GENERAL

Article 1
Juridical status of the territorial sea, of the air space over
the territorial sea and of its bed and subsoil

1. The sovereignty of a coastal State extends beyond its land territory and internal waters, and in the case of an archipelagic State, its archipelagic waters, over an adjacent belt of sea described as the territorial sea.

2. This sovereignty extends to the air space over the territorial sea as well as to its bed and subsoil.

3. The sovereignty over the territorial sea is exercised subject to the present Convention and to other rules of international law.

SECTION 2. LIMITS OF THE TERRITORIAL SEA

Article 2
Breadth of the territorial sea

Every State has the right to establish the breadth of its territorial sea up to a limit not exceeding 12 nautical miles, measured from baselines determined in accordance with the present Convention.

Article 3
Outer limit of the territorial sea

The outer limit of the territorial sea is the line every point of which is at a distance from the nearest point of the baseline equal to the breadth of the territorial sea.

Article 4
Normal baseline

Except where otherwise provided in the present Convention, the normal baseline for measuring the breadth of the territorial sea is the low-water line along the coast as marked on large-scale charts officially recognized by the coastal State.

Article 5
Reefs

In the case of islands situated on atolls or of islands having fringing reefs, the baseline for measuring the breadth of the territorial sea shall be the seaward low-water line of the reef, as shown by the appropriate symbol on official charts.

Article 6
Straight baselines

1. In localities where the coastline is deeply indented and cut into, or if there is a fringe of islands along the coast in its immediate vicinity, the method of straight baselines joining appropriate points may be employed in drawing the baseline from which the breadth of the territorial sea is measured.

2. Where because of the presence of a delta and other natural conditions the coastline is highly unstable, the appropriate points may be selected along the furthest seaward extent of the low-water line and, nothwithstanding subsequent regression of the low-water line, such baselines shall remain effective until changes by the coastal State in accordance with the present Convention.

3. The drawing of such baselines must not depart to any appreciable extent from the general direction of the coast, and the sea areas lying within the lines must be sufficiently closely linked to the land domain to be subject to the regime of internal waters.

4. Straight baselines shall not be drawn to and from low-tide elevations, unless lighthouses or similar installations which are permanently above sea level have been built on them or except in instances where the drawing of baselines to and from such elevations has received general international recognition.

5. Where the method of straight baselines is applicable under paragraph 1 account may be taken, in determining particular baselines, of economic interests peculiar to the region concerned, the reality and the importance of which are clearly evidenced by a long usage.

6. The system of straight baselines may not be applied by a State in such a manner as to cut off from the high seas or the exclusive economic zone the territorial sea of another State.

Article 7
Internal waters

1. Except as provided in Chapter VII, waters on the landward side of the baseline of the territorial sea form part of the internal waters of the State.

2. Where the establishment of a straight baseline in accordance with article 6 has the effect of enclosing as internal waters areas which had not previously been considered as such, a right of innocent passage as provided in the present Convention shall exist in those waters.

Article 8
Mouths of rivers

If a river flows directly into the sea, the baseline shall be a straight line across the mouth of the river between points on the low-tide line of its banks.

Article 9
Bays

1. This article relates only to bays the coasts of which belong to a single State.

2. For the purposes of the present Convention, a bay is a well-marked identation whose penetration is in such proportion to the width of its mouth as to contain land-locked waters and constitute more than a mere curvature of the coast. An indentation shall not, however, be regarded as a bay unless its area is as large as, or larger than, that of the semi-circle whose diameter is a line

drawn across the mouth of that indentation.

3. For the purpose of measurement, the area of an indentation is that lying between the low-water mark around the shore of the indentation and a line joining the low-water mark of its natural entrance points. Where, because of the presence of islands, an indentation has more than one mouth, the semi-circle shall be drawn on a line as long as the sum total of the lengths of the lines across the different mouths. Islands within an indentation shall be included as if they were part of the water area of the indentation.

4. If the distance between the low-water marks of the natural entrance points of a bay does not exceed twenty-four miles a closing line may be drawn between these two low-water marks, and the waters enclosed thereby shall be considered as internal waters.

5. Where the distance between the low-water marks of the natural entrance points of a bay exceeds twenty-four miles a straight baseline of twenty-four miles shall be drawn within the bay in such a manner as to enclose the maximum area of water that is possible with a line of that length.

6. The foregoing provisions do not apply to so-called "historic" bays, or in any case where the system of straight baselines provided for in article 6 is applied.

Article 10
Ports

For the purpose of delimiting the territorial sea, the outermost permanent harbour works which form an integral part of the harbour system are regarded as forming part of the coast. Offshore installations and artificial islands shall not be considered as permanent harbour works.

Article 11
Roadsteads

Roadsteads which are normally used for the loading, unloading, and anchoring of ships, and which would otherwise be situated wholly or partly outside the outer limit of the territorial sea, are included in the territorial sea.

Article 12
Low-tide elevations

1. A low-tide elevation is a naturally formed area of land which is surrounded by and above water at low tide but submerged at high tide. Where a low-tide elevation is situated wholly or partly at a distance not exceeding the breadth of the territorial sea from the mainland or an island, the low-water line on that elevation may be used as the baseline for measuring the breadth of the territorial sea.

2. Where a low-tide elevation is wholly situated at a distance exceeding the breadth of the territorial sea from the mainland or an island, it has no territorial sea of its own.

Article 13
Combination of methods for determining baselines

The coastal State may determine baselines in turn by any of the methods provided for in the foregoing articles to suit different conditions.

Article 14
Delimitation of the territorial sea between States with opposite or adjacent coasts

Where the coasts of two States are opposite or adjacent to each other, neither of the two States is entitled, failing agreement between them to the contrary, to extend its territorial sea beyond the median line every point of which is equidistant from the nearest points on the baselines from which the breadth of the territorial seas of each of the two States is measured. This article does not apply, however, where it is necessary by reason of historic title or other special circumstances to delimit the territorial seas of the two States in a way which is at variance with this provision.

Article 15
Charts and lists of geographical co-ordinates

1. The baselines for measuring the breadth of the territorial sea determined in accordance with articles 6, 8 and 9, or the limits derived therefrom, and the lines of delimitation drawn in accordance with articles 11 and 14, shall be shown on charts on a scale or scales adequate for determining them. Alternatively, a list of geographical co-ordinates of points, specifying the geodetic datum, may be substituted.

2. The coastal State shall give due publicity to such charts or lists of geographical co-ordinates and shall deposit a copy of each such chart or list with the Secretary-General of the United Nations.

SECTION 3. INNOCENT PASSAGE IN THE TERRITORIAL SEA
SUBSECTION A. RULES APPLICABLE TO ALL SHIPS

Article 16
Right of innocent passage

Subject to the present Convention, ships of all States, whether coastal or landlocked, enjoy the right of innocent passage through the territorial sea.

Article 17
Meaning of passage

1. Passage means navigation through the territorial sea for the purpose of:

(a) Traversing that sea without entering internal waters or calling at a roadstead or port facility outside internal waters; or

(b) Proceeding to or from internal waters or a call at such roadstead or port facility.

2. Passage shall be continuous and expeditious. However, passage includes stopping and anchoring, but only in so far as the same are incidental to ordinary navigation or are rendered necessary by *force majeure* or distress or for the purpose of rendering assistance to persons, ships or aircraft in danger or distress.

Article 18
Meaning of innocent passage

1. Passage is innocent so long as it is not prejudicial to the peace, good order or security of the coastal State. Such passage shall take place in conformity with the present Convention and with other rules of international law.

2. Passage of a foreign ship shall be considered to be prejudicial to the peace, good order or security of the coastal State, if in the territorial sea it engages in any of the following activities:

(a) Any threat or use of force against the sovereignty, territorial integrity or political independence of the coastal State, or in any other manner in violation of the principles of international law embodied in the Charter of the United Nations;

(b) Any exercise or practice with weapons of any kind;

(c) Any act aimed at collecting information to the prejudice of the defence or security of the coastal State;

(d) Any act of propaganda aimed at affecting the defense or security of the coastal State;

(e) The launching, landing or taking on board of any aircraft;

(f) The launching, landing or taking on board of any military device;

(g) The embarking or disembarking of any commodity, currency or person contrary to the customs, fiscal, immigration or sanitary regulations of the coastal State;

(h) Any act of wilful and serious pollution, contrary to the present Convention;

(i) Any fishing activities;

(j) The carrying out of research or survey activities;

(k) Any act aimed at interfering with any systems of communication or any other facilities or installations of the coastal State.

(l) Any other activity not having a direct bearing on passage.

Article 19
Submarines and other underwater vehicles

In the territorial sea, submarines and other underwater vehicles are required to navigate on the surface and to show their flag.

Article 20
Laws and regulations of the coastal State relating to innocent passage

1. The coastal State may make laws and regulations, in conformity with the provisions of the present Convention and other rules of international law, relating to innocent passage through the territorial sea, in respect of all or any of the following:

(a) The safety of navigation and the regulation of marine traffic

(b) The protection of navigational aids and facilities and other facilities or installations;

(c) The protection of cables and pipelines;

(d) The conservation of the living resources of the sea;

(e) The prevention of infringement of the fisheries regulations of the coastal State;

(f) The preservation of the environment of the coastal State and the prevention of pollution thereof;

(g) Marine scientific research and hydrographic surveys;

(h) The prevention of infringement of the customs, fiscal, immigration, or sanitary regulations of the coastal State.

2. Such laws and regulations shall not apply to or affect the design, construction, manning or equipment of foreign ships or matters regulated by generally accepted international rules unless specificaly authorized by such rules.

3. The coastal State shall give due publicity to all such laws and regulations.

4. Foreign ships exercising the right of innocent passage through the territorial sea shall comply with all such laws and regulations and all generally accepted international regulations relating to the prevention of collisions at sea.

Article 21
Sea lanes and traffic separation schemes in the territorial sea

1. The coastal State may, where necessary having regard to the safety of navigation, require foreign ships exercising the right of innocent passage through its territorial sea to use such sea lanes and traffic separation schemes as it may designate or prescribe for the regulation of the passage of ships.

2. In particular, tankers, nuclear-powered ships and ships carrying nuclear or other inherently dangerous or noxious substances or materials may be required to confine their passage to such sea lanes.

3. In the designation of sea lanes and the prescription of traffic separation schemes under this article the coastal State shall take into account:

(a) The recommendations of competent international organizations;

(b) Any channels customarily used for international navigation;

(c) The special characteristics of particular ships and channels; and

(d) The density of traffic.

4. The coastal State shall clearly indicate such sea lanes and traffic separation schemes in charts to which due publicity shall be given.

Article 22
Foreign nuclear-powered ships and ships carrying nuclear or other inherently dangerous or noxious substances

Foreign nuclear-powered ships and ships carrying nuclear or other inherently dangerous or noxious nuclear substances shall, when exercising the right of innocent passage through the territorial sea, carry documents and observe special precautionary measures established for such ships by international agreements.

Article 23
Duties of the coastal State

1. The coastal State shall not hamper the innocent passage of foreign ships through the territorial sea except the accordance with the present Convention. In particular, in the application of the present Convention or of any laws or regulations made under the present Convention, the coastal State shall not:

(a) Impose requirements on foreign ships which have the practical effect of denying or impairing the right of innocent passage; or

(b) Discriminate in form or in fact against the ships of any State or aginst ships carrying cargoes to, from or on behalf of any State.

2. The coastal State shall give appropriate publicity to any dangers to navigation, of which it has knowledge, within its territorial sea.

Article 24
Rights of protection of the coastal State

1. The coastal State may take the necessary steps in its territorial sea to prevent passage which is not innocent.

2. In the case of ships proceeding to internal waters or a call at a port facility outside internal waters, the coastal State also has the right to take the necessary steps to prevent any breach of the conditions to which admission of those ships to internal waters or such a call is subject.

3. The coastal State may, without discrimination amongst foreign ships, suspend temporarily in specified areas of its territorial sea the innocent passage of foreign ships if such suspension is essential for the protection of its security. Such suspension shall take effect only after having been duly published.

Article 25
Charges which may be levied upon foreign ships

1. No charge may be levied upon foreign ships by reason only of their passage through the territorial sea.

2. Charges may be levied upon a foreign ship passing through the territorial sea as payment only for specific services rendered to the ship. These charges shall be levied without discrimination.

SUBSECTION B. RULES APPLICABLE TO MERCHANT SHIPS AND GOVERNMENT SHIPS OPERATED FOR COMMERCIAL PURPOSES

Article 26
Criminal jurisdiction on board a foreign ship

1. The criminal jurisdiction of the coastal State should not be exercised on board a foreign ship passing through the territorial sea to arrest any person or to conduct any investigation in connection with any crime committed on board the ship during its passage, save only in the following cases:

(a) If the consequences of the crime extend to the coastal State;

(b) If the crime is of a kind to distrub the peace of the country or the good order of the territorial sea;

(c) If the assistance of the local authorities has been requested by the captain of the ship or by the diplomatic agent or consular officer of the flag State; or

(d) If such measures are necessary for the suppression of illicit traffic in narcotic drugs or psychotropic substances.

2. The above provisions do not affect the right of the coastal State to take any steps authorized by its laws for the purpose of an arrest or investigation on board a foreign ship passing through the territorial sea after leaving internal waters.

3. In the cases provided for in paragraphs 1 and 2, the coastal State shall, if the captain so requests, advise the diplomatic agent or consular officer of the flag State before taking any steps, and shall facilitate contact between such agent or officer and the ship's crew. In cases of emergency this notification may be communicated while the measures are being taken.

4. In considering whether or how an arrest should be made, the local authorities shall pay due regard to the interests of navigation.

5. The coastal State may not take any steps on board a foreign ship passing through the territorial sea to arrest any person or to conduct any investigation in connexion with any crime committed before the ship entered the territorial sea, if the ship, proceeding from a foreign port, is only passing through the territorial sea without entering internal waters.

Article 27
Civil jurisdiction in relation to foreign ships

1. The coastal State should not stop or divert a foreign ship passing through the territorial sea for the purpose of

exercising civil jurisdiction in relation to a person on board the ship.

2. The coastal State may not levy execution against or arrest the ship for the purpose of any civil proceedings, save only in respect of obligations or liabilities assumed or incurred by the ship itself in the course or for the purpose of its voyage through the waters of the coastal State.

3. Paragraph 2 is without prejudice to the right of the coastal State, in accordance with its laws, to levy execution against or to arrest, for the purpose of any civil proceedings, a foreign ship lying in the territorial sea or passing through the territorial sea after leaving internal waters.

SUBSECTION C. RULES APPLICABLE TO WARSHIPS AND OTHER GOVERNMENT SHIPS OPERATED FOR NONCOMMERCIAL PURPOSES

Article 28
Definition of warships

For the purposes of the present Convention, "warships" means a ship belonging to the armed forces of a State bearing the external marks distinguishing such ships of its nationality, under the command of an officer duly commissioned by the Government of the State and whose name appears in the appropriate service list or its equivalent, and manned by a crew which is under regular armed forces discipline.

Article 29
Nonobservance by warships of the laws and regulations of the coastal State

If any warship does not comply with the laws and regulations of the coastal State concerning passage through the territorial sea and disregards any request for compliance which is made to it, the coastal State may require it to leave the territorial sea immediately.

Article 30
Responsibility of the flag State for damage caused by a warship or other government ship used for noncommercial purposes

The flag State shall bear international responsibility for any loss or damage to the coastal State resulting from the non-compliance by warship or other government ship operated for non-commercial purposes with the laws and regulations of the coastal State concerning passage through the territorial sea or with the provisions of the present Convention or other rules of international law.

Article 31
Immunities of warships and other government ships used for non-commercial purposes

With such exceptions as are contained in subsection A and in article 29 and 30, nothing in the present Convention affects the immunities of warships and other government ships operated for non-commercial purposes.

SECTION 4. CONTIGUOUS ZONE

Article 32
Contiguous zone

1. In a zone contiguous to its territorial sea, described as the contiguous zone, the coastal State may exercise the control necessary to:

(a) Prevent infringement of its customs, fiscal, immigration or sanitary regulations within its territory or territorial sea;

(b) Punish infringement of the above regulations committed within its territory or territorial sea.

2. The contiguous zone may not extend beyond 24 nautical miles from the baselines from which the breadth of the territorial sea is measured.

Chapter II: Straits used for international navigation

SECTION 1. GENERAL

Article 33
Juridical status of waters forming straits used for international navigation

1. The régime of passage through straits used for international navigation established in this Chapter shall not in other respects affect the status of the waters forming such straits nor the exercise by the State bordering the straits of their sovereignty or jurisdiction over such waters and their air space, bed and subsoil.

2. The sovereignty or jurisdiction of the States bordering the straits is exercised subject to this Chapter and to other rules of international law.

Article 34
Scope of this Chapter

Nothing in this Chapter shall affect:

(a) Any areas of internal waters within a strait, except where the establishment of a straight baseline in accordance with article 6 has the effect of enclosing as internal waters areas which had not previously been considered as such;

(b) The status of the waters beyond the territorial seas of States bordering straits as exclusive economic zones or high seas; or

(c) The legal régime in straits in which passage is regulated in whole or in part by long-standing international conventions in force specifically relating to such straits.

Article 35
High seas routes or routes through exclusive economic zones through straits used for international navigation

This Chapter does not apply to a strait used for international navigation if a high seas route or a route through an exclusive economic zone of similar convenience with respect to navigational and hydrographical characteristics exists through the strait.

SECTION 2. TRANSIT PASSAGE

Article 36
Scope of this section

This section applies to straits which are used for international navigation between one area of the high seas or an exclusive economic zone and another area of the high seas or an exclusive economic zone.

Article 37
Right of transit passage

1. In straits referred to in article 36, all ships and aircraft enjoy the right of transit passage, which shall not be impeded, except that if the strait is formed by an island of a State bordering the strait and its mainland, transit passage shall not apply if a high seas route or a route in an exclusive economic zone of similar convenience with respect to navigational and hydrographical characteristics exists seaward of the island.

2. Transit passage is the exercise in accordance with this Chapter of the freedom of navigation and overflight solely for the purpose of continuous and expeditious transit of the strait between one area of the high seas or an exclusive economic zone and another area of the high seas or an exclusive economic zone. However, the requirement of continuous and expeditious transit does not preclude passage through the strait for the purpose of entering, leaving or returning from a State bordering the strait, subject to the conditions of entry to that State.

3. An activity which is not an exercise of the right of transit passage through a strait remains subject to the other applicable provisions of the present Convention.

Article 38
Duties of ships and aircraft during their passage

1. Ships and aircraft, while exercising the right of transit passage, shall:

(a) Proceed without delay through or over the strait;

(b) Refrain from any threat or use of force against the sovereignty, territorial integrity or political independence of States bordering straits, or in any other manner in violation of the principles of international law embodied in the Charter of the United Nations;

(c) Refrain from any activities other than those incident to their normal modes of continuous and expeditious transit unless rendered necessary by *force majeure* or by distress;

(d) Comply with other relevant provisions of this Chapter.

2. Ships in transit shall:

(a) Comply with generally accepted international regulations, procedures and practices for safety at sea, including the International Regulations for Preventing Collisions at Sea;

(b) Comply with generally accepted international regulations, procedures and practices for the prevention and control of pollution from ships.

3. Aircraft in transit shall:

(a) Observe the Rules of the Air established by the International Civil Aviation Organization as they apply to civil aircraft; State aircraft will normally comply with such safety measures and will at all times operate with due regard for the safety of navigation;

(b) At all times monitor the radio frequency assigned by the appropriate internationally designated air traffic control authority or the appropriate international distress radio frequency.

Article 39
Sea lanes and traffic separation schemes in straits used for international navigation

1. In conformity with this Chapter, States bordering straits may designate sea lanes and prescribe traffic separation schemes for navigation in straits where necessary to promote the safe passage of ships.

2. Such State may, when circumstances require, and after giving due publicity thereto, substitute other sea lanes or traffic separation schemes for any sea lanes or traffic separation schemes previously designated or prescribed by them.

3. Such sea lanes and traffic separation schemes shall conform to generally accepted international regulations.

4. Before designating or substituting sea lanes or prescribing or substituting traffic separation schemes, States bordering straits shall refer proposals to the competent international organization with a view to their adoption. The organization may adopt only such sea lanes and traffic separation schemes as may be agreed with the States bordering the straits, after which the States may designate, prescribe or substitute them.

5. In respect of a strait where sea lanes or traffic separation schemes are proposed through the waters of two or more States bordering the strait, the States concerned shall co-operate in formulating proposals in consultation with the organization.

6. States bordering straits shall clearly indicate all sea lanes and traffic separation schemes designated or prescribed by them on charts to which due publicity shall be given.

7. Ships in transit shall respect applicable sea lanes and traffic separation schemes established in accordance with this article.

Article 40
Laws and regulations of States bordering straits
relating to transit passage

1. Subject to the provisions of this section, States bordering straits may make laws and regulations relating to transit passage through straits, in respect of all or any of the following:

(a) The safety of navigation and the regulation of marine traffic, as provided in article 39;

(b) The prevention of pollution by giving effect to applicable international regulations regarding the discharge of oil, oily waters and other noxious substances in the strait;

(c) With respect to fishing vessels, the prevention of fishing, including the stowage of fishing gear;

(d) The taking on board or putting overboard of any commodity, currency or person in contravention of the customs, fiscal, immigration or sanitary regulations of States bordering straits.

2. Such laws and regulations shall not discriminate in form or fact amongst foreign ships, nor in their application have the practical effect of denying, hampering or impairing the right of transit passage as defined in this section.

3. States bordering straits shall give due publicity to all such laws and regulations.

4. Foreign ships exercising the right of transit passage shall comply with such laws and regulations.

5. The flag State of a ship or aircraft entitled to sovereign immunity which acts in a manner contrary to such laws and regulations or other provisions of this Chapter shall bear international responsibility for any loss or damage which results to States bordering straits.

Article 41
Navigation and safety aids and other improvements and the prevention and control of pollution

User States and States bordering a strait should by agreement co-operate:

(a) In the establishment and maintenance in a strait of necessary navigation and safety aids or other improvements in aid of international navigation; and

(b) For the prevention and control of pollution from ships.

Article 42
Duties of States bordering straits

States bordering straits shall not hamper transit passage and shall give appropriate publicity to any danger to navigation or overflight within or over the strait of which it has knowledge. There shall be no suspension of transit passage.

SECTION 3. INNOCENT PASSAGE

Article 43
Innocent passage

1. The régime of innocent passage, in accordance with section 3 of Chapter I, shall apply in straits used for international navigation;

(a) Excluded under paragraph 1 of article 37, from the application of the régime of transit passage; or

(b) Between one area of the high seas or an exclusive economic zone and the territorial sea of a foreign State.

2. There shall be no suspension of innocent passage through such straits.

Chapter III: The exclusive economic zone

Article 44
Rights, jurisdiction and duties of the coastal State in the exclusive economic zone

1. In an area beyond and adjacent to its territorial sea, described as the exclusive economic zone, the coastal State has:

(a) Sovereign rights for the purpose of exploring and exploiting, conserving and managing the natural resources, whether living or non-living, of the bed and subsoil and the superjacent waters;

(b) Exclusive rights and jurisdiction with regard to the establishment and use of artificial islands, installations and structures;

(c) Exclusive jurisdiction with regard to:

    (i) Other activities for the economic exploitation and exploration of the zone, such as the production of energy from the water, currents and winds; and

    (ii) Scientific research;

(d) Jurisdiction with regard to the preservation of the marine environment, including pollution control and abatement;

(e) Other rights and duties provided for in the present Convention   in the exclusive economic zone, the coastal State shall have due regard to the rights and duties of other States.

3. The rights set out in this article with respect to the bed and subsoil shall be exercised in accordance with Chapter IV.

Article 45
Breadth of the exclusive economic zone

The exclusive economic zone shall not extend beyond 200 nautical miles from the baselines from which the breadth of the territorial sea is measured.

Article 61
Enforcement of laws and regulations of the coastal State

1. The coastal State may, in the exercise of its sovereign rights to explore, exploit, conserve and manage the living resources in the exclusive economic zone, take such measures, including boarding, inspection, arrest and judicial proceedings, as may be necessary to ensure compliance with the laws and regulations enacted by it in conformity with the present Convention.

2. Arrested vessels and their crews shall be promptly released upon the posting of reasonable bond or other security.

3. Coastal State penalties for violations of fisheries regulations in the exclusive economic zone may not include imprisonment, in the absence of agreement to the contrary by the States concerned, or any other form of corporal punishment.

4. In cases of arrest or detention of foreign vessels the coastal State shall promptly notify, through appropriate channels, the flag State of the action taken and of any penalties subsequently imposed.

Chapter V: High Seas

SECTION 1. GENERAL

Article 75
Definition of the high seas

The term "high seas" as used in the present Convention means all parts of the sea that are not included in the exclusive economic zone, in the territorial sea or in the internal waters of a State, or in the archipelagic waters of an archipelagic State.

Article 76
Freedom of the high seas

1. The high seas are open to all States, whether coastal or land-locked. Accordingly, no State may validly purport

to subject any part of them to its sovereignty. Freedom of the high seas is exercised under the conditions laid down by the present Convention and by other rules of international law. It comprises, *inter alia,* both for coastal and land-locked States:

(a) Freedom of navigation;

(b) Freedom of overflight;

(c) Freedom to lay submarine cables and pipelines, subject to Chapter IV;

(d) Freedom to construct artificial islands and other installations permitted under international law, subject to Chapter IV;

(e) Freedom of fishing, subject to the conditions laid down in section 2;

(f) Freedom of scientific research, subject to Chapters IV and . . . (Marine scientific research).

2. These freedoms shall be exercised by all States, with due consideration for the interests of other States in their exercise of the freedom of the high seas, and also with due consideration for the rights under the present Convention with respect to activities in the International Area.

Article 77
Reservation of the high seas for peaceful purposes
The high seas shall be reserved for peaceful purposes.

Article 78
Right of navigation
Every State, whether coastal or land-locked, has the right to sail ships under its flag on the high seas.

Article 79
Nationality of ships
1. Each State shall fix the conditions for the grant of its nationality to ships, for the registration of ships in its territory and for the right to fly its flag. Ships have the nationality of the State whose flag they are entitled to fly.

There must exist a genuine link between the State and the ship.

2. Each State shall issue to ships to which it has granted the right to fly its flag documents to that effect.

Article 80
Status of ships

1. Ships shall sail under the flag of one State only and, save in exceptional cases expressly provided for in international treaties or in the present Convention, shall be subject to its exclusive jurisdiction on the high seas. A ship may not change its flag during a voyage or while in a port of call, save in the case of a real transfer of ownership or change of registry.

2. A ship which sails under the flags of two or more States, using them according to convenience, may not claim any of the nationalities in question with respect to any other State, and may be assimilated to a ship without nationality.

Article 81
Ships flying the flag of the United Nations, its specialized agencies and the International Atomic Energy Agency

The preceding articles do not prejucide the question of ships employed on the official service of the United Nations, its specialized agencies or the International Atomic Energy Agency flying the flag of the organization.

Article 82
Duties of the flag State

1. Every State shall effectively exercise its jurisdiction and control in administrative, technical and social matters over ships flying its flag.

2. In particular every State shall:

(a) Maintain a register of shipping containing the names and particulars of ships flying its flag, except those which are excluded from generally accepted international regulations on account of their small size; and

(b) Assume jurisdiction under its internal law over each ship flying its flag and its master, officers and crew in respect of administrative, technical and social matters concerning the ship.

3. Every state shall take measures for ships flying its flag as are necessary to ensure safety at sea with regard, *inter alia,* to:

(a) The construction, equipment and seaworthiness of ships;

(b) The manning of ships, labour conditions and the training of crews, taking into account the applicable international instruments;

(c) The use of signals, the maintenance of communications and the prevention of collisions.

4. Such measures shall include those necessary to ensure:

(a) That each ship, before registration and thereafter at appropriate intervals, is surveyed by a qualified surveyor of ships, and has on board such charts, nautical publications and navigational equipment and instruments as are appropriate for the safe navigation of the ship;

(b) That each ship is in the charge of a master and officers who possess appropriate qualifications, in particular in seamanship, navigation, communications and marine engineering, and that the crew is appropriate in qualification and numbers for the type, size, machinery and equipment of the ship;

(c) That the master, officers and, to the extent appropriate, the crew are fully conversant with and required to observe the applicable international regulations concerning the safety of life at sea, the prevention of collisions, the prevention and control of marine pollution and the maintenance of communications by radio.

5. In taking the measures called for in paragraphs 3 and 4 each State is required to conform to generally accepted international regulations, procedures and practices and to take any steps which may be necessary to secure their observance.

6. A State which has clear grounds to believe that proper jurisdiction and control with respect to a ship have not been exercised may report the facts to the flag State. Upon receiving such a report, the flag State shall investigate the matter and, if appropriate, take any action necessary to remedy the situation.

7. Each State shall cause an inquiry to be held by or before a suitably qualified person or persons into every marine casualty or incident of navigation on the high seas involving a ship flying its flag and causing loss of life or serious injury to nationals of another State or serious damage to shipping or installations of another State or to the marine environment. The flag State and the other State shall co-operate in the conduct of any inquiry held by that other State into any such marine casualty or incident of navigation.

Article 83
Immunity of war ships on the high seas
Warships on the high seas have complete immunity from the jurisdiction of any State other than the flag State.

Article 84
Immunity of ships used only on government non-commercial service
Ships owned or operated by a State and used only on government noncommercial service shall, on the high seas, have complete immunity from the jurisdiction of any State other than the flag State.

Article 85
Penal jurisdiction in matters of collision

1. In the event of a collision or any other incident of navigation concerning a ship on the high seas, involving the penal or disciplinary responsibility of the master or of any other person in the service of the ship, no penal or disciplinary proceedings may be instituted against such person except before the judicial or administrative authorities either of the flag State or of the State of which such person is a national.

2. In disciplinary matters, the State which has issued a master's certificate or a certificate of competence or license shall alone be competent, after due legal process, to pronounce with withdrawal of such certificates, even if the holder is not a national of the State which issued them.

3. No arrest or detention of the ship, even as a measure of investigation, shall be ordered by any authorities other than those of the flag State.

Article 86
Duty to render assistance

1. Every State shall require the master of a ship sailing under its flag, insofar as he can do so without serious danger to the ship, the crew or the passengers:

(a) To render assistance to any person found at sea in danger of being lost;

(b) To proceed with all possible speed to the rescue of persons in distress if informed of their need of assistance, insofar as such action may reasonably be expected of him;

(c) After a collision, to render assistance to the other ship, its crew and its passengers and, where possible, to inform the other ship of the name of his own ship, its port of registry and the nearest port at which it will call.

2. Every coastal State shall promote the establishment, operation and maintenance of an adequate and effective

search and rescue service regarding safety on and over the sea and, where circumstances so require, by way of mutual regional arrangements co-operate with neighboring States for this purpose.

Article 88
Duty to co-operate in the repression of piracy

All States shall co-operate to the fullest possible extent in the repression of piracy on the high seas or in any other place outside the jurisdiction of any State.

Article 89
Definition of piracy

Piracy consists of any of the following acts:

(a) Any illegal acts of violence, detention or any act of depredation, committed for private ends by the crew or the passengers of a private ship or a private aircraft, and directed:

> (i) On the high seas, against another ship or aircraft, or against persons or property on board such ship or aircraft;
>
> (ii) Against a ship, aircraft, persons or property in a place outside the jurisdiction of any State;

(b) Any act of voluntary participation in the operation of a ship or of an aircraft with knowledge of facts making it a pirate ship or aircraft;

(c) Any act of inciting or of intentionally facilitating an act described in sub-paragraphs (a) and (b).

Article 90
Piracy by a warship, government ship or government aircraft whose crew has mutinied

The acts of piracy, as defined in article 89, committed by a warship, government ship or government aircraft whose crew has mutinied and taken control of the ship or aircraft are assimilated to acts committed by a private ship.

Article 91
Definition of a pirate ship or aircraft

A ship or aircraft is considered a pirate ship or aircraft if it is intended by the persons in dominant control to be used for the purpose of committing one of the acts referred to in article 89. The same applies if the ship or aircraft has been used to commit any such act, so long as it remains under the control of the persons guilty of that act.

Article 92
Retention or loss of the nationality of a pirate ship or aircraft

A ship or aircraft may retain its nationality although it has become a pirate ship or aircraft. The retention or loss of nationality is determined by the law of the State from which such nationality was derived.

Article 93
Seizure of a pirate ship or aircraft

On the high seas, or in any other place outside the jurisdiction of any State, every State may seize a pirate ship or aircraft, or a ship taken by piracy and under the control of pirates, and arrest the persons and seize the property on board. The courts of the State which carried out the seizure may decide upon the penalties to be imposed, and may also determine the action to be taken with regard to the ships, aircraft or property, subject to the rights of third parties acting in good faith.

Article 94
Liability of seizure without adequate grounds

Where the seizure of a ship or aircraft on suspicion of piracy has been effected without adequate grounds, the State making the seizure shall be liable to the State the nationality of which is possessed by the ship or aircraft, for any loss or damage caused by the seizure.

Article 95
Ships and aircraft which are entitled to seize on account of piracy

A seizure on account of piracy may only be carried out by warships or military aircraft, or other ships or aircraft clearly marked and identifiable as being on government service and authorized to that effect.

Article 98
Right of visit

1. Except where acts of interference derive from powers conferred by treaty, a warship which encounters on the high seas a foreign ship, other than a ship entitled to complete immunity in accordance with articles 83 and 84, is not justified in boarding her unless there is reasonable ground for suspecting:

(a) That the ship is engaged in piracy;

(b) That the ship is engaged in the slave trade;

(c) That the ship is engaged in unauthorized broadcasting and the warship has jurisdiction under article 97;

(d) That the ship is without nationality; or

(e) That, though flying a foreign flag or refusing to show its flag, the ship is, in reality, of the same nationality as the warship.

2. In the cases provided for in paragraph 1, the warship may proceed to verify the ship's right to fly its flag. To this end, it may send a boat, under the command of an officer, to the suspected ship. If suspicion remains after the documents have been checked, it may proceed to a further examination on board the ship, which must be carried out with all possible consideration.

3. If the suspicions prove to be unfounded, and provided that the ship boarded has not committed any act justifying them, it shall be compensated for any loss or damage that may have been sustained.

4. These provisions shall apply *mutatis mutandis* to military aircraft.

5. These provisions shall also apply to any other duly authorized ships or aircraft clearly marked and identifiable as being on government service.

Article 99
Right of hot pursuit

1. The hot pursuit of a foreign ship may be undertaken when the competent authorities of the coastal State have good reason to believe that the ship has violated the laws and regulations of that State. Such pursuit must be commenced when the foreign ship or one of its boats is within the internal waters, the territorial sea or the contiguous zone of the pursuing State, and may only be continued outside the territorial sea or the contiguous zone if the pursuit has not been interrupted. It is not necessary that, at the time when the foreign ship within the territorial sea or the contiguous zone receives the order to stop, the ship giving the order should likewise be within the territorial sea or the contiguous zone. If the foreign ship is within a contiguous zone, as defined in article 32, the pursuit may only be undertaken if there has been a violation of the rights for the protection of which the zone was established.

2. The right of hot pursuit shall apply *mutatis mutandis* to violations in the exclusive economic zone or on the continental shelf, including safety zones areound continental shelf installations, of the laws and regulations of the coastal State applicable in accordance with the present Convention to the exclusive economic zone or the continental shelf, including such safety zones.

3. The right of hot pursuit ceases as soon as the ship pursued enters the territorial sea of its own country or of a third State.

4. Hot pursuit is not deemed to have begun unless the pursuing ship has satisfied itself by such practicable means as may be available that the ship pursued or one of its boats or other craft working as a team and using the

ship pursued as a mother ship are within the limits of the territorial sea, or as the case may be, within the contiguous zone or the exclusive economic zone or above the continental shelf. The pursuit may only be commenced after a visual or auditory signal to stop has been given at a distance which enables it to be seen or heard by the foreign ship.

5. The right of hot pursuit may be exercised only by warships or military aircraft, or other ships or aircraft clearly marked and identifiable as being on government service and specially authorized to that effect.

6. Where hot pursuit is effected by an aircraft:

(a) The provisions of paragraphs 1 to 4 shall apply *mutatis mutandis*;

(b) The aircraft giving the order to stop must itself actively pursue the ship until a ship or aircraft of the coastal State, summoned by the aircraft, arrives to take over the pursuit, unless the aircraft is itself able to arrest the ship. It does not suffice to justify an arrest outside the territorial sea that the ship was merely sighted by the aircraft as an offender or suspected offender, if it was not both ordered to stop and pursued by the aircraft itself or other aircraft or ships which continue the pursuit without interruption.

7. The release of a ship arrested within the jurisdiction of a State and escorted to a port of that State for the purposes of an inquiry before the competent authorities may not be claimed solely on the ground that the ship, in the course of its voyage, was escorted across a portion of the exclusive economic zone or the high seas, if the circumstances rendered this necessary.

8. Where a ship has been stopped or arrested outside the territorial sea in circumstances which do not justify the exercise of the right of hot pursuit, it shall be compensated for any loss or damage that may have been thereby sustained.

Article 116
Equal treatment in maritime ports

Ships flying the flag of land-locked States shall enjoy treatment equal to that accorded to other foreign ships in maritime ports.

Article 117
Grant of greater transit facilities

The present Convention does not entail in any way the withdrawal of transit facilities which are greater than those provided for in the present Convention and which are agreed between States parties to the present Convention or granted by a State party. The present Convention also does not preclude such grant of greater facilities in the future.

Chapter VII. Archipelagic States

Article 118
Use of Terms

For the purposes of the present Convention:

(a) "Archipelagic State" means a State constituted wholly by one or more archipelagos and may include other islands;

(b) "Archipelago" means a group of islands, including parts of islands, inter-connecting waters and other natural features which are so closely interrelated that such islands, waters and other natural features form an intrinsic geographical, economic and political entity, or which historically have been regarded as such.

Article 119
Archipelagic baselines

1. An archipelagic State may draw straight archipelagic baselines joining the outermost points of the outermost islands and drying reefs of the archipelago provided that within such baselines are included the main islands and an area in which the ratio of the area of the water to

the area of the land, including atolls, is between one to one and nine to one.

2. The length of such baselines shall not exceed 80 nautical miles, except that up to one per cent of the total number of baselines enclosing any archipelago may exceed that length, up to a maximum length of 125 nautical miles.

3. The drawing of such baselines shall not depart to any appreciable extent from the general configuration of the archipelago.

4. Such baselines shall not be drawn to and from low-tide elevations, unless lighthouses or similar installations which are permanently above sea level have been built on them or where a low-tide elevation is situated wholly or partly at a distance not exceeding the breadth of the territorial sea from the nearest island.

5. The system of such baselines shall not be applied by an archipelagic State in such a manner as to cut off from the high seas or the exclusive economic zone the territorial sea of another State.

6. The archipelagic State shall clearly indicate such baselines on charts of a scale or scales adequate for determining them. The archipelagic State shall give due publicity to such charts and shall deposit a copy of each such chart with the Secretary-General of the United Nations.

7. If the drawing of such baselines encloses a part of the sea which has traditionally been used by an immediately adjacent neighbouring State for direct access and all forms of communication, including the laying of submarine cables and pipelines, between two or more parts of the territory of such State, the archipelagic State shall continue to recognize and guarantee such rights of direct access and communication.

8. For the purposes of computing the ratio of water to land under paragraph 1, land areas may include waters lying within the fringing reefs of islands and atolls,

including that part of a steep-sided oceanic plateau which is enclosed or nearly enclosed by a chain of limestone islands and drying reefs lying on the perimeter of the plateau.

Article 120
Measurement of the breadth of the territorial sea, the contiguous zone, the exclusive economic zone and the continental shelf

The breadth of the territorial sea, the contiguous zone, the exclusive economic zone and the continental shelf shall be measured from the baselines drawn in accordance with article 119.

Article 121
Juridical status of archipelagic waters, of the air space over archipelagic waters and of their bed and subsoil

1. The sovereignty of an archipelagic State extends to the waters enclosed by the baselines, described as archipelagic waters, regardless of their depth or distance from the coast.

2. This sovereignty extends to the air space over the archipelagic waters, the bed and subsoil thereof, and the resources contained therein.

3. This sovereignty is exercised subject to this Chapter.

Article 122
Delimitation of internal waters

Within its archipelagic waters, the archipelagic State may draw closing lines for the delimitation of internal waters, in accordance with articles 8 9 and 10.

Article 123
Existing agreements, traditional fishing rights and existing submarine cables

1. Without prejudice to article 120, archipelagic States shall respect existing agreements with other States and shall recognize traditional fishing rights and other legitimate activities of the immediately adjacent neighbouring

States in certain areas falling within archipelagic waters. The terms and conditions of the exercise of such rights and activities, including the nature, the extent and the areas to which they apply, shall, at the request of any of the States concerned, be regulated by bilateral agreements between them. Such rights shall not be transferred to or shared with third States or their national.

2. Archipelagic States shall respect existing submarine cables laid by other States and passing through their waters without making a landfall. Archipelagic States shall permit the maintenance and replacement of such cables upon receiving due notice of the location of such cables and the intention to repair or replace them.

Article 124
Right of innocent passage

1. Subject to article 125, ships of all States enjoy the right of innocent passage through archipelagic waters, in accordance with section 3 of Chapter I.

2. The archipelagic State may, without discrimination in form or in fact amongst foreign ships, suspend temporarily in specified areas of its archipelagic waters the innocent passage of foreign ships if such suspension is essential for the protection of its security. Such suspension shall take effect only after having been duly published.

Article 125
Right of archipelagic sea lanes passage

1. An archipelagic State may designate sea lanes and air routes suitable for the safe, continuous and expeditious passage of foreign ships and aircraft through or over its archipelagic waters and the adjacent territorial sea.

2. All ships and aircraft enjoy the right of archipelagic sea lanes passage in such sea lanes and air routes.

3. Archipelagic sea lanes passage is the exercise in accordance with the present Convention of the rights of navigation and overflight in the normal mode for the pur-

pose of continuous and expeditious transit between one part of the high seas or an exclusive economic zone and another part of the high seas or an exclusive economic zone.

4. Such sea lanes and air routes shall traverse the archipelago and the adjacent territorial sea and shall include all normal passage routes for international navigation or overflight through the archipelago, and, within such routes, so far as ships are concerned, all normal navigational channels, provided that duplication of routes of similar convenience between the same entry and exit points shall not be necessary.

5. The width of a sea lane shall not be less than . . . nautical miles or . . . per cent of the distance between the nearest points on islands bordering the sea lane.

6. An archipelagic State which designates sea lanes under this article may also prescribe traffic separation schemes for the safe passage of ships through narrow channels in such sea lanes.

7. An archipelagic State may, when circumstances require, after giving due publicity thereto, substitute other sea lanes or traffic separation schemes for any sea lanes or traffic separation schemes previously designated or prescribed by it.

8. Such sea lanes or traffic separation schemes shall conform to generally accepted international regulations.

9. Before designating or substituting sea lanes or prescribing or substituting traffic separation schemes, an archipelagic State shall refer proposals to the competent international organization with a view to their adoption. The organization may adopt only such sea lanes and traffic separation schemes as may be agreed with the archipelagic State, after which the archipelagic State may designate, prescribe or substitute them.

10. The archipelagic State shall clearly indicate all sea lanes and traffic separation schemes designated or pre-

scribed by it on charts to which due publicity shall be given.

11. Ships in transit shall respect applicable sea lanes and traffic separation schemes established in accordance with this article.

12. If an archipelagic State does not designate sea lanes or air routes, the right of archipelagic sea lanes passage may be exercised through the routes normally used for international navigation.

Article 126
Duties of ships and aircraft during their passage, duties of the archipelagic State and laws and regulations of the archipelagic State relating to archipelagic sea lanes passage

Articles 38, 40 and 42 apply *mutatis mutandis* to archipelagic sea lanes passage.

Article 127
Research and survey activities

During their passage through archipelagic waters, foreign ships, including marine research and hydrographic survey ships, may not carry out any research or survey activities without the prior authorizaton of the archipelagic State.

Chapter VIII: Regime of Islands

Article 128
Regime of islands

1. An island is a naturally formed area of land, surrounded by water, which is above water at high tide.

2. Except as provided for in paragraph 3, the territorial sea, the contiguous zone, the exclusive economic zone and the continental shelf of an island are determined in accordance with the provisions of the present Convention applicable to other land territory.

3. Rocks which cannot sustain human habitation or

economic life of their own shall have no exclusive economic zone or continental shelf.

Chapter IX: Enclosed or Semi-Enclosed Seas

Article 129
Definition

For the purposes of this Chapter, "enclosed or semi-enclosed sea" means a gulf, basin, or sea surrounded by two or more States and connected to the open seas by a narrow outlet or consisting entirely or primarily of the territorial seas and exclusive economic zones of two or more coastal States.

Article 130
Co-operation of States bordering enclosed or semi-enclosed seas

States bordering enclosed or semi-enclosed seas should co-operate with each other in the exercise of their rights and duties under the present Convention. To this end they shall endeavour, directly or through an appropriate regional organization:

(a) To co-ordinate the management, conservation, exploration and exploitation of the living resources of the sea;

(b) To co-ordinate the implementation of their rights and duties with respect to the preservation of the marine environment;

(c) To co-ordinate their scientific research policies and undertake where appropriate joint programmes of scientific research in the area;

(d) To invite, as appropriate, other interested States or international organizations to co-operate with them in furtherance of the provisions of this article . . . .

APPENDIX 5

Remarks and Selected Provisions of the Informal Composite Negotiating Text

15 July 1977
A/CONF.62/WP.10

The Informal Composite Negotiating Text is both an extension and a revision of the Revised Single Negotiating Text (See Appendix 4). Although many of the sections are basically the same—with slight variations in phraseology—there have nonetheless been significant revisions in both organization and substance. The changes from the Revised Single Negotiating Text in the Informal Composite Negotiating Text that are relevant to this present inquiry are noted below within square brackets. Because of the introduction of a Use of Terms article in Part I, Article I, of the Informal Composite Text, the article numbers here do not exactly correspond with those in the Revised Single Negotiating Text. Changes in article numbers are also noted in comments enclosed in square brackets.

Among other changes in the Informal Composite Negotiating Text are:

1. Part II of the Composite Text is entitled, "Territorial Sea and Contiguous Zone," and follows in large part the provisions in this area set out under the previous Revised Single Negotiating Text.

2. Article 26 of the Revised Single Negotiating Text entitled, "Criminal Jurisdiction on board of a foreign ship," is Article 27 with the same title in the Composite Text; paragraph 5 of the original article received a new introductory clause in the Composite Text, "Except as provided in Part XII or with respect to violations of laws and regulations enacted in accordance with Part IV . . . ."

3. A new Article 40 in the Composite Text forbids ships from carrying out marine research during their passage through straits without first obtaining authorization from the states bordering the straits. Article 40 in the Revised Single Negotiating Text is numbered as Article 42 in the Composite Text, but it remains entitled, "Laws and regulations of States bordering straits relating to transit passage." Yet, in the new Article 42, paragraph 1 (b) two new words are inserted: "reduction and control." The opening clause thus reads: "The prevention, reduction and control of pollution, ..." Obviously this addition makes for a much stronger position.

Chapter III of the Revised Single Negotiating Text, entitled "Exclusive Economic Zone," retains the same title in the Composite Text, but is numbered Part V. Part V is, however, extensively reorganized; its provisions are printed below. The basic provision of the exclusive economic zone — that it not extend beyond 200 nautical miles — remains the same as in Article 45 of the Revised Single Negotiating Text.

The Preamble to the Informal Composite Negotiating Text states:

The States Parties to the present Convention,

Considering that the General Assembly of the United Nations, by its resolution 2749 (XXV) of 17 December 1970, adopted the Declaration of Principles Governing the Sea-Bed and the Ocean Floor, and the Subsoil Thereof, beyond the Limits of National Jurisdiction,

Believing that the codification and progressive development of the law of the sea achieved in the present Convention will contribute to the maintenance of international peace and security, in accordance with the purposes and principles of the United Nations as set forth in the Charter,

Having regard to the Declaration on Principles of International Law concerning Friendly Relations and Co-operation among States in accordance with the Charter of the United Nations,

Affirming that the rules of customary international law continue to govern matters not expressly regulated by the provision of the present Convention,

Have agreed as follows: . . . .
             The Composite Text provides

PART IV. ARCHIPELAGIC STATES

Article 46
Use of terms
For the purposes of the present Convention:

(a) "Archipelagic State" means a State constituted wholly by one or more archipelagos and may include other islands;

(b) "Archipelago" means a group of islands, including parts of islands, interconnecting waters and other natural features which are so closely interrelated that such islands, waters and other natural features form an intrinsic geographical, economic and political entity, or which historically have been regarded as such.

Article 47
Archipelagic baselines

1. An archipelagic State may draw straight archpelagic baselines joining the outermost points of the outermost islands and drying reefs of the archipelago provided that within such baselines are included the main islands and an area in which the ratio of the area of the water to the area of the land, including atolls, is between one to one and nine to one.

2. The length of such baselines shall not exceed 100 nautical miles, except that up to three per cent of the total number of baselines enclosing any archipelago may exceed that length, up to a maximum length of 125 nautical miles.

3. The drawing of such baselines shall not depart to any appreciable extent from the general configuration of the archipelago.

4. Such baselines shall not be drawn to and from low-tide elevations, unless lighthouses or similar installations which are permanently above sea level have been built on them or where a low-tide elevation is situated wholly or partly at a distance not exceeding the breadth of the territorial sea from the nearest island.

5. The system of such baselines shall not be applied by an archipelagic State in such a manner as to cut off from the high seas or the exclusive economic zone the territorial sea of another State.

6. The archipelagic State shall clearly indicate such baselines on charts of a scale or scales adequate for determining them. The archipelagic State shall give due publicity to such charts and shall deposit a copy of each such chart with the Secretary-General of the United Nations.

7. If a certain part of the archipelagic water of an archipelagic State lies between two parts of an immediately adjacent neighbouring State, existing rights and all other legitimate interests which the latter State has traditionally

exercised in such waters and all rights stipulated under agreement between those States shall continue and be respected.

8. For the purposes of computing the ratio of water to land under paragraph 1, land areas may include waters lying within the fringing reefs of islands and atolls, including that part of a steep-sided oceanic plateau which is enclosed or nearly enclosed by a chain of limestone islands and drying reefs lying on the perimeter of the plateau.

Article 48
Measurement of the breadth of the territorial sea, the the contiguous zone, the exclusive economic zone and the continental shelf

The breadth of the territorial sea, the contiguous zone, the exclusive economic zone and the continental shelf shall be measured from the baselines drawn in accordance with article 47.

Article 49
Juridical status of archipelagic waters, of the air space over archipelagic waters and of their bed and subsoil

1. The sovereignty of an archipelagic State extends to the waters enclosed by the baselines, described as archipelagic waters, regardless of their depth or distance from the coast.

2. This sovereignty extends to the air space over the archipelagic waters, the bed and subsoil threof, and the resources contained therein.

3. This sovereignty is exercised subject to this Part.

4. The regime of archipelagic sea lanes passage established in this Part shall not in other respects affect the status of the archipelagic waters, including the sea lanes, or the exercise of the archipelagic State of its sovereignty over such waters and their air space, bed and subsoil, and the resources contained therein.

Article 52
Right of innocent passage

1. Subject to article 53 and without prejudice to article 50 ships of all States enjoy the right of innocent passage through archipelagic waters, in accordance with section 3 of Part II.

2. The archipelagic State may, without discrimination in form or in fact amongst foreign ships, suspend temporarily in specified areas of its archipelagic waters the innocent passage of foreign ships if such suspension is essential for the protection of its security. Such suspension shall take effect only after having been duly published.

Article 53
Rights of archipelagic sea lanes passage

1. An archipelagic State may designate sea lanes and air routes thereabove, suitable for the safe, continuous and expeditious passage of foreign ships and aircraft through or over its archipelagic waters and the adjacement territorial sea.

2. All ships and aircraft enjoy the right of archipelagic sea lanes passage in such sea lanes and air routes.

3. Archipelagic sea lanes passage is the exercise in accordance with the present Convention of the rights of navigation and overflight in the normal mode solely for the purpose of continuous, expeditious and unobstructed transit between one part of the high seas or an exclusive economic zone and another part of the high seas or an exclusive economic zone.

4. Such sea lanes and air routes shall traverse the archipelagic waters and the adjacent territorial sea and shall include all normal passage routes used as routes for international navigation or overflight through the archipelagic waters and, within such routes, so far as ships are concerned, all normal navigational channels, provided that duplication of routes of similar convenience between the same entry and exit points shall not be necessary.

5. Sea lanes shall be defined by a series of continuous axis lines from the entry points of passage routes to the exit points. Ships and aircraft in archipelagic sea lanes passage shall not deviate more than 25 nautical miles to either side of such axis lines during passage, provided that ships and aircraft shall not navigate closer to the coasts than 10 per cent of the distance between the nearest points on islands bordering the sea lane.

6. An archipelagic State which designates sea lanes under this article may also prescribe traffic separation schemes for the safe passage of ships through narrow channels in such sea lanes.

7. An archipelagic State may, when circumstances require, after giving due publicity thereto, substitute other sea lanes or traffic separation schemes for any sea lanes or traffic separation schemes previously designated or prescribed by it.

8. Such sea lanes and traffic separation schemes shall conform to generally accepted international regulations.

9. In designating or substituting sea lanes or prescribing or substituting traffic separation schemes, an archipelagic State shall refer proposals to the competent international organization with a view to their adoption. The organization may adopt only such sea lanes and traffic separation schemes as may be agreed with the archipelagic State may designate, prescribe or substitute them.

10. The archipelagic State shall clearly indicate the axis of the sea lanes and the traffic separation schemes designated or prescribed by it on charts to which due publicity shall be given.

11. Ships in transit shall respect applicable sea lanes and traffic separation schemes established in accordance with this article.

12. If an archipelagic State does not designate sea lanes or air routes, the right of archipelagic sea lanes passage may be exercised through the routes normally used for international navigation.

PART V. EXCLUSIVE ECONOMIC ZONE

Article 55
Specific legal regime of the exclusive economic zone

The exclusive economic zone is an area beyond and adjacent to the territorial sea, subject to the specific legal régime established in this Part, under which the rights and jurisdictions of the coastal State and the rights and freedoms of other States are governed by the relevant provisions of the present Convention.

Article 56
Rights, jurisdiction and duties of the coastal State in in the exclusive economic zone

1. In the exclusive economic zone, the coastal State has:

(a) sovereign rights for the purpose of exploring and exploiting, conserving and managing the natural resources, whether living or non-living, of the sea-bed and subsoil and the superjacent waters, and with regard to other activities for the economic exploitation and exploration of the zone, such as the production of energy from the water, currents and winds;

(b) jurisdiction as provided for in the relevant provisions of the present Convention with regard to:

(i) the establishment and use of artificial islands, installations and structures;

(ii) marine scientific research;

(iii) the preservation of the marine environment;

(c) other rights and duties provided for in the present Convention.

2. In exercising its rights and performing its duties under the present Convention in the exclusive economic zone, the coastal State shall have due regard to the right and duties of other States and shall act in a manner compatible with the provisions of the present Convention.

3. The rights set out in this article with respect to the

sea-bed and subsoil shall be exercised in accordance with Part VI.

Article 57
Breadth of the exclusive economic zone

The exclusive economic zone shall not extend beyond 200 nautical miles from the baselines from which the bredth of the territorial sea is measured.

Article 58
Rights and duties of other States in the exclusive economic zone

1. In the exclusive economic zone, all States, whether coastal or land-locked, enjoy, subject to the relevant provisions of the present Convention, the freedoms referred to in article 87 of navigation and overflight and of the laying of submarine cables and pipelines, and other internationally lawful uses of the sea related to these freedoms such as those associated with the operation of ships, aircraft and submarine cables and pipelines, and compatible with the other provisions of the present Convention.

2. Articles 88 to 115 and other pertinent rules of international law apply to the exclusive economic zone in so far as they are not incompatible with this Part.

3. In exercising their rights and performing their dutties under the present Convention in the exclusive economic zone, States shall have due regard to the rights and duties of the coastal State and shall comply with the laws and regulations established by the coastal State in accordance with the provisions of this Convention and other rules of international law in so far as they are not incompatible with this Part.

Article 59
Basis for the resolution of conflicts regarding the attribution of rights and jurisdiction in the exclusive economic zone

In cases where the present Convention does not attribute rights or jurisdiction to the coastal State or to other States within the exclusive economic zone, and a conflict arises between the interests of the coastal State and any other State or States, the conflict should be resolved on the basis of equity and in the light of all the relevant circumstances, taking into account the respective importance of the interests involved to the parties as well as to the international community as a whole.

[Article 61 entitled, "Enforcement of laws and regulations of coastal States," in the Revised Single Negotiating Text, is Article 73 in the Composite Text and is preserved *in toto.*]

Article 74
Delimitation of the exclusive economic zone between adjacent or opposite States

1. The delimitation of the exclusive economic zone between adjacent or opposite States shall be effected by agreement in accordance with equitable principles, employing, where appropriate, the median or elquidistance line, and taking account of all the relevant circumstances.

2. If no agreement can be reached within a reasonable period of time, the States concerned shall resort to the procedures provided for in Part XV.

3. Pending agreement or settlement, the States concerned shall make provisional arrangements, taking into account the provisions of paragraph 1.

4. For the purposes of the present Convention, "median or equidistance line" means the line every point of which is equidistant from the nearest points of the baselines from which the breadth of the territorial sea of each State is measured.

5. Where there is an agreement in force between the States concerned, questions relating to the delimitation of the exclusive economic zone shall be determined in accordance with the provisions of that agreement.

[Chapter V entitled, "High Seas," in the Revised Single Negotiating Text is Part VII in the Composite Text, and Article 75 is now Article

86; a qualifying proviso has been added to the second sentence in Article 86.]

Article 86
Application of the provisions of this Part

The provisions of this Part apply to all parts of the sea that are not included in the exclusive economic zone, in the territorial sea or in the internal waters of a State, or in the archipelagic waters of an archipelagic State. This article does not entail any abridgement of the freedoms enjoyed by all States in the exclusive economic zone in accordance with article 58.

Article 87
Freedom of the high seas

1. The high seas are open to all States, whether coastal or land-locked. Freedom of the high seas is exercised under the conditions laid down by the present Convention and by other rules of international law. It comprises, *inter alia*, both for coastal and land-locked States:

(a) Freedom of navigation;

(b) Freedom of overflight;

(c) Freedom to lay submarine cables and pipelines, subject to Part VI;

(d) Freedom to construct artificial islands and other installations permitted under international law, subject to Part VI;

(e) Freedom of fishing, subject to the conditions laid down in section 2;

(f) Freedom of scientific research, subject to Parts VI and XII.

2. These freedoms shall be exercised by all States, with due consideration for the interests of other States in their exercise of the freedom of the high seas, and also with due consideration for the rights under the present Convention with respect to activities in the Area.

[An important sentence has been deleted from the Revised Single Negotiating Text as presented in the Composite Text. Under Article

76 of the Revised Text, the second sentence read, "Accordingly, no State may validly purport to subject any part of them to its sovereignty." To give greater significance and indeed importance to the principle here, this sentence has been isolated as Article 89.]

Article 88
Reservation of the high seas for peaceful purposes
The high seas shall be reserved for peaceful purposes.

Article 89
Invalidity of claims of sovereignty over the high seas
No State may validly purport to subject any part of the high seas to its sovereignty.

[Former Article 78 in the Revised Single Negotiating Text, guaranteeing the right of navigation is, *in toto,* Article 90 in the Composite Text.

In the Revised Single Negotiating Text, Paragraph 2 of Article 119, "Archipelagic baselines," read: "The length of such baselines shall not exceed 80 nautical miles, except that up to one per cent of the total number of baselines enclosing any archipelago may exceed that length, up to a maximum length of 125 nautical miles."

In the Composite Text, Article 47 entitled, "Archipelagic baselines," states that the *maximum* length of such baselines is set at *100* nautical miles, "except that up to three per cent of the total number of baselines enclosing any archipelago may exceed that length, up to a maximum length of 125 nautical miles."

Paragraph 7 of former Article 119 of the Revised Text, now Article 47 in the Composite Text, was rewritten as follows:

"If a certain part of the archipelagic water of an archipelagic State lies between two parts of an immediately adjacent neighbouring State, existing rights and all other legitimate interests which the latter State has traditionally exercised in such waters and all rights stipulated under agreement between those States shall continue and be respected."

A fourth paragraph has been added to former Article 121 of the Revised Text, now Article 49 of the Composite Text, entitled "Juridical status of archipelagic waters, of the air space over archipelagic waters and of their bed and subsoil." It reads:

"The régime of archipelagic sea lanes passage established in this Part shall not in other respects affect the status of the archipelagic waters, including the sea lanes, or the exercise by the archipelagic State of its sovereignty over such waters and their airspace, bed and subsoil, and the resources contained therein."

Article 54, entitled "Right of Archipelagic sea lanes passage," formerly Article 125 in the Revised Single Negotiating Text, has inserted one important word to paragraph 3: "unobstructed." Reference was previously made only to "continuous and expeditious transit." Now "continuous, expeditious and unobstructed" transit is discussed in relation to archipelagic sealanes passage.

Article 53 of the Composite Text rewrites paragraph 5 of former Article 125 of the Revised Negotiating Text to read:

"Sea lanes shall be defined by a series of continuous axis lines from the entry points of passage routes to the exist points. Ships and aircraft in archipelagic sea lanes passage shall not deviate more than 25 nautical miles to either side of such axis lines during passage, provided that ships and aircraft shall not navigate closer to the coasts than 10 per cent of the distance between the nearest points on island bordering the sea lane."

Paragraph 9 of former Article 125 of the Revised Text opened with the phrase, "In designating or substituting sea lanes or prescribing or substituting traffic separation schemes . . . ." The word, "Before," is substituted for "In" in paragraph 9 of former Article 125; it appears in the Composite Text as Article 53.

Paragraph 10 of former Article 125 of the Revised Text required the archipelagic state to "clearly indicate all sea lanes and traffic separation schemes designated or prescribed by it on charts to which due publicity shall be given." Under redrafted paragraph 10 of Article 53 in the Composite Text, the archipelagic state, "shall clearly indicate the axis of the sea lanes and the traffic separation schemes . . . ."

Former Article 127 of the Revised Single Negotiating Text prohibited foreign ships from carrying out research activities during their passage through archipelagic waters without prior authorization from the archipelagic state. This article is retained as Article 40 in the Composite Text, but made applicable to "States bordering straits" rather than specific archipelagic states. By making Articles 39, 40, 42 and 44 in the Composite Text applicable *mutatis mutandis* to archipelagic sealanes passage, the basic prohibition of former Article 127 of the Revised Text is broadened and retained.

Former Chapter VIII on "Régime of Islands" is reorganized as Part VIII, starting with Article 121 in the Informal Composite Negotiating Text.

Article 125 of the Composite Negotiating Text is entitled, "Right of access to and from the sea and freedom of transit." It reads:

"1. Land-locked States shall have the right of access to and from the sea for the purpose of exercising the rights provided for in the present Convention including those relating to the freedom of the high seas and the common heritage of mankind. To this end, land-locked States shall enjoy freedom of transit through the territories of transit States by all means of transport.

"2. The terms and modalities for exercising freedom of transit shall be agreed between the land-locked States and the transit States concerned through bilateral, subregional or regional agreement.

"3. Transit States, in the exercise of their full sovereignty over their territory, shall have the right to take all necessary measures to ensure that the rights and facilities, provided for in this Part for land-locked States shall in no way infringe their legitimate interests."

Article 128 of the Composite Text is entitled, "Free zones and other customs facilities." It reads:

"For the convenience of traffic in transit, free zones or other customs facilities may be provided at the ports of entry and exit in the transit States, by agreement between those States and the land-locked States."

Article 130 of the Composite Text is entitled, "Measures to avoid or eliminate delay or other difficulties of a technical nature in traffic in transit." It reads:

"1. Transit states shall take all appropriate measures to avoid delays or other difficulties of a technical nature in traffic in transit.

"2. Should such delays or difficulties occur, the competent authorities of the transit States and of land-locked States shall cooperate toward their expeditious elimination."]

Article 211
Dumping

1. States shall establish national laws and regulations to prevent, reduce and control pollution of the marine environment from dumping.

2. States shall also take other measures as may be necessary to prevent, reduce and control such pollution.

3. Such laws, regulations and measures shall ensure that dumping is not carried out without the permission of the competent authorities of States.

4. States, acting in particular through competent international organizations or diplomatic conference, shall endeavor to establish global and regional rules, standards and recommended practices and procedures to prevent, reduce and control pollution of the marine environment by dumping. Such rules, standards and recommended

practices and procedures shall be re-examined from time to time as necessary.

5. Dumping, within the territorial sea and the exclusive economic zone or onto the continental shelf shall not be carried out without the express prior approval of the coastal State, which has the right to permit, regulate and control such dumping after due consultation with other States which by reason of their geographical situation may be adversely affected thereby.

6. National laws, regulations and measures shall be no less effective in preventing, reducing and controlling pollution from dumping than global rules and standards.

Article 212
Pollution from vessels

1. States, acting through the competent international organization or general diplomatic conference, shall establish international rules and standards for the prevention, reduction and control of pollution of the marine environment from vessels. Such rules and standards shall, in the same manner, be re-examined from time to time as necessary.

2. States shall establish laws and regulations for the prevention, reduction and control of pollution of the marine environment from vessels flying their flag or vessels of their registry. Such laws and regulations shall at least have the same effect as that of generally accepted international rules and standards established through the competent international organization or general diplomatic conference.

3. Coastal States may, in the exercise of their sovereignty within their territorial sea, establish national laws and regulations for the prevention, reduction and control of marine pollution from vessels. Such laws and regulations shall, in accordance with section 3 of Part II not hamper innocent passage of foreign vessels.

4. Coastal States, for the purpose of enforcement as provided for in section 6 of this Part of the present Convention, may in respect of their economic zones establish laws and regulations for the prevention, reduction and control of pollution from vessels conforming to and giving effect to generally accepted international rules and standards established through the competent international organization or general diplomatic conference.

Article 217
Enforcement with respect to dumping

1. Laws and regulations adopted in accordance with the present Convention and applicable international rules and standards established through competent international organizations or diplomatic conference for the prevention, reduction and control of pollution of the marine environment from dumping shall be enforced:

(a) by the coastal State with regard to dumping within its territorial sea or its exclusive economic zone or onto its continental shelf;

(b) by the flag State with regard to vessels and aircraft registered in its territory or flying its flag.;

(c) by any state with regard to acts of loading of wastes or other matter occurring within its territory or at its off-shore terminals.

2. This article shall not impose on any State an obligation to institute proceedings when such proceedings have already been commenced by another State in accordance with this article.

Article 218
Enforcement by flag States

1. States shall ensure compliance with applicable international rules and standards established through the competent international organization or general diplomatic conference and with their laws and regulations established in accordance with the present Convention for

the prevention, reduction and control of pollution of the marine environment, by vessels flying their flag or vessels of their registry and shall adopt the necessary legislative, administrative and other measures for their implementation. Flag States shall provide for the effective enforcement of such rules, standards, laws and regulations, irrespective of where the violation occurred.

2. Flag States shall, in particular, establish appropriate measures in order to ensure that vessels flying their flags or vessels of their registry are prohibited from sailing, until they can proceed to sea in compliance with the requirements of international rules and standards referred to in paragraph 1 for the prevention, reduction and control of pollution from vessels, including the requirements in respect of design, construction, equipment and manning of vessels.

3. States shall ensure that vessels flying their flags or of their registry carry on board certificates required by and issued pursuant to international rules and standards referred to in paragraph 1. Flag States shall ensure that their vessels are periodically inspected in order to verify that such certificates are in conformity with the actual condition of the vessels. These certificates shall be accepted by other States as evidence of the condition of the vessel and regarded as having the same force as certificates issued by them, unless there are clear grounds for believing that the condition of the vessel does not correspond substantially with the particulars of the certificates.

4. If a vessel commits a violation of rules and standards established through the competent international organization or general diplomatic conference, the flag State, without prejudice to articles 28, 30 and 38 shall provide, for immediate investigation and where appropriate cause proceedings to be taken in respect of the alleged violation irrespective of where the violation occurred or where the

pollution caused by such violation has occurred or has been spotted.

5. Flag States may seek in conducting investigation of the violation of the assistance of any other State whose co-operation could be useful in clarifying the circumstances of the case. States shall endeavor to meet the appropriate request of flag States.

6. Flag States shall, at the written request of any State, investigate any violation alleged to have been committed by their vessels. If satisfied that sufficient evidence is available to enable proceedings to be brought in respect of the alleged violations, flag States shall without delay cause such proceedings to be taken in accordance with their laws.

7. Flag States shall promptly inform the requesting State and the competent international organization of the action taken and its outcome. Such information shall be available to all States.

8. Penalties specified under the legislation of flag States for their own vessels shall be adequate in severity to discourage violations wherever the violations occur.

Article 221
Enforcement by coastal States

1. When a vessel is voluntarily within a port or at an off-shore terminal of a State, that State may, subject to the provisions of section 7 of this Part of the Convention cause proceedings to be taken in respect of any violation of national laws and regulations established in accordance with the present Convention of applicable international rules and standards for the prevention, reduction and control of pollution from vessels when the violation has occurred within the territorial sea or the exclusive economic zone of that State.

2. Where there are clear grounds for believing that a vessel navigating in the territorial sea of a State has, during its passage therein, violated national laws and regula-

tions established in accordance with the present Convention or applicable international rules and standards for the prevention, reduction and control of pollution from vessels, that State, without prejudice to the application of the relevant provisions of section 3 of Part II may undertake physical inspection of the vessel relating to the violation and may, when warranted by the evidence of the case, cause proceedings, including arrest of the vessel, to be taken in accordance with its laws, subject to the provisions of section 7 of this Part of the present Convention.

3. Where there are clear grounds for believing that a vessel navigating in the exclusive economic zone or the territorial sea of a State has, in the exclusive economic zone, violated applicable international rules and standards or national laws and regulations conforming and giving effect to such international rules and standards for the prevention, reduction and control of pollution from vessels, that State may require the vessel to give information regarding the identification of the vessel and its port of registry, its last and next port of call and other relevant information required to establish whether a violation has occurred.

4. Flag States shall take legislative, administrative and other measures so that their vessels comply with requests for information as set forth in paragraph 3.

5. Where there are clear grounds for believing that a vessel navigating in the exclusive economic zone or the territorial sea of a State has, in the exclusive economic zone, violated applicable international rules and standards or national laws and regulations conforming and giving effect to such international rules and standards for the prevention, reduction and control of pollution from vessels and the violation has resulted in a substantial discharge into and, insignificant pollution of, the marine environment, the State may undertake physical inspection of the vessel for matters relating to the violation if the vessel has refused to give information or if the informa-

tion supplied by the vessel is manifestly at variance with the evident factual situation and if the circumstances of the case justify such inspection.

6. Where there are clear grounds for believing that a vessel navigating in the exclusive economic zone or the territorial sea of a State has, in the exclusive economic zone, committed a flagrant or gross violation of applicable international rules and standards or national laws and regulations conforming and giving effect to such international rules and standards for the conforming and giving effect to such international rules and standards for the prevention, reduction and control of pollution from vessels, resulting in discharge causing major damage or threat of major damage to the coastline or related interests of the coastal State, or to any resources of its territorial sea or exclusive economic zone, that State may, subject to the provisions of Section 7 of this Part of the Convention provided that the evidence so warrants, cause proceedings to be taken in accordance with its laws.

7. Notwithstanding the provisions of paragraph 6, whenever appropriate procedures have been established either through the competent international organization or as otherwise agreed, whereby compliance with requirements for bonding or other appropriate financial security has been assured, the coastal State if bound by such procedures shall allow the vessel to proceed.

8. The provisions of paragraphs 3, 4, 5, 6 and 7 shall apply correspondingly in respect of national laws and regulations established pursuant to paragraph 5 of article 212.

Article 224
Measures to facilitate proceedings

In proceedings pursuant to this Chapter, States shall take measures to facilitate the hearing of witnesses and the admission of evidence submitted by authorities of another State, or by the competent international organization and shall facilitate the attendance at such proceedings of official representatives of the competent international organization or of the flag State, or of any State affected by pollution arising out of any violation. The official representatives attending such proceedings shall enjoy such rights and duties as may be provided under national legislation or applicable international law.

Article 225
Exercise of powers of enforcement

The powers of enforcement against foreign vessels under this Part of the present Convention may only be exercised by officials or by warships or military aircraft or other ships or aircraft clearly marked and identifiable as being on government service and authorized to that effect.

Article 226
Duty to avoid adverse consequences in the exercise of the powers of enforcement

In the exercise of their powers of enforcement against foreign vessels under the present Convention, States shall not endanger the safety of navigation or otherwise cause any hazard to a vessel, or bring it to an unsafe port or anchorage, or cause an unreasonable risk to the marine environment.

Article 227
Investigation of foreign vessels

1. States shall not delay a foreign vessel longer than is essential for purposes of investigation provided for in Articles 217, 219 and 221 of this Part of the present Convention. If the investigation indicates a violation of applicable laws and regulations of international rules and standards for the preservation of the marine environment release shall be made subject to reasonable procedures such as bonding or other appropriate financial security. Without prejudice to applicable international rules and

standards relating to the seaworthiness of ships, the release of a vessel may, whenever it would present an unreasonable threat of damage to the marine environment, be refused or made conditional upon proceeding to the nearest appropriate repair yard.

2. States shall co-operate to develop procedures for the avoidance of unnecessary physical inspection of vessels at sea.

Article 228
Non-discrimination of foreign vessels

In exercising their right and carrying out their duties under this Part of the present Convention, States shall not discriminate in form or in fact against vessels of any other State.

Article 230
Institution of civil proceedings

Nothing in the present Convention shall affect the institution of civil proceedings in respect of any claim for loss or damage resulting from pollution of the marine environment.

Article 231
Monetary penalties and the observance of recognized rights of the accused

1. Only monetary penalties may be imposed with respect to violations of national laws and regulations, or applicable international rules and standards, for the prevention, reduction and control of pollution from vessels committed by foreign vessels beyond the internal waters.

2. In the conduct of proceedings to impose penalties in respect of such violations committed by a foreign vessel, recognized rights of the accused shall be observed.

Article 232
Notification to flag States and other States concerned

States shall promptly notify the flag State and any

other State concerned of any measures taken pursuant to section 6 of this Part of the Convention against foreign vessels, and shall submit to the flag State all official reports concerning such measures. However, with respect to violations committed in the territorial sea, the foregoing obligations of the coastal State shall apply only to such measures as are taken in proceedings. The consular officers or diplomatic agents, and where possible the maritime authority of the flag State, shall be immediately informed of any such measures.

Article 233
Liability of States arising from enforcement measures

States shall be liable for damage or loss attributable to them arising from measures taken pursuant to section 6 of this Part of the Convention, when such measures were unlawful or exceeded those reasonably required in the light of available information. States shall provide for recourse in their courts for actions in respect of such damage or loss.

Article 234
Safeguards with respect to straits used for international navigation

Nothing in sections 5, 6, and 7 of this Part of the Convention shall affect the legal regine of straits used for international navigation. However, if a foreign ship other than those referred to in section 10 of this Part of the present Convention has committed a violation of the laws regulations referred to in subparagraphs 1 (a) and (b) of Article 42 of Part III of the present Convention causing or threatening major damage to the maritime environment of the straits, the States bordering the straits may take appropriate enforcement measures and if so shall respect *mutatis mutandis* the provisions of section 7 of this Part of the Convention.

Article 235
Ice-covered areas

Coastal States have the right to establish and enforce non-discriminatory laws and regulations for the prevention, reduction and control of marine pollution from vessels in ice-covered areas within the limits of the exclusive economic zone, where particularly severe climatic conditions and the presence of ice covering such areas for most of the year create obstructions or exceptional hazards to navigations, and pollution of the marine environment could cause major harm to or irreversible disturbance of the ecological balance. Such laws and regulations shall have due regard to navigation and the protection of the marine environment based on the best available scientific evidence.

Article 236
Responsibility and liability

1. States are responsible for the fulfillment of their international obligations concerning the protection and preservation of the marine environment. They shall be liable in accordance with international law for damage attributable to them resulting from violations of these obligations.

2. States shall ensure that recourse is available in accordance with their legal systems for prompt and adequate compensaton or other relief in respect of damage caused by pollution of the marine environment by persons, natural or juridical, under their jurisdiction.

3. States shall co-operate in the development of international law relating to criteria and procedures for the determination of liability, the assessment of damage, the payment of compensation and the settlement of related disputes.

Article 237
Sovereign immunity

The provisions of the present Convention regarding pollution of the marine environment shall not apply to any warship, naval auxiliary, other vessels or aircraft owned or operated by a State and used, for the time being, only on government non-commercial service. However, each State shall ensure by the adoption of appropriate measures not impairing operations or operational capabilities of such vessels or aircraft owned or operated by it, that such vessels or aircraft act in a manner consistent, so far as is reasonable and practicable, with the present Convention.

APPENDIX 6

Remarks and Selected Provisions of the
Informal Composite Negotiating Text, Rev. 1
28 April 1979
A/CONF.62/WP.10/Rev.1

At the conclusion of the first part of the eighth session of the Conference in Geneva, certain revisions were made to the Informal Composite Negotiating Text. Basically, these revisions were concerned with the following areas: the exploration and exploitation of resources from the deep seabed; financial arrangements; organization of the International Sea-Bed Authority; the right of access of landlocked states and certain developing coastal states in a subregion or region to the living resources of the exclusive economic zone; the right of access of landlocked and geographically disadvantaged states to the living resources of the economic zone; the settlement of disputes relating to the exercise of the sovereign rights of coastal states in the exclusive economic zone; defining the outer limits of the continental shelf together with the question of payments and contributions with respect to the exploitation of the continental shelf beyond two hundred miles and revenue sharing; and the delimitation of maritime boundaries between adjacent and opposite states and the settlement of disputes thereon.

Printed here are those sections of the Informal Composite Negotiating Text which complement the principal areas where revisions were undertaken.

PART V. EXCLUSIVE ECONOMIC ZONE

Article 55
Specific legal regime of the exclusive economic zone

The exclusive economic zone is an area beyond and adjacent to the territorial sea, subject to the specific legal regime established in this Part, under which the rights and jurisdictions of the coastal State and the rights and freedoms of other States are governed by the relevant provisions of this Convention.

Article 56
Rights, jurisdiction and duties of the coastal State in the exclusive economic zone

1. In the exclusive economic zone, the coastal State has:

(a) sovereign rights for the purpose of exploring and exploiting, conserving and managing the natural resources, whether living or non-living of the sea-bed and subsoil and the superjacent waters, and with regard to other activities for the economic exploitation and exploration of the zone, such as the production of energy from the water, currents and winds:

(b) jurisdiction as provided for in the relevant provisions of this Convention with regard to:

    (i) the establishment and use of artificial island installations and structures;

    (ii) marine scientific research;

    (iii) the preservation of the marine environment.

(c) other rights and duties provided for in this Convention.

2. In exercising its rights and performing its duties under this Convention in the exclusive economic zone, the coastal State shall have due regard to the rights and duties of other States and shall act in a manner compatible with the provisions of this Convention.

3. The rights set out in this article with respect to the sea-bed and subsoil shall be exercised in accordance with Part VI.

Article 57
Breadth of the exclusive economic zone

The exclusive economic zone shall not extend beyond 200 nautical miles from the baselines from which the breadth of the territorial sea is measured.

Article 58
Rights and duties of other States in the exclusive economic zone

1. In the exclusive economic zone, all States, whether coastal or land-locked, enjoy, subject to the relevant provisions of this Convention, the freedoms referred to in article 87 of navigation and overflight and of the laying of submarine cables and pipelines, and other internationally lawful uses of the sea related to these freedoms such as those associated with the operations of ships, aircraft and submarine cables and pipelines, and comptatible with the other provisions of this Convention.

2. Articles 88 to 115 and other pertinent rules of international law apply to the exclusive economic zone in so far as they are not incompatible with this Part.

3. In exercising their rights and performing their duties under this Convention in the exclusive economic zone, States shall have due regard to the rights and duties of the coastal State and shall comply with the laws and regulations established by the coastal State in accordance with the provisions of this Convention and other rules of inter-

national law in so far as they are not incompatible with this Part.

Article 59
Basis for the resolution of conflicts regarding the attribution of rights and jurisdiction in the exclusive economic zone

In cases where this Convention does not attribute rights or jurisdiction to the coastal State or to other States within the exclusive economic zone, and a conflict arises between the interests of the coastal State and any other State or States, the conflict should be resolved on the basis of equity and in the light of all the relevant circumstances, taking into account the respective importance of the interests involved to the parties as well as to the international community as a whole.

Article 60
Artificial island, installations and structures in the exclusive economic zone

1. In the exclusive economic zone, the coastal State shall have the exclusive right to construct and to authorize and regulate the construction, operation and use of:

(a) Artificial islands;

(b) Installations and structures for the purposes provided for in article 56 and other economic purposes;

(c) Installations and structures which may interfere with the exercise of the rights of the coastal State in the zone.

2. The coastal State shall have exclusive jurisdiction over such artificial islands, installations and structures, including jurisdicition with regard to customs, fiscal, health, safety and immigration regulations.

3. Due notice must be given of the construction of such artificial island, installations or structures, and permanent means for giving warning of their presence must be maintained. Any installations or structures which are abandoned or disused must be entirely removed.

4. The coastal State may, where necessary, establish reasonable safety zones around such artificial islands, installations and structures in which it may take appropriate measures to ensure the safety both of navigation and of the artificial islands, installations and structures.

6. All ships must respect these safety zones and shall comply with generally accepted international standards regarding navigation in the vicinity of artificial islands, installations, structures and safety zones. Due notice shall be given of the extent of safety zones.

Article 61
Conservation of the living resources

1. The coastal State shall determine the allowable catch of the living resources in its exclusive economic zone.

2. The coastal State, taking into account the best scientific evidence available to it, shall ensure through proper conservation and management measures that the maintenance of the living resources in the exclusive economic zone is not endangered by over-exploitation. As appropriate, the coastal State and relevant subregional, regional and global organizations shall co-operate to this end.

3. Such measures shall also be designed to maintain or restore populations of harvested species at levels which can produce the maximum sustainable yield, as qualified by relevant environmental and economic factors, including the economic needs of coastal fishing communities and the special requirements of developing countries, and taking into account fishing patterns, the interdependence of stocks and any generally recommended subregional, regional or global minimum standards.

4. In establishing such measures the coastal State shall take into consideration the effects on species associated with or dependent upon harvested species with a view to maintaining or restoring populations of such associated or

dependent species above levels at which their reproduction may become seriously threatened.

Article 62
Utilization of the living resources

1. The coastal State shall promote the objective of optimum utilization of the living resources in the exclusive economic zone without prejudice to article 61.

2. The coastal State shall determine its capacity to harvest the living resources of the exclusive economic zone. Where the coastal State does not have the capacity to harvest the entire allowable catch, it shall, through agreements or other arrangements and pursuant to the terms, conditions and regulations referred to in paragraph 4, give other States access to the surplus of the allowable catch having particular regard to the provisions of articles 69 and 70, especially in relation to the developing States mentioned therein.

3. In giving access to other States to its exclusive economic zone under this article, the coastal State shall take into account all relevant factors, including, *inter alia,* the significance of the living resources of the area to the economy of the coastal State concerned and its other national interests, the provisions of articles 69 and 70, the requirements of developing countries in the subregion or region in harvesting part of the surplus and the need to minimize economic dislocation in States whose nationals have habitually fished in the zone or which have made substantial efforts in research and identification of stocks.

4. Nationals of other States fishing in the exclusive economic zone shall comply with the conservation measures and with the other terms and conditions established in the regulations of the coastal State. These regulations shall be consistent with this Convention and may relate, *inter alia,* to the following:

(a) Licensing of fishermen, fishing vessels and equipment . . .

(b) Determining the species which may be caught, and fixing quotas of catch . . .

(c) Regulating seasons and areas of fishing, the types, sizes and amount of gear, and the numbers, sizes and types of fishing vessels that may be used;

Article 69
Right of land-locked States

1. Land-locked States shall have the right to participate, on an equitable basis, in the exploitation of an appropriate part of the surplus of the living resources of the exclusive economic zones of coastal States of the same subregion or region, taking into account the relevant economic and geographical circumstances of all the States concerned and in conformity with the provisions of this article and of articles 61 and 62.

2. The terms and modalities of such participation shall be established by the States concerned through bilateral, subregional or regional agreements taking into account *inter alia*:

(a) the need to avoid effects detrimental to fishing communities or fishing industries of the coastal State;

(b) the extent to which the land-locked State, in accordance with the provisions of this article, is participating or is entitled to participate under existing bilateral, subregional or regional agreements in the exploitation of living resources of the exclusive economic zones of other coastal States;

(c) the extent to which other land-locked States and States with special geographical characteristics are participating in the exploitation of the living resources of the exclusive economic zone of the coastal State and the consequent need to avoid a particular burden for any single coastal State or a part of it;

(d) the nutritional needs of the populations of the respectives States.

3. When the harvesting capacity of a coastal State ap-

proaches a point which would enable it to harvest the entire allowable catch of the living resources in its exclusive economic zone, the coastal State and other States concerned shall operate in the establishment of equitable arrangements on bilateral, subregional or regional bases to allow for participation of developing land-locked States of the same subregion or region in the exploitation of the living resources of the exclusive economic zones of coastal States or the subregion or region, as may be appropriate in the circumstances and on terms satisfactory to all parties. In the implementation of this provision the factors mentioned in paragraph 2 shall also be taken into account.

4. Developed land-locked States shall, under the provisions of this article, be entitled to participate in the exploitation of living resources only in the exclusive economic zones of developed coastal States of the same subregion or region having regard to the extent to which the coastal State in giving access to other States to the living resources of its exclusive economic zone has taken into account the need to minimize detrimental effects on fishing communities and economic dislocation in States whose nationals have habitually fished in the zone.

5. The above provisions are without prejudice to arrangements agreed upon in subregions or regions where the coastal States may grant to land-locked States of the same subregion or region equal or preferential rights for the exploitation of the living resources in the exclusive economic zones.

Article 74
Delimitation of the exclusive economic zone between adjacent or opposite States

1. The delimitation of the exclusive economic zone between adjacent or opposite States shall be effected by agreement in accordance with equitable principles, employing, where appropriate, the median or

equidistance line, and taking account of all the relevant circumstances.

2. If no agreement can be reached within a reasonable period of time, the States concerned shall resort to the procedures provided for in Part XV.

3. Pending agreement or settlement, the States concerned shall make provisional arrangements, taking into account the provisions of paragraph 1.

4. For the purposes of this Convention, "median or equidistance line" means the line every point of which is equidistant from the nearest points of the baselines from which the breadth of the territorial sea of each State is measured.

5. Where there is an agreement in force between the States concerned, questions relating to the delimitation of the exclusive economic zone shall be determined in accordance with the provisions of that agreement.

PART VI. CONTINENTAL SHELF

Article 76
Definition of the continental shelf

1. The continental shelf of a coastal State comprises the sea-bed and subsoil of the submarine areas that extend beyond its territorial sea throughout the natural prolongation of its land territory to the outer edge of the continental margin, or to a distance of 200 nautical miles from the baselines from which the breadth of the territorial sea is measured where the outer edge of the continental margin does not extend to that distance.

2. The continental shelf of a coastal State shall not extend beyond the limits provided for in paragraphs 4 and 5.

3. The continental margin comprises the submerged prolongation of the land mass of the coastal State, and consists of the sea-bed and subsoil of the shelf, the slope

and the rise. It does not include the deep ocean floor or the subsoil thereof.

4. (a) For the purposes of this Convention, the coastal State shall establish the outer edge of the continental margin wherever the margin extends beyond 200 nautical miles from the baselines from which the breadth of the territorial sea is measured, by either:

(i) A line delineated in accordance with paragraph 6 by reference to the outermost fixed points at each of which the thickness of sedimentary rocks is at least 1 per cent of the shortest distance from such point to the foot of the continental slope; or,

(ii) A line delineated in accordance with paragraph 6 by reference to fixed points not more than 60 nautical miles from the foot of the continental slope.

(b) In the absence of evidence to the contrary, the foot of the continental slope shall be determined as the point of maximum change in the gradient at its base.

5. The fixed points comprising the line of the outer limits of the continental shelf on the sea-bed, drawn in accordance with paragraph 4 (a) (i) and (ii), either shall not exceed 350 miles from the baseline from which the breadth of the territorial sea is measured or shall not exceed 100 nautical miles from the 2,500 metre isobath, which is a line connecting the depth of 2,500 metres.

6. The coastal State shall delineate the seaward boundary of its continental shelf where that shelf extends beyond 200 nautical miles from the baselines from which the breadth of the territorial sea is measured by straight lines not exceeding 60 nautical miles in length, connecting fixed points, such points to be defined by co-ordinates of latitude and longitude.

7. Information on the limits of the continental shelf beyond the 200 nautical mile exclusive economic zone shall be submitted by the coastal State to the Commission

on the Limits of the Continental Shelf set up under annex on the basis of equitable geographic representation. The Commission shall make recommendations to coastal States on matters related to the establishment of the outer limits of their continental shelf. The limits of the shelf established by a coastal State taking into account these recommendations shall be final and binding . . . .

Article 77
Rights of the coastal State over the continental shelf

1. The coastal State exercises over the continental shelf sovereign rights for the purpose of exploring it and exploiting its natural resources.

2. The rights referred to in paragraph 1 are exclusive in the sense that if the coastal State does not explore the continental shelf or exploit its natural resources, no one may undertake these activities without the express consent of the coastal State.

3. The rights of the coastal State over the continental shelf do not depend on occupation, effective or notional, or on any express proclamation.

4. The natural resources referred to in this Part consist of the mineral and other non-living resources of the sea-bed and subsoil together with living organisms belonging to sedentary species, that is to say, organisms which, at the harvestable stage, either are immobile on or under the sea-bed or are unable to move except in constant physical contact with the sea-bed or the subsoil.

Article 78
Legal status of the superjacent waters and airspace and the rights and freedoms of other States

1. The rights of the coastal State over the continental shelf do not affect the legal status of the superjacent waters or of the air space above those waters.

2. The exercise of the rights of the coastal State over the continental shelf must not infringe, or result in any unjustifiable interference with navigation other rights

and freedoms of other States as provided for in the Convention.

Article 81
Drilling on the continental shelf

The coastal State shall have the exclusive right to authorize and regulate drilling on the continental shelf for all purposes.

Article 82
Payments and contributions with respect to the exploitation of the continental shelf beyond 200 miles

1. The coastal State shall make payments or contributions in kind in respect of the exploitation of the non-living resources of the continental shelf beyond 200 nautical miles from the baselines from which the breadth of the territorial sea is measured.

2. The payments and contributions shall be made annually with respect to all production at a site after the first five years of production at that site. For the sixth year, the rate of payment or contribution shall be one per cent of the value or volume of production at the site. The rate shall increase by one percent for each subsequent year until the twelfth year and shall remain at seven per cent thereafter. Production does not include resources used in connection with exploitation.

3. A developing country which is a net importer of a mineral resource produced from its continental shelf is exempt from making such payments or contributions in respect of that mineral resource.

4. The payments or contributions shall be made through the Authority, which shall distribute them to States Parties to this Convention, on the basis of equitable sharing criteria, taking into account the interests and needs of developing countries, particularly the least developed and the land-locked amongst them.

Article 83
Delimitation of the continental shelf between adjacent or opposite States

1. The delimitation of the continental shelf between adjacent or opposite States shall be effected by agreement in accordance with equitable principles, employing, where appropriate, the median or equidistance line, and taking account of all the relevant circumstances.

2. If no agreement can be reached within a reasonable period of time, the States concerned shall resort to the procedures provided for in Part XV.

3. Pending agreement or settlement, the States concerned shall make provisional arrangements, taking into account the provisions of paragraph 1.

4. Where there is an agreement in force between the States concerned, questions relating to the delimitation of the continental shelf shall be determined in accordance with the provisions of the agreement.

SECTION 2. MANAGEMENT AND CONSERVATION OF THE LIVING RESOURCES OF THE HIGH SEAS

Article 116
Right to fish on the high seas

All States have the right for their nationals to engage in fishing on the high seas subject to:

(a) Their treaty obligations;

(b) The rights and duties as well as the interests of coastal States provided for, *inter alia,* in article 63, paragraph 2 and articles 64 and 67; and

(c) The provisions of this section.

Article 117
Duty of States to adopt with respect to their nationals measures for the conservation of the living resources of the high seas

All States have the duty to adopt, or to co-operate with

other States in adopting, such measures for their respective nationals as may be necessary for the conservation of the living resources of the high seas.

Article 118
Co-operation of States in the management and conservation of living resources

States shall co-operate with each other in the management and conservation of living resources in the areas of the high seas. States whose nationals exploit identical resources, or different resources in the same area, shall enter into negotiations with a view to adopting the means necessary for the conservation of the living resources concerned. They shall, as appropriate, co-operate to establish subregional fisheries organizations to this end.

Article 119
Conservation of the living resources of the high seas

1. In determining the allowable catch and establishing other conservation measures for the living resources in the high seas, States shall:

(a) Adopt measures which are designed, on the best scientific evidence available to the States concerned, to maintain or restore populations of harvested species at levels which can produce the maximum sustainable yield, as qualified by relevant environmental and economic factors, including the special requirements of developing countries, and taking into account fishing patterns, the interdependence of stocks and any generally recommended subregional, regional or global minimum standards;

(b) Take into consideration the effects on species associated with or dependent upon harvested species with a view to maintaining or restoring populations of such associated or dependent species above levels at which their reproduction may become seriously threatened.

2. Available scientific information, catch and fishing

effort statistics, and other data relevant to the conservation of fish stocks shall be contributed and exchanged on a regular basis through subregional, regional and global organizations where appropriate and with participation by all States concerned.

3. States concerned shall ensure that conservation measures and their implementation do not discriminate in form or in fact against the fishermen of any State.

PART IX. ENCLOSED OR SEMI-ENCLOSED SEAS

Article 122
Definition

For the purposes of this Part, "enclosed or semi-enclosed sea" means a gulf, basin, or sea surrounded by two or more States and connected to the open seas by a narrow outlet or consisting entirely or primarily of the territorial seas and exclusive economic zones of two or more coastal States.

Article 123
Co-operation of States bordering enclosed or semi-enclosed seas

States bordering enclosed or semi-enclosed seas should co-operate with each other in the exercise of their rights and duties under this Convention. To this end they shall endeavour, directly or through an appropriate regional organization:

(a) To co-ordinate the management, conservation, exploration and exploitation of the living resources of the sea;

(b) To co-ordinate the implementation of their rights and duties with respect to the preservation of the marine environment;

(c) To co-ordinate their scientific research policies and undertake where appropriate joint programmes of scientific research in the area;

(d) To invite, as appropriate, other interested States or

international organizations to co-operate with them in furtherance of the provision of this article.

Article 125
Right of access to and from the sea and freedom of transit

1. Land-locked States shall have the right of access to and from the sea for the purpose of exercising the rights provided for in this Convention including those relating to the freedom of the high seas and the common heritage of mankind. To this end, land-locked States shall enjoy freedom of transit through the territory of transit States by all means of transport.

2. The terms and modalities for exercising freedom of transit shall be agreed between the land-locked States and the transit States concerned through bilateral, sub-regional or regional agreements.

3. Transit States, in the exercise of their full sovereignty over their territory, shall have the right to take all necessary measures to ensure that the rights and facilities, provided for in this Part for land-locked States shall in no way infringe their legitimate interests.

PART XI. THE AREA

SECTION 1. GENERAL

For the purpose of this Part

(a) "Activities in the Area" means all activities of exploration for, and exploitation of, the resources of the Area.

(b) "Resources" means mineral resources *in situ*. When recovered from the Area, such resources shall, for the purposes of this Part, be regarded as minerals . . . .

Article 135
Legal status of the superjacent waters and air space

Neither the provisions of this Part nor any rights granted or exercised pursuant thereto shall affect the legal status of the waters superjacent to the Area or that of the air space above those waters.

Article 137
Legal status of the Area and its resources

1. No state shall claim or exercise sovereignty or sovereign rights over any part of the Area or its resources, nor shall any State or person, natural or juridical, appropriate any part thereof. No such claim or exercise of sovereignty or sovereign rights, nor such appropriation shall be recognized.

2. All rights in the resources of the Area are vested in mankind as a whole, on whose behalf the Authority shall act. These resources are not subject to alienation. The minerals derived from the Area, however, may only be alienated in accordance with this Part and the rules and regulations adopted thereunder.

3. No State or person, natural or juridical, shall claim, acquire or exercise rights with respect to the minerals of the Area except in accordance with the Provisions of this Part. Otherwise, no such claim, acquisition or exercise of such rights shall be recognized.

Article 142
Rights and legitimate interests of coastal States

1. Activities in the Area, with respect to resource deposits in the Area which lie across limits of national jurisdiction, shall be conducted with due regard to the rights and legitimate interests of any coastal State across whose jurisdiction such resources lie.

2. Consultations, including a system of prior notification, shall be maintained with the State concerned, with a view to avoiding infringement of such rights and interests. In cases where activities in the Area may result in the exploitation of resources lying within national jurisdiction, the prior consent of the coastal State concerned shall be required.

3. Neither the provisions of this Part nor any rights granted or exercised pursuant thereto shall affect the rights of coastal States to take such measures consistent with the relevant provisions of Part XII as may be necessary to prevent, mitigate or eliminate grave and imminent danger to their coastlines, or related interests from pollution or threat thereof or from other hazardous occurrences resulting from or caused by any activities in the Area.

SECTION 3. CONDUCT OF ACTIVITIES IN THE AREA

Article 143
Marine scientific research

1. Marine scientific research in the Area shall be carried out exclusively for peaceful purposes and for the benefit of mankind as a whole, in accordance with Part XIII.

2. The Authority may carry out marine scientific research concerning the Area and its resources, and may enter into contracts for that purpose. The Authority shall promote and encourage the conduct of marine scientific research in the Area, and shall co-ordinate and disseminate the results of such research and analysis when available.

3. States Parties may carry out marine scientific research in the Area. States Parties shall promote international co-operation in marine scientific research in the Area by:

(a) Participation in international programmes and encouraging co-operation in marine scientific research by personnel of different countries and of the Authority;

(b) Ensuring that programmes are developed through the Authority or other international bodies as appropriate for the benefit of developing countries and technologically less developed countries with a view to

(i)   Strengthening their research capabilities;

(ii) Training their personnel and the personnel of the Authority in the techniques and applications of research;

(iii) Fostering the employment of their qualified personnel in activities of research in the Area.

(c) Effective dissemination of the results of research and analysis when available, through the Authority or other international channels when appropriate.

Article 144
Transfer of technology

1. The Authority shall take measure in accordance with this Convention:

(a) to acquire technology and scientific knowledge relating to activities in the Area; and

(b) to promote and encourage the transfer to developing countries of such technology and scientific knowledge so that all States Parties benefit therefrom.

2. To this end the Authority and the States Parties shall co-operate in promoting the transfer of technology and scientific knowledge relating to activities in the Area so that the Enterprise and all States Parties may benefit therefrom. In particular they shall initiate and promote:

(a) Programmes for the transfer of technology to the Enterprise and to developing countries with regard to activities in the Area, including, *inter alia,* facilitating the access of the Enterprise and of developing countries to the relevant technology, under fair and reasonable terms and conditions;

(b) Measures directed towards the advancement of the technology of the Enterprise and the domestic technology of developing countries, particularly through the opening of opportunities to personnel from the Enterprise and from developing countries for training in marine science and technology and their full participation in activities in the Area.

SECTION 4. DEVELOPMENT OF RESOURCES OF THE AREA

Article 150
Policies relating to
activities in the Area

Activities in the Area shall be carried out in accordance with the provisions of this Part in such a manner as to foster healthy development of the world economy and balanced growth of international trade, and to promote international co-operation for the over-all development of all countries, especially the developing countries and with a view to ensuring:

(a) orderly and safe development and rational management of the resources of the Area, including the efficient conduct of activities in the Area and, in accordance with sound principles of conservation, the avoidance of unnecessary waste;

(b) the expanding of opportunities for participation in such activities consistent particularly with articles 144 and 148;

(c) participation in revenues by the Authority and the transfer of technology to the Enterprise and developing countries as provided for in this Convention;

(d) increasing availability of the minerals produced from the resources of the Area as needed, in conjunction with minerals produced from other sources, to ensure supplies to consumer of such minerals;

(e) just and stable prices remunerative to producers and fair to consumers for minerals produced both from the resources of the Area and from other sources, and promoting equilibrium between supply and demand;

(f) the enhancing of opportunities for all States Parties, irrespective of their social and economic systems or geographical location, to participate in the development of the resources of the Area and preventing monopolization of the exploration and exploitation of the resources of the Area; and

(g) the protection of developing countries from adverse effects on their economies or on their export earnings resulting from a reduction in the price of affected mineral, or in the volume of that mineral exported, to the extent that such reductions are caused by activities in the Area, as provided in article 151.

Article 151
Production policies
Without prejudice to the objectives set forth in article 150, and for the purpose of implementing the provisions of article 150, paragraph (g)

1. Acting through existing forums or such new arrangements or agreements as may be appropriate, and in which all interested parties participate, the Authority shall take measures necessary to promote the growth, efficiency and stability of markets for those commodities produced from the resources of the Area, at prices remunerative to producers and fair to consumers. All States Parties shall co-operate to this end. The Authority shall have the right to participate in any commodity conference dealing with those commodities. The Authority shall have the right to become a party to any such arrangement or agreement resulting from such conferences as are referred to above . . . .

2. During an interim period specified in subparagraph (a), the Authority shall not approve any plan of work covering exploitation if the level of production of minerals from nodules as specified in that plan of work will cause the nickel production ceiling, as calculated pursuant to subparagraphs (b) and (d) during the year of approval of the plan of work, to be exceeded during any year of planned production. Should the level of planned produc-

tion not cause the ceiling to be so exceeded, the level of nickel production specified in that plan of work shall be authorized.

(a) The interim period shall begin five years prior to 1 January of the year in which the earliest commercial production is planned to commence under an approved plan of work. In the event that the earliest commercial production is delayed beyond the year originally planned, the beginning of the interim period and the production ceiling originally calculated shall be adjusted accordingly. The interim period shall last 25 years or until the day when such new arrangements or agreements as are referred to in paragraph 1 enter into force, whichever is earlier. The Authority shall resume the power to limit the production of minerals from nodules as provided in this article for the remainder of the 25 year period if the said arrangements or agreements should lapse or become ineffective for any reason whatsoever.

(b) The production ceiling for any year, beginning with the year of the earliest commercial production shall be the sum of (i) and (ii):

    (i) The difference between the trend line values for annual nickel consumption, as calculated pursuant to subparagraph (c) for the year immediately prior to the year of the earliest commercial production, and the year immediately prior to the commencement of the interim period;

    (ii) Sixty per cent of the difference between trend line values for nickel consumption, as calculated pursuant to subparagraph (c), for the year for which the ceiling is being calculated, and the year immediately prior to the year of the earliest commercial production.

(c) Trend line values used for computing the nickel production ceiling shall be those annual nickel consumption values on a trend line computed during the year in which a plan of work is approved. The trend line shall be derived from a linear regression of the logarithms of actual annual nickel consumption for the most recent 15 year period for which such data are available, time being the independent variable.

3. The Authority shall regulate production of minerals from the Area, other than mineral from nodules, under such conditions and applying such methods as may be appropriate . . . .

4. Following recommendations from the Council on the basis of advice from the Economic Planning Commission, the Assembly shall establish a system of compensation for developng countries which suffer adverse effects on their export earnings or economics resulting from a reduction in the price of an affected mineral or the volume of the mineral exported, to the extent that such reduction is caused by activities in the Area.

Article 153
System of exploration and exploitation

1. Activities in the Area shall be organized, carried out and controlled by the Authority on behalf of mankind as a whole in accordance with the provisions of this Article as well as other relevant provisions of this Part and its annexes, and the rules, regulations and procedures of the Authority.

2. Activities in the Area shall be carried out as prescribed in paragraph 3:

(a) by the Enterprise, and

(b) in association with the Authority by States Parties or State Entities, or persons natural or juridical which possess the nationality of States Parties or are effectively controlled by them or their nationals, when sponsored by such States, or any group of the foregoing which meets the requirements provided in this Part including annex II.

3. Activities in the Area shall be carried out in accordance with a formal written plan of work drawn up in accordance with annex II and approved by the Council after review by the Technical Commission. In the case of activities in the Area carried out as authorized by the Authority by the entities specified in paragraph 2(b), such a plan of work shall in accordance with article 3 of annex II be in the form of a contract. Such contract may provide for joint arrangements in accordance with article 10 of annex II.

4. The Authority shall exercise such control over activities in the Area as is necessary for the purpose of securing compliance with the relevant provisions of this Part including its annexes, and the rules, regulations and procedures of the Authority, and the plans of work approved in accordance with paragraph 3. States Parties shall assist the Authority by taking all measures necessary to ensure such compliance, in accordance with article 139.

5. The Authority shall have the right to take at any time any measures provided for under this Part to ensure compliance with its terms, and the performance of the control and regulatory functions assigned to it thereunder or under any contract. The Authority shall have the right to inspect all facilities in the Area used in connexion with activities in the Area.

6. A contract under paragraph 3 shall provide for security of tenure. Accordingly, it shall not be revised, suspended or terminated except in accordance with articles 17 and 18 of annex II.

Article 155
The Review Conference

1. Twenty years from the approval of the first contract or plan of work under this Convention the Assembly shall convene a conference for the review of those provisions of this Part and the annexes thereto which govern the system

or exploration and exploitation of the resources of the Area . . . .

2. In particular, the Conference shall consider whether, during the 20 year period, reserved areas have been exploited in an effective and balanced way in comparison with non-reserved areas.

3. The Conference shall ensure that the principles of the common heritage of mankind, the international regime designed to ensure its equitable exploitation for the benefit of all countries, especially the developing countries, and an Authority to conduct, organize and control activities in the Area are maintained. It shall also ensure the maintenance of the principles laid down in this Part with regard to the exclusion of claims or exercise of sovereignty over any part of the Area, the rights of States and their general conduct in relation to the Area, the prevention of monopolization of activities in the Area, the use of the Area exclusively for peaceful purposes, economic aspects of activities in the Area, scientific research, transfer of technology, protection of the marine environment, and of human life, rights of coastal States, the legal status of the superjacent waters and air space and accommodation as between the various forms of activities in the Area and in the marine environment.

4. The Conference shall establish its own rules of procedure.

5. Decisions adopted by the Conference under the provisions of this article shall not affect the rights acquired under existing contracts.

6. Five years after the commencement of the Review Conference, and until an agreement on the system of exploration and exploitation of the resources of the Area enters into force, the Assembly may decide, by the majority required for questions of substance, that no new contracts or plans of work for activities in the Area shall be approved. However, such decision shall not affect contracts already approved, or contracts and plans of work

for the conduct of activities in the areas already reserved in accordance with article 8 of annex II.

SECTION 5. THE AUTHORITY
SUBSECTION A. GENERAL

Article 156
Establishment of the Authority

1. There is hereby established the International Sea-Bed Authority which shall function in accordance with the provisions of this Part.

2. All States parties are *ipso facto* members of the Authority.

3. The seat of the Authority shall be at Jamaica.

4. The Authority may establish such regional centres or offices as it deems necessary for the performance of its functions.

Article 157
Nature and fundamental principles of the Authority

1. The Authority is the organization through which States Parties shall organize and control activities in the Area, particularly with a view to administering the resources of the Area, in accordance with this Part.

2. The Authority is based on the principle of the sovereign equality of all its members.

3. All members, in order to ensure to all of them the rights and benefits resulting from membership, shall fulfill in good faith the obligations assumed by them in accordance with this Part.

PART XII. PROTECTION AND PRESERVATION OF THE MARINE ENVIRONMENT

SECTION 1. GENERAL PROVISIONS

Article 192
General obligation

States have the obligation to protect and preserve the marine environment.

Article 193
Sovereign right of States to exploit their natural resources

States have the sovereign right to exploit their natural resources pursuant to their environmental policies and in accordance with their duty to protect and preserve the marine environment.

Article 194
Measures to prevent, reduce and control pollution of the marine environment

1. States shall take all necessary measures consistent with this Convention to prevent, reduce and control pollution of the marine environment from any source using for this purpose the best practicable means at their disposal and in accordance with their capabilities, individually or jointly as appropriate, and they shall endeavour to harmonize their policies in this connexion.

2. States shall take all necessary measures to ensure that activities under their jurisdiction or control are so conducted that they do not cause damage by pollution to other States and their environment, and that pollution arising from incidents or activities under their jurisdiction or control does not spread beyond the areas where they exercise sovereign rights in accordance with this Convention.

3. The measures taken pursuant to this Part shall deal with all sources of pollution of the marine environment. These measures shall include, *inter alia,* those designed to minimize to the fullest possible extent:

   (a) Release of toxic, harmful and noxious substances, especially those which are persistent:
   (i)   from land-based sources;
   (ii) from or through the atmosphere;
   (iii) by dumping.

   (b) Pollution from vessels, in particular for preventing accidents and dealing with emergencies, ensuring the safety of operations at sea, preventing intentional and un-intentional discharges, and regulating the design, construction, equipment, operation and manning of vessels;

(c) Pollution from installations and devices used in exploration or exploitation of the natural resources of the sea-bed and subsoil, in particular for preventing accidents and dealing with emergencies, ensuring the safety of operations at sea, and regulating the design, construction, equipment, operation and manning of such installations or devices;

(d) Pollution from other installations and devices operating in the marine environment, in particular for preventing accidents and dealing with emergencies, ensuring the safety of operations at sea, and regulating the design, construction, equipment, operation and manning of such installations or devices.

4. In taking measures to prevent, reduce or control pollution of the marine environment, States shall refrain from unjustifiable interference with activities in pursuance of the rights and duties of other States exercised in conformity with this Convention.

5. The measures taken in accordance with this Part shall include those necessary to protect and preserve rare or fragile ecosystems as well as the habitat of depleted, threatened or endangered species and other marine life.

SECTION 5. INTERNATIONAL RULES AND NATIONAL LEGISLATION TO PREVENT, REDUCE AND CONTROL POLLUTION OF THE MARINE ENVIRONMENT

Article 230
Monetary penalties and the observance of recognized rights of the accused

1. Only monetary penalties may be imposed with respect to violations of national laws and regulations or applicable international rules and standards, for the pre-

vention, reduction and control of pollution of the marine environment from vessels committed by foreign vessels beyond the territorial sea.

2 Only monetary penalties may be imposed with respect to violations of national laws and regulations or applicable international rules and standards for the prevention, reduction and control of pollution of the the marine environment from vessels committed by foreign vessels in the territorial sea, except in the case of a wilfull and serious act of pollution in the territorial sea.

3. In the conduct of proceedings to impose penalties in respect of such violations committed by a foreign vessel, recognized rights of the accused shall be observed.

Article 231
Notification to flag States and other
States concerned

States shall promptly notify the flag State and any other State concerned of any measures taken pursuant to section 6 against foreign vessels, and shall submit to the flag State all official reports concerning such measures. However, with respect to violations committed in the etrritorial sea, the foregoing obligations of the coastal State shall apply only to such measures as are taken in proceedings. The consular officers or diplomatic agents, and where possible the maritime authority of the flag State, shall be immediately informed of any such measure.

Article 232
Liability of States arising from
enforcement measures

States shall be liable for damage or loss attributable to them arising from measures taken pursuant to section 6 when such measures were unlawful or exceeded those reasonably required in the light of available information. States shall provide for recourse in their courts for actions in respect of such damage or loss.

PART XIV. DEVELOPMENT AND TRANSFER OF MARINE TECHNOLOGY

SECTION 1. GENERAL PROVISIONS

Article 266
Promotion of development and transfer of marine technology

1. States, directly or through appropriate international organizations, shall co-operate within their capabilities to promote actively the development and transfer of marine science and marine technology on fair and reasonable terms and conditions.

2. States shall promote the development of the marine scientific and technological capacity of States which may need and request technical assistance in this field, particularly developing States, including land-locked and geographically disadvantaged States, with regard to the exploration, exploitation, conservation and management of marine resources, the preservation of the marine environment, marine scientific research and other uses of the marine environment compatible with this Convention, with a view to accelerating the social and economic development of the developing States.

3. States shall endeavour to foster favourable economic and legal conditions for the transfer of marine technology for the benefit of all parties concerned on an equitable basis.

Article 268
Basic objectives

States, directly or through competent international organizations, shall promote:

(a) the acquisition, evaluation and dissemination of marine technological knowledge and facilitate access to such information data;

(b) the development of appropriate marine technology;

(c) the development of the necessary technological infrastructure to facilitate the transfer of marine technology;

(d) the development of human resources through training and education of nationals of developing States and countries and especially of the least developed among them; and

(e) international co-operation at all levels, particularly at the regional, subregional and bilateral levels.

Article 269
Measures to achieve the basic objectives

In order to achieve the above-mentioned objectives, States, directly or through competent international organizations, shall, *inter alia,* endeavour to:

(a) establish programmes of technical co-operation for the effective transfer of all kinds of marine technology to States which may need and request technical assistance in this field, particularly the developing land-locked and other geographically disadvantaged States, as well as other developing States which have not been able either to establish or develop their own technological capacity in marine science and in the exploration and exploitation of the marine resources, and to develop the infrastructure of such technology;

(b) promote favourable conditions for the conclusion of agreements, contracts and other similar arrangements, under equitable and reasonable conditions;

(c) hold conferences, seminars and symposia on scientific and technological subjects, in particular, on policies and methods for the transfer of marine technology;

(d) promote the exchange of scientists, technologists and other experts;

(e) undertake projects, promote joint ventures and other forms of bilateral and multilateral co-operation.

SECTION 2. INTERNATIONAL CO-OPERATION

Article 270
Ways and means of international co-operation

International co-operation for the development and transfer of marine technology shall, where feasible and appropriate, be carried out through existing bilateral, regional or multilateral programmes, and also through expanded and new programmes in order to facilitate marine scientific research and the transfer of marine technology, particularly in new fields and appropriate international funding for ocean research and development.

Article 274
Objectives of the Authority with respect to the transfer of technology

Subject to all legitimate interests including, *inter alia*, the rights and duties of holders, suppliers and recipients of technology, the Authority shall, with regard to the exploration of the Area and the exploitation of its resources, ensure:

(a) that on the basis of the principle of equitable geographical distribution, nationals of developing States, whether coastal, land-locked or geographically disadvantaged, shall be taken on for the purposes of training as members of the managerial, research and technical staff constituted for its undertaking;

(b) that the technical documentation on the relevant equipment, machinery, devices and processes be made available to all States, in particular developing States which may need and request technical assistance in this field;

(c) that adequate provision is made by the Authority to facilitate the acquisition by States which may need and request technical assistance in the field of marine technology, in particular developing States and the acquisition by their nationals of the necessary skills and know-how, including professional training;

(d) that States which may need and request technical assistance in this field, in particular developing States, are assisted in the acquisition of necessary equipment, processes, plans and other technical know-how through any financial arrangements provided for in this Convention.